Global Families

Second Edition

Contemporary Family Perspectives

Series Editor

Susan J. Ferguson
Grinnell College

Volumes in the Series

Families: A Social Class Perspective
Shirley A. Hill

Making Families Through Adoption
Nancy E. Riley and Krista E. Van Vleet

Family Policy and the American Safety Net
Janet Z. Giele

Families and Health
Janet R. Grochowski

Families and Work
Stephen Sweet

Gay and Lesbian Families
Nancy J. Mezey

Families and Aging in the 21st Century
Patricia Drentea

Global Families

Second Edition

MEG WILKES KARRAKER

University of St. Thomas

SUSAN J. FERGUSON, SERIES EDITOR

Los Angeles | London | New Delhi
Singapore | Washington DC

Los Angeles | London | New Delhi
Singapore | Washington DC

For information:

SAGE Publications, Inc.
2455 Teller Road
Thousand Oaks, California 91320
E-mail: order@sagepub.com

SAGE Publications Ltd.
1 Oliver's Yard
55 City Road
London, EC1Y 1SP
United Kingdom

SAGE Publications India Pvt. Ltd.
B 1/I 1 Mohan Cooperative Industrial Area
Mathura Road, New Delhi 110 044
India

SAGE Publications Asia-Pacific Pte. Ltd.
3 Church Street
#10-04 Samsung Hub
Singapore 049483

Printed in the United States of America

Library of Congress Cataloging-in-Publication Data

Karraker, Meg Wilkes.
Global families / Meg Wilkes Karraker. — 2nd ed.

p. cm. — (Contemporary family perspectives)
Includes bibliographical references and index.

ISBN 978-1-4129-9863-5 (pbk.)

1. Families—Study and teaching. I. Title.

HQ10.K37 2013
306.8509—dc23   2012004125

This book is printed on acid-free paper.

Acquisitions Editor: David Repetto
Editorial Assistant: Lauren Johnson
Production Editor: Eric Garner
Copy Editor: Megan Granger
Typesetter: C&M Digitals (P) Ltd.
Proofreader: Joyce Li
Indexer: J. Naomi Linzer
Cover Designer: Janet Kiesel
Marketing Manager: Erica DeLuca
Permissions Editor: Karen Ehrmann

12 13 14 15 16 10 9 8 7 6 5 4 3 2 1

Contents

Series Preface

Contemporary Family Perspectives

Susan J. Ferguson
Grinnell College

The family is one of the most private and pervasive social institutions in U.S. society. At the same time, public discussions and debates about the institution of the family persist. Some scholars and public figures claim that the family is declining or dying, or that the contemporary family is morally deficient. Other scholars argue that the family is caught in the larger culture wars currently taking place in the United States. The recent debates on same sex marriage are one example of this larger public discussion about the institution of the family. Regardless of one's perspective that the family is declining or caught in broader political struggles, scholars agree that the institution has undergone dramatic transformations in recent decades. U.S. demographic data reveal that fewer people are married, divorce rates remain high at almost 50 percent, and more families are living in poverty. In addition, people are creating new kinds of families via Internet dating, cohabitation, single-parent adoption, committed couples living apart, donor insemination, and polyamorous relationships. The demographic data and ethnographic research on new family forms require that family scholars pay attention to a variety of family structures, processes, ideologies, and social norms. In particular, scholars need to address important questions about the family, such as, what is the future of marriage? Is divorce harmful to individuals, to the institution of the family, and/or to society? Why are rates of family violence so high? Are we living in a post-dating culture? How do poverty and welfare policies affect families? How is child rearing changing now that so many parents work outside the home, and children spend time with caretakers other than their parents? Finally, how are families socially constructed in different societies and cultures?

Most sociologists and family scholars agree that the family is a dynamic social institution that is continually changing as other social structures and individuals in society change. The family also is a social construction with complex and shifting age, gender, race, and social class meanings. Many excellent studies are currently investigating the changing structures of the institution of the family and the lived experiences and meanings of families. **Contemporary Family Perspectives** is a series of short texts and research monographs that provides a forum for the best of this burgeoning scholarship The series aims to recognize the diversity of families that exist in the United States and globally. A second goal is for the series to better inform pedagogy and future family scholarship about this diversity of families. The series also seeks to connect family scholarship to a broader audience beyond the classroom by informing the public and by ensuring that family studies remain central to contemporary policy debates and to social action. Each short text contains the most outstanding current scholarship on the family from a variety of disciplines, including sociology, demography, policy studies, social work, human development, and psychology. Moreover, each short text is authored by a leading family scholar or scholars who bring their unique disciplinary perspective to an understanding of contemporary families.

Contemporary Family Perspectives provides the most advanced scholarship and up-to-date findings on the family. Each volume provides a brief overview of significant scholarship on that family topic, including critical current debates or areas of scholarly disagreement. In addition to providing an assessment of the latest findings related to their family topic, authors also examine the family utilizing an intersectional framework of race-ethnicity, social class, gender, and sexuality. Much of the research is interdisciplinary, with a number of theoretical frameworks and methodological approaches presented. Several of the family scholars use a historical lens as well to ground their contemporary research. A particular strength of the series is that the short texts appeal to undergraduate students as well as to family scholars, but they are written in a way that makes them accessible to a larger public.

About This Volume

To understand the institution of the family in the twenty-first century, we need to understand how globalization affects families across the world. *Global Families* investigates scholarship from sociology, economics, political science, history, anthropology, and even from literature to assess the complex effects of globalization on contemporary families. The author, Meg Wilkes

Karraker (University of St. Thomas), argues that this interdisciplinary approach is necessary because the scholarship on global families is just developing and somewhat fragmented. In this volume, Karraker begins with an overview of the concepts and theories related to globalization. Karraker also reviews several debates related to globalization and suggests the utility of feminist theory for understanding global families in this introductory chapter. After providing this background, Karraker investigates specific topic areas that demonstrate the complex effects of globalization on families. These topics include demography, employment, violence, and culture. The last chapter looks at national and international policies that are attempting to address issues affecting global families. Throughout this volume, Karraker compassionately illustrates the consequences of globalization on families in both developing and developed countries.

A unique feature of this book is Karraker's use of original essays at the end of each chapter. These essays convey the issues presented in the chapters in a more specific and intimate matter. The authors of these essays, whether they are academics or social service professionals, provide additional perspectives, which enhance our understanding of global families.

Global Families is appropriate for use in any class concerned with family structure, social inequality, gender, and how globalization affects families in terms of employment, migration, and well being. This book is a valuable resource to teachers and students in beginning and advanced courses in sociology, family studies, women's studies, global studies, political science, social work, public policy, and other disciplines. It also finds an audience among any person interested in comparative family studies or among those who work in various human services fields, including human development, social work, education, counseling, health services, and the government. This last statement is particularly true for social service employees who work with immigrant or refugee populations. This volume can help them to better understand the dramatic economic and social forces that transnational labor and migration have on families.

Author Preface

Meg Wilkes Karraker

In 2006 Susan Ferguson initiated a new series to illuminate critical issues facing families in the 21st century. *Contemporary Family Perspectives* offers a powerful synthesis of quantitative and qualitative data around such pressing family issues as adoption, families and health, elder care, families and social inequality, family policy, and families and work.

Global Families is the third book in the series. Of necessity, *Global Families* draws on sociology and family studies but also on economics and political science as well as anthropology, criminology, geography, history, and even literature. The result is an interdisciplinary approach to a complex but increasingly critical issue facing societies and families today: the impact of globalization on families.

Changes to the second edition of course include updated research and statistics throughout. Data from the Organisation for Economic Co-operation and Development, the United Nations, the World Health Organization, and other international organizations feature prominently in each chapter. This edition draws on research and theory published in scholarly books and journals, as well as on studies conducted by organizations such as the Pew Research Center and Rand. The second edition gives more space to up-to-the-minute print and online news sources from around the world (e.g., the BBC, *The Economist*, *The New York Times*) and references reports from organizations such as Human Rights Watch and Minnesota Advocates for Human Rights.

Global Families opens with an introduction to the field, situating an authentic global approach to families in the context of a long-standing comparative tradition. I offer a summary of the concepts, debates, and theories of globalization, along with a discussion of how globalization increases the potential for risk in a postmodern world. The first chapter also addresses the value of a feminist perspective for understanding the impacts of globalization on families. Each of the subsequent four chapters—Chapters 2 through

5—addresses a key area of families in global context: demography, culture, violence, and employment. The final chapter reviews some of the international and supranational policies that are "positioning families in global landscapes."

I remain fortunate to be part of a network of academic and other professionals who not only have specialized expertise on global families but communicate their knowledge in the most compelling, graceful, passionate prose. Each chapter ends with an original essay authored by one of these discerning scholars.

Writing on globalization is a sobering business. As I wrote these chapters, however, I had before me the many images of the old and new immigrant families I encounter every day in Minneapolis/St. Paul—a globalizing city if ever there was one! I also had in mind students, colleagues, and friends whose own family experiences with globalization inspire in me a sense of respect and admiration for their resilient valor. To Ani, Awa, Bao, Barbara, Boonmae, Dina, Elena, Henry, Jacquez, Jessica, Jim, Jonathan, Jose, Lashere, Lea, Liam, Luis, Mathew, Mayem, Paola, Pedro, Putt, Richard, Thanos, Xia, Xong, and many others of Argentina, Armenia, Cambodia, Croatia, Cyprus, Egypt, Germany, Ireland, Israel, Italy, Liberia, Puerto Rico, Romania, Sierra Leone, Somalia, Thailand, Vietnam, and so many societies around the world: I pray this book honors your global family stories.

Acknowledgments

The original call to participate in this promising series came from Susan Ferguson of Grinnell College. My first earnest thanks, therefore, goes to Susan, general editor for the series *Contemporary Family Perspectives,* who offered me substantive and editorial criticism that sustained the preparation of this manuscript. Susan, as well as David Repetto, senior editor at SAGE, saw the potential of a manuscript that went beyond the usual comparative perspective on families to a work that breaks new ground. I also prize the editorial assistance extended first by Maggie Stanley and then by Lydia Balian, as well as Meg Granger's copyediting. This edition also reflects criticisms offered by five thoughtful, anonymous reviewers.

Early in my career at the University of St. Thomas, my colleagues in the International Education Program enriched my experience with global families. I am grateful for the exceptional support of that office over the years: funds to participate in international seminars, grants to research teaching and learning abroad, symposia and workshops (often accompanied by delicious international cuisine), as well as opportunities to take sociology "on the road" and across the sea.

Likewise, in the Luann Dummer Center for Women at the University of St. Thomas I have an enthusiastic community that has buoyed my development as a feminist scholar for almost two decades. The Luann Dummer Center provided me with curriculum and professional development grants that served as both the seed from which this book sprouted and the support to sustain my scholarship in the field. The center continues to serve as a sounding board for my professional work.

I continue to benefit from colleagues who have extended themselves as critical, enthusiastic readers, resources, and the most supportive friends. These include Paola Ehrmantraut (University of St. Thomas), Morten Ender (United States Military Academy), Amelia Wilkes Karraker (University of Wisconsin), Sister Margaret Kvasnicka (Sister of St. Joseph), and Susan Smith-Cunnien (University of St. Thomas). Reference librarian Jan Orf provided exceptional reference, technical, and clerical assistance. Cara Molinari assisted me with fact-checking. As always, Mark, Miriam, and Gretel patiently assisted in checking citations and references, reading the occasional passage, and repeatedly indulging me in "just 10 more minutes. . . ."

Finally, I have been blessed to be enmeshed in a loving, if geographically dispersed, family. My parents, Mary Gold Mitchell Wilkes and Herbert W. Wilkes, Jr., introduced me to global travel before I could walk. My favorite global travel partner, Mark Karraker, is always ready for another trip. Finally, in this book I honor Amelia Wilkes Karraker and Miriam Wilkes Karraker, two young women whose respectful consciousness of societies and cultures and efforts to build relationships across borders inspire me and give me hope for this world even on a day with the saddest global headlines.

While any errors are my own, I extend my sincere gratitude to all named above for their support in this work.

About the Author

Since 1990 I have been on the faculty at the University of St. Thomas in St. Paul, Minnesota, where I am Professor of Sociology and Criminal Justice and Family Business Center Fellow. I earned a Doctor of Philosophy at the University of Minnesota, following a Master of Science at North Carolina State University and a Bachelor of Arts at Clemson University. My degrees are all in sociology, with supporting coursework in anthropology, education, history, international development, psychology, and women's studies.

My interest in the effects of globalization on families is rooted in my own life experience. I grew up in a military family, spending the majority of my childhood and adolescence in Germany with travels through Europe and the former Soviet Union. I have always been drawn to research questions around the impacts of social structure—gender, race, social class, and global location—on quality of life. Currently, I am studying social networks and social capital, especially across religious organizations and civil society, with a particular interest in family businesses ("family values, business virtues"). I teach undergraduate courses in sociology, family studies, and women's studies. In addition to courses on the sociology of marriages and families and the capstone course in family studies, I teach a course on global perspectives on gender, one on sociological theory, and the introductory course in sociology (the last with a community-based learning emphasis).

I am honored to have received my university's Aquinas Scholars Honors Program Teacher of the Year Award. I am past president of Alpha Kappa Delta, the international sociology honor society. With Janet R. Grochowski, I am coauthor of *Families With Futures: A Survey of Family Studies Into the Twenty-First Century* (2012, Routledge).

I live in Minneapolis, Minnesota, with Mark Karraker, Gretel the sheltie, and a fine circle of friends. (Daughters Amelia and Miriam are graduate and undergraduate college students, respectively.) Besides cooking, gardening, and enjoying music and theatre in the Twin Cities, I would still rather be no other place than on a terrazzo in Assisi, sipping a glass of wine while meditating on the Umbrian plain.

1

Introduction

Families in Global Context

In 1960, the 6-year-old daughter of a career officer in the U.S. Army watched as dirty, shabbily dressed children about her age pulled discarded items from the garbage cans surrounding the apartment building where she lived in Nürmberg, Germany. She observed the same children, who appeared to be unsupervised by any adults, stash away some of the retrieved items and, to her revulsion, eat bits of food they found in the cans.

More than four decades later, the same woman, now a college professor in her 50s, stood in the Piazza di Santa Marie Trastevere in Rome, Italy, fending off two very persistent Roma (more familiarly known by the derogatory term *gypsy*) boys begging for money. A colleague who works with children in Rome later told her that the marks she noticed on the children's faces and hands were cigarette burns, most likely inflicted by their parents. In the transient, nationless communities of the Roma—despised by much of the Italian society in which they live for the moment—when children return home with less than what they were expected to beg (or steal) for the day, they are harshly punished (P. S. Moffett, personal communication, 2000).

What puts families in positions in which their most vulnerable members must scavenge for basic necessities in others' refuse? Under what kinds of social conditions must children approach strangers with pitiful appeals for money or suffer the consequences from their own families?

I know other, more heartening stories of families traversing global milieus. An increasing number of my university students come from Armenia, China, or Kuwait to study at our campus. Others from Guatemala,

1

Korea, or Romania have been adopted into American families. Some of my students' families were economically displaced from former East Germany, Lithuania, or Mexico. Others have fled embattled countries such as Croatia, Sierra Leone, and Somalia. Along the way, some have been refugees and asylees, passing through Europe, North America, and Southeast Asia.

These students may represent the first generation in their families to speak English or to complete high school, let alone pursue a college degree. Their families arrived in the United States seeking what immigrants to this country have always sought: freedom and opportunity. I cherish little more than stories of their successes and happiness as they share news of their career achievements and postgraduate plans, but I also find joy in their continued connections with extended kin and the new families they form as they move into adulthood.

A More Global Milieu

These students and their stories provide firsthand evidence that the world is not only an international but also a transnational place. A visit to a public high school, a trip to a shopping mall, or a stroll down a street in even a Midwestern city in the United States reveals how globally diverse American society is becoming. A walk across my own campus (a private, Catholic college in St. Paul, Minnesota—often noted as one of the "whitest" states in the nation) is like a convocation at the United Nations, with a scattering of voices speaking not only American English but also Arabic, Hmong, Karekare (a language of Nigeria), Spanish, Russian, and English with an Irish lilt.

What then are the impacts of international, transnational, and global forces on families? What is the quality of family life in a world in which national borders are so permeable and global forces directly affect families in profound ways?

In the western hemisphere at least, as trade barriers have been lowered the wealthiest nations have become more integrated in a worldwide economy. Innovations in information technologies make rapid movement of capital and services across borders ever more possible. These changes in the global milieu certainly benefit the most privileged societies and their families through lower prices on luxury goods and services, from the latest flat-screen television to strawberries enjoyed during a Minnesota winter.

In Western nations, the competition fostered by global markets can also increase the purchasing power of low-income families, while extending a check on inflation and boosting returns in the stock market. In poorer countries, globalization has generally increased family wealth, thus decreasing the incentive for parents to put their children to work and increasing the inducement for children to be in school (Bhagwati 2004). In places such as

China and India, globalization has created new markets for goods and services while reducing poverty for some. If those changes make nations more interdependent and the world a more stable place, perhaps some families' exposure to war and other armed conflicts can be reduced.

However, some scholars paint a grimmer picture of the effects of globalization on societies and families. They see nations, communities, families, and individuals shrouded under an increasingly oppressive, even malevolent, global cloud. They see the market forces of globalization facilitating exploitation of the most vulnerable members of society on an even larger scale than previously possible.

For example, according to the International Labor Organization, 100 million to 200 million children under 15 years of age are working—most (almost 95 percent) working children are in poor countries, and half are in Asia (Bhagwati 2004). As companies outsource and relocate offshore, wage growth stagnates and health and retirement costs and risks are shifted to workers (Obama 2006). Workers compelled to cross borders to meet growing demands for agricultural and industrial labor often work under the most inhumane conditions. Some women and children are trafficked and enslaved into prostitution.

Bhagwati (2004) acknowledges the "perils of gung-ho international financial capitalism" (p. 30). However, he sees the hazards of globalization as exaggerated and critics of globalization as "alarmist." He offers a "defense of globalization" in his book of that title and argues that antiglobalization sentiments mask anticapitalist, anticorporate, and anti-American (or at least anti-Western) prejudices.

As the author of *Global Families,* I disagree. Even some supporters of globalization find specious the argument that increased global competition will reduce structural inequalities in society, for example by ensuring that prejudice and discrimination will be too competitively costly for firms (Bhagwati 2004). To the contrary, capitalist employers seeking to minimize costs and maximize profits while operating in global markets can effectively outbid employers in home countries for cheap labor. Further, the supply of workers, especially women, willing to work for exploitative wages inadequate to support themselves and their dependents still far exceeds the supply of positions at the bottom of the employment ladder (i.e., those with the lowest wages, the least security, and the most dangerous working conditions). Also, as discussed in Chapter 4, I offer human trafficking as the epitome of the worst side of global economics. Consequently, the broad consequences of these and other risky global practices are disproportionately borne by workers and their families in the least-advantaged societies.

Thus, a primary thesis of *Global Families* is that, in the 21st century, economic, political, cultural, and other social forces trespass national, regional, and other borders in profound ways unanticipated even a few decades ago. Legal and illegal migration between nations means that families may call multiple countries or even continents "home." Worldwide revolutions in mass media and consumerism raise the specter of cultural homogenization and challenge traditional family norms and values. Families continue to inherit the legacies of colonialism, armed conflict, and other violence. Transnational commerce and differences in life chances between the most- and least-advantaged societies create wide discrepancies in the supply of and demand for human labor, including the care work of families. Increasingly, policymakers must contend with the effects of economic, political, cultural, and other social development on families around the globe.

In the first pages of this first chapter, I call for scholarship on families to be framed around an inclusive definition of family that takes into account social change while moving beyond a comparative to a global perspective. I define globalization and explore three competing "debates" on globalization. I offer a sketch of theories drawn from sociology and family studies that, when coupled with postmodern theory and feminism, help us describe, explain, and possibly predict something about the effects of globalization on families. I close this first chapter with an overview of the material to come in the following five chapters and an essay authored by a scholar who serves as an "expert witness" on global families in Australia.

Family: From Comparative to Global Perspectives

For all the variation in cultures and societies across the globe, families provide certain widespread experiences for their members and meet some common requirements for societies. Murdock (1949) offered the classic articulation of a comparative perspective in the middle of the past century. From his analysis of the institution of family across hundreds of societies, Murdock concluded that every society contains family units organized around common residence, economic cooperation, and sexual reproduction. Thus structured, the family meets critical needs/functions for both family members and societies, including the care and socialization of infants and children.

Murdock's (1949) functional analysis can be criticized on a number of fronts. First, his traditional definition of family as two or more adults in a sexual relationship fails to capture the rich variety in the intimate bonds that function as family. Second, societies vary in the centrality of the family in meeting critical social needs. In many societies the family extends to a wide network of kith and kin and shares the production and distribution of goods and services, the regulation of sexualities, and the socialization and care of children and other family members with religion, government, education, and other institutions.

I favor a more inclusive definition of family, one that better captures family diversity. In *Global Families, family* refers to a small group organized around kinship, often (but not always) involving some form of marriage, which is often (but, again, not always) between one man and one woman. In my definition, families may also include more extended networks of what Stack (1974) called fictive kin. Like families under Murdock's definition, families in my definition can provide emotional and physical care for their members, including the youngest members of society—newborns and children—but also elders, the disabled, the infirm, and other dependents. These families are a primary (but not the only) means of performing socialization and other functions in society.

Global Families stretches the definition of family beyond a shared household and bonds formed by marriage, blood, or adoption (the definition favored by the U.S. Bureau of the Census). As described in Karraker and Grochowski's (2012) *Families With Futures: A Survey of Family Studies Into the Twenty-First Century,* my definition includes intimate relationships among individuals who play significant roles of support in one another's lives over extended periods of time, often over a lifetime. We are all familiar with these relationships: the girlfriend you can call on anytime, the man who has been your friend since preschool, the "aunts" and "uncles" who have no such official status but nonetheless have rights and responsibilities regarding you and yours. While this definition may be messier than traditional definitions, such a dynamic definition of family enables scholars to encompass the kinds of relationships increasingly found not only across but within societies.

Although social scientists debate the definition of the family and the precise functions the institution of the family fills in society, virtually everyone agrees that the family is in transition. Further, social scientists recognize that the velocity of social change around the globe in the 21st century is shaping the family as an institution in revolutionary ways. With the tremendous divergences in structure and function exhibited by families worldwide, societies in the 21st century are undergoing what Giddens (2001) has termed a "global revolution in family and personal life" (p. 17).

Silverstein and Auerbach (2005) identified five major trends regarding families in the past century:

1. A movement from homogeneity to diversity

2. A movement from stability to change

3. A movement from gendered parenting to transgendered families

4. A movement from male dominance to greater egalitarianism

5. A movement from homogeneity to diversity

Silverstein and Auerbach applied those trends primarily to families in the United States, but the same trends can be applied to families in many parts of the world today. Throughout the world, diversity in family forms is expanding to include new patterns of cohabitation and childbearing, as well as extended family forms. Unmarried cohabitation is supplanting marriage, even with the presence of children, in many parts of the world. Extended kin relations are becoming less central in many societies, perhaps dangerously so in places where governments have reduced or never supported social safety nets for the increasing numbers of people living alone or living longer. Finally, "queerness is now global" (Cruz-Malavé and Manalansan 2002:1). The globalization of lesbian and gay politics and the increasing visibility of queer sexualities and cultures worldwide (Adam, Duyvendak, and Krouwel 1999a; Binnie 2004) challenges the old assumption of a married man and woman and their biological offspring as the elemental family unit.

As parenting relationships in some parts of the world shift from traditional gender and sexual roles to include dual-work couples and those led by LGBTQ (lesbian, gay, bisexual, transgender, or questioning) parents, greater role sharing and even degendered parenting characterize an increasing proportion of families. Changes in women's education, employment, and other roles and movements for children's rights proceed apace with the erosion of patriarchy, the ideological framework that has characterized human societies throughout history.

Thus, transitions into, within, and from relationships vary both across and within societies. Changes such as later age at first marriage, as well as increased rates of marital dissolution (separation and divorce), indicate not only elasticity within individual families but also less social predictability in family structures. Further, socioeconomic factors, including gender, class, and other inequalities, and social policies (discussed in Chapter 6) all have a significant bearing on variations in families both across and within societies (Cooke and Baxter 2010).

The viewpoint of families as shifting from stability to change—sometimes conceptualized as one of the "culture wars" because of the highly charged, political nature of the debate (Berger and Berger 1983)—reflects greater realism in popular views of families. But romance about the family dies hard.

Skolnick and Skolnick (2001) argue that four myths contribute to a romantic view of the family as a safe, secure haven for children and adults: (1) the myth of the universal nuclear family, (2) the myth of family harmony, (3) the myth of parental determinism, and (4) the myth of a stable, harmonious past. Such myths have been discounted by historian Stephanie Coontz in her series of best-selling books, *The Way We Never Were* (1992), *The Way We Really Are* (1997), and *Marriage, a History: How Love Conquered Marriage* (2005). In contrast to simplistic views of family, social historians—among them

Phillipe Aries (1960) in *L'Enfant et la Vie Familiale sous l'Ancien Régime* (published in the United States under the title *Centuries of Childhood: A History of Family Life*)—have revealed that childhood and family life in Western Europe have often been anything but blissful and innocent. In case any doubt remains, news accounts of families across the world disrupted and rendered ineffective by famine, natural disaster, war, and social crises, as well as those that willfully exploit and oppress their own members, leave only the most naïve to adhere to the popular image of the traditional family as an integrated unit that functions successfully as in some mythical, simpler time.

In the essay at the end of Chapter 6, Freeman argues that one of the most important tasks of supranational organizations is to hold societies accountable for the well-being of families and their members. Doing so requires seeing "the way we really are," to use Coontz's (1997) phrase. The comparative tradition on families can be a significant aid in that regard.

The Comparative Tradition

Interest in the effects of globalization on families is a relatively late development among family scholars, but family scholarship has a long-standing tradition of comparative study across space and time in anthropology, history, sociology, and other social sciences. Family and kinship structures were keystones in Murdock's (1949) Cross-Cultural Survey (cited earlier) and the foundation for the later Human Relations Area Files (Murdock 1982). Also, the work of the late Tamara Hareven (1977, 1982, 2000) and others further reveals the value to family sociology of the study of historical forces, especially in areas such as the family and individual life course.

Goode's (1963) *World Revolution and Family Patterns* serves as a classic scholarly effort on world families, a tradition continued through Hutter's (1981) *The Changing Family: Comparative Perspectives*, Bryceson and Vuorela's (2002) *The Transnational Family*, Adams and Trost's (2005) *Handbook of World Families*, and others. In the first decade, textbooks and readers such as Leeder's (2004) *The Family in Global Perspective: A Gendered Journey*, Roopnarine and Gielen's (2005) *Families in Global Perspectives*, Ingoldsby and Smith's (2006) *Families in Global and Multicultural Perspective*, Trask and Hamon's (2007) *Cultural Diversity and Families*, and Hennon and Wilson's (2008) *Families in a Global Context* are witness to the value of comparative approaches in family studies.

Special issues on international perspectives on families in the *Journal of Marriage and the Family* (2004), as well as the establishment of dedicated journals (e.g., *International Family Studies, Journal of Comparative Family Studies*) affirm the value family studies scholars place on international and comparative approaches. Likewise, specialized divisions in professional associations (e.g., the International Section of the National Council on Family Relations) affirm that these approaches have become institutionalized in the social–scientific study of families.

Among textbooks, volumes such as Scott, Treas, and Richards's (2004) *The Blackwell Companion to the Sociology of Families* have included large sections on "Families in a Global World." Yet the focus remains on North American and European families. Other works, such as Kamerman and Kahn's (1997) *Family Change and Family Policies in Great Britain, Canada, New Zealand, and the United States*, are typical of much of the comparative writing on families. Only more recently have volumes, such as Robila's (2004) *Families in Eastern Europe*, examined families in non-Western regions of the world. Still, many nationalities, especially those in Africa and Southeast Asia, remain less frequently represented in the literature.

Part of the reason for the inattention to non-Western families lies in the nationality of family scholars and their institutions. Adams (2004) notes that productive family scholars are plentiful in Western societies, as well as India, Japan, and Taiwan, along with a "scattering of professionals throughout the Middle East, Sub-Saharan Africa, Russia, China, and Latin America" (p. 1077). In other regions of the world, family scholars are considerably less abundant. Adams suggests that this underrepresentation relates to communication, money, and values. Family scholars may be active and even publishing in their own venues in underrepresented societies, but their work does not enter into the larger stream of family scholarship if those scholars are not in communication with outside, especially Western, scholars. Also, research— from research design and collection through data analysis and dissemination— is expensive and thus limited by local fiscal constraints, especially in non-Western countries. Finally, research may be restricted in more subtle ways by conservative political, religious, or social values that constrain analysis of families and family problems in many parts of the world.

Not surprisingly, then, family sociology gives the appearance of having a decidedly Western bias. Further, Edgar (2004) charges that study of the family has increasingly come to emphasize individualism and free-market liberalism, as represented by the personal psychology and concern with self-actualization characteristic of Western societies. According to Edgar, even scholars such as Beck (1998, 2001) and Giddens (1992), whose work represents postmodern and often global concerns, are "too dismissive of the still-important collective contexts in which the risks of biography are mastered" (Edgar 2004:7).

Beyond national and regional gaps, research is sparse on certain categories of families. Families of the very wealthy and those living in rural areas offer researchers challenges in terms of social or geographic accessibility, but our knowledge also is limited concerning the families of poor urbanites and other oppressed groups, as well as the families of refugees and other nomads (Adams 2004). Such omissions and bias reflect not only Western viewpoints but also white privilege, serving to effectively silence the voices of families on the margins. This costs family scholars understanding of the influence of legal, religious, and other social–structural forces and economic and other status inequalities on families and their members.

Hollinger (2007) reminds us that the road to an authentically global view of families is difficult.

> The most seasoned of diplomats, anthropologists, and development workers are often caught by surprise at the stubborn persistence of their own ethnocentric beliefs and judgments. Even after such individuals have rationally and cognitively rejected their own judgmental thinking, they may still find themselves repelled when encountering certain traditional family practices. . . . It is easy for westerners to dismiss them out of hand. Indeed, few of us ever fully transcend the delimiting vision of own cultures. (P. 245)

As depicted in Figure 1.1, cultural competence and sensitivity is a long developmental process, requiring that one recognize and claim one's own ethnocentrism, adopt a position of cultural relativism, and reflect on ethical engagement before initiating social change.

Figure 1.1 Developmental Model for Ethical Reflection Across Cultures

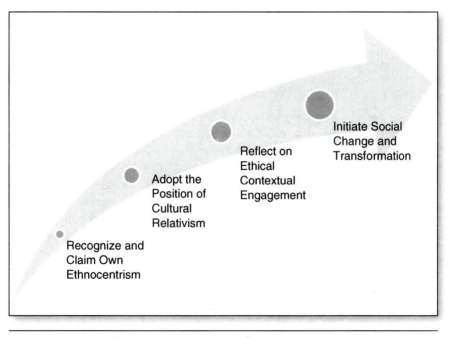

SOURCE: Adapted with permission from Hollinger (2007).

Although scholarship on non-Western societies is scarce and ethnocentrism remains a persistent hazard, cross-cultural, historical, and other comparative studies enhance our knowledge of the macro social forces that shape the family across societies. Such studies deepen our understanding of both that which is unique about some families within specific societies and that which is common about families across societies. In other words, comparative research promises to reveal both variations among and contrasts within cultures, while providing insights into familial and societal influences on individuals. A global approach can complement and extend the strong comparative tradition in family studies.

Toward a Global Perspective

While the institution is undergoing dramatic change across the globe, the family remains a—arguably, *the*—central force in social life in every society. The family is vital to the operation of society and critical to the formation of economic capital, human capital, cultural capital, and social capital. However, comparative studies or even a cross-cultural or cross-national approach do not do justice to the need for a critical synthesis of family scholarship that addresses the effects of globalization on family systems. Too often even compendia such as Quah's (2008) *Families in Asia* provide rich comparative analyses of families (which we know are touched by global forces) but make little or no reference to the processes of globalization.

Such neglect of globalization in family studies is unfortunate. "When family research remains fixed to the container model of the nation-state, it becomes increasingly unable to understand and explain the situation of families in today's interconnected world" (Beck and Beck-Gernsheim 2010:401).

Global Families begins to remedy a gap in scholarly literature by focusing on the effects of global processes on families across societies.

Family structures may be relatively more traditional in the more remote regions of the planet (Gielen 1993). Families are affected by modernization, as when populations migrate from rural to urban areas. (Migration across national boundaries is discussed in Chapter 2 and revealed in Kvasnicka's essay on women seeking refuge in a home for immigrant women in St. Paul, Minnesota.) However, strains toward assimilation into Western society may be contested by individuals and families who fear alienation from values and norms that traditionally guided family life. (Chapter 3 and the essay by Abdi at the end of that chapter address such challenges among Somali families who find themselves in North America.) Modernization shapes other aspects of family life, for example, as employment patterns become more complex.

(Transnational employment is discussed in Chapter 5 and illustrated by Dreby's essay on the life of a Mexican mother working in the United States.) Such are the forces of globalization.

Global Families contends that the changes facing families today are not only national; they are also global, encompassing social forces that transcend national and even broader regional or continental borders. These forces have the potential to advance and empower or exploit and oppress families and their members, as well as whole societies. As described in the United Nations (1999b) Human Development Report *Globalization With a Human Face*:

> Global markets, global technology, global ideas and global solidarity can enrich the lives of people everywhere. . . . Globalization has swung open the door to opportunities. . . . But markets can go too far and squeeze the non-market activities so vital for human development. . . . Globalization is also increasing human insecurity as the spread of global crime, disease and financial volatility outpaces actions to tackle them. (P. 1)

In *Global Families,* I explore issues through which globalization can enrich but also too often squeeze families, increasing their risk even in the face of national, international, and transnational policies to assist them.

This global perspective on families has many strata. On the one hand, the families that are the subject of this book are *transnational*. Transnationalism is "a social process in which . . . social fields cross geographic, cultural, and political borders" (Schiller, Basch, and Blanc-Szanton 1992a:ix). Taking a cue from Bose and Kim's (2009) transnational approach to gender research, a transnational approach to families emphasizes the similarities and differences in research on families across the globe. Transnational families are those that span borders as a result of immigration or dislocation, sometimes enabled by technology. Members of transnational families act, decide, feel, and express identities across social networks that traverse two (or more) societies, often simultaneously.

At another, broader level, families are *global*. That is, every family on earth is more or less touched by global economic and political realities but also by the globalization of culture and other social systems. For example, in the essay that follows this chapter, "Globalization and Family Down Under," Janet Grochowski offers an illustration of the particular ways in which globalization is revealed in Australian families. Using data from the Centre for Social Research at the Australian National University, Grochowski describes Australia as a society with a uniquely global history, both confronting and embracing the global forces acting on Australian families.

Grochowski discusses how Australians' attitudes toward family diversity in particular are linked to their society's complex global context.

Globalization as an Analytical Framework

Consideration of global families requires an understanding of globalization. Because globalization is a relatively new paradigm for family scholars, in the following section, I outline the definitions and debate surrounding globalization. First, I provide some background on the treatment of global concerns in sociology.

The consequences of macro social change for the quality of social life have long been major themes in sociology. For example, Durkheim (1897/1951) noted the extent to which rapid social changes, such as those caused either by sudden disaster or unexpected prosperity, compromise social solidarity and contribute to social instability. *Anomia*[1] is the resulting sense that familiar customs and standards can no longer be relied on to give meaning to and control everyday life (Karraker [Wilkes] 1975).

Other frameworks also provide a backdrop for examination of social change on a worldwide scale. Classic modernization theory (e.g., Rostow 1961) views traditional norms and values as inhibiting or repressing social change. From this perspective, families in a society in the earliest stages of demographic transition (a concept discussed in Chapter 2)—one with a high birth rate but also a high death rate—have difficulty putting resources aside for the future. When coupled with high infant and other mortality rates, members of such societies may hold a fatalistic outlook on hardship and resist conserving resources, including "saving for a rainy day." In those societies, the "rainy day" is outside the window and, to be sure, will be there again tomorrow. This theory holds that societies must surrender traditional ways of life in favor of modern culture, institutions, and technologies, which in turn favor economic and social investment and are premised on values favoring optimism, a Western work ethic, and, most of all, capitalism.

As demonstrated in the dramatic economic growth in some East Asian nations, including some former European colonies, political stability,

---

[1]While many contemporary writers use the term *anomie* (most prominent among them Merton, 1968; Durkheim, 1897/1951; and some more recent scholars, including Srole, 1956, who developed the Srole Anomia Scale), Mizruchi (1960), Miller and Butler (1966), Karraker [Wilkes] (1975), Fischer and Srole (1978), Bilsen and de Witte (2001), Rippi (2003), and others have preferred the term *anomia* to refer to this persistent sense of interpersonal alienation and normlessness.

centralized planning, and social programming may be critical for modernization (Giddens, Duneier, and Appelbaum 2006). Wealthy nations support modernization in other countries through such supranational organizations as the International Monetary Fund and the World Bank, which finances programs aimed at economic and social development in less-developed nations. Economic policies are often linked to policies targeting families, often specifically through requirements aimed at population control. As less-developed nations reduce population growth, they are better able to invest in economic development while institutionalizing values and norms common to more-developed (and capitalist) societies. What follows is a push toward the high standard of living and high levels of mass consumption characteristic of more-developed, high-income societies, but perhaps at the cost of turmoil in family relationships (Rostow 1961).

World systems theory takes another view on global change and the relations among less- and more-developed societies. In particular, Wallerstein (1996) emphasizes the global interdependence of economic systems, viewing the world as divided into those who own and control the means of production and the distribution of goods and services (capitalists) and those who do not. From this perspective, goods and labor operate in world markets shaped by economic and political competition (and sometimes cooperation) among the most powerful nations. These processes result in a three-tiered world system: (1) core nations, which reap the greatest benefits; (2) periphery, mostly agricultural nations, which are exploited to the advantage of the core nations; and (3) semiperiphery, semi-industrialized nations, which sit at a point of wealth between the core and the periphery.

Historically, global capitalism created economic and political systems through which the most powerful nations colonized weaker nations in order to secure raw materials, as well as slave and wage labor, and monopolize industrial production and markets. Further, as described in Chapter 4, colonialism and the often ensuing violence and exploitation have had significant, often tragic consequences for the sexual, marital, and other social orders that shape family life. In the 20th century, colonization was replaced by multinational and transnational corporations that still exploit resources and labor in poor countries, often with the collaboration of powerful economic and political interests. Local economies in poor countries cannot compete in such a global market, and so poor countries are maintained in a state of economic and political dependency on the wealthier countries. The result is a world system of dependency, in which nations are linked in exploitative global commodity chains of labor, production, and consumption. In Chapter 5, I describe one such type of chain, global care, which occurs when women from periphery countries leave their own families to care for families in core countries.

The effects of rapid social change on a global scale are evident at both macrosocial and microsocial levels, in both institutions and everyday life (Ray 2006).

> Changes in intimate aspects of personal life . . . are directly tied to the establishment of social connections of very wide scope. . . . For the first time in human history, self and society are interrelated in a global milieu. (Giddens 1991:32)

Global Families articulates the far-reaching effects of globalization on that most primary aspect of social and personal life—family. However, with rare exception (e.g., Trask 2010), the vernacular of globalization theory has not yet permeated family sociology or family studies. In the following section I define globalization as a critical concept for family scholars. I also delineate the debate among those who remain skeptical about the place of globalization on the world stage, those who embrace globalization as a critical paradigm, and those who recognize the significance of global forces, yet acknowledge the extent to which regional, national, and even local forces continue to shape social life.

Globalization Defined

Globalization conventionally refers to the development of economic, political, and cultural systems that extend worldwide. These systems and the consequent relationships result in a world system that, in turn, can be seen as constituting a single social order (Giddens et al. 2006). Such a global social order is autonomous and independent of any single nation or region (Appadurai 1996; Bauman 1998).

Globalization theorists (e.g., Ritzer 2007, 2010) often emphasize one of three frames: economic, political, or cultural. Table 1.1 summarizes these three dimensions of globalization theory.

Economic theories often focus on transnational capitalism, including transnational corporations, and the labor markets they create. For example, Sklair (2002) takes a neo-Marxist economic approach, examining how globalization promotes the formation of a transnational capitalist class and a worldwide culture of consumption.

Political theorists, such as Rosenau (2003), see globalization as advancing both "distant proximities" (a sense of that which is remote is also nearby) and "fragmentation" (a situation in which the world is simultaneously globalizing, centralizing, and integrating as it is localizing, decentralizing,

Table 1.1   Economic, Political, and Cultural Dimensions of Globalization

Dimension	Key Concepts and Generalizations
Economic	Transnational capitalism, including transnational corporations, transnational class structure, and the culture-ideology of consumption is contributing to emerging global socialism (Sklair 2002).
	Capitalist imperialism will be replaced by global empire (Hardt and Negri 2000, 2004).
Political/institutional	The world is increasingly decentralizing, fragmenting, and localizing while simultaneously centralizing, integrating, and globalizing (Rosenau 2003).
Cultural differentialism	Lasting differences among cultures are little affected by globalization (Huntington 1996).
Cultural convergence	Globalization is leading to increasing homogeneity among world cultures through greater emphasis on efficiency, calculability, predictability, control, and rationality (Nederveen Pieterse 2004; Ritzer 2004a).
Cultural hybridization	Glocalization and creolization contribute to cultural hybridization (Appadurai 1996).

and fragmenting). Political theorists see these seemingly contradictory processes as facilitated by new microelectronic technologies, the erosion of territoriality, and increasing subgroup formation across historic political boundaries (Ritzer 2007).

Some cultural theorists underscore cultural differentialism. They argue that globalization has little effect on the deep differences that exist within and between societies. Other cultural theorists highlight cultural convergence, the idea that globalization is resulting in an increasing cultural similarity among societies. They are reflected in Ritzer's (2004b) "McDonaldization" thesis, which emphasizes the efficiency in production and the predictability of product (such as a McDonald's hamburger). Still other cultural theorists (e.g., Nederveen Pieterse 2004) see not differentialism or convergence but, rather, cultural hybridization in globalization. For these theorists, globalization contributes to the generation of new cultures composed of creative mixtures of different cultures brought into contact with one another (Appadurai 1996).

Some feminist scholars are challenging the economic, political, and cultural emphasis in globalization studies. In her book subtitled *Rethinking Globalization,* Desai (2009) calls attention to the microlevel aspects of globalization to better understand the effect of individuals on globalization. She argues that "it is women, as cross-border traders, transnational activists, and *Modemmujers,* who are shaping processes of globalization in a specifically gendered way" (p. 3). Desai is optimistic that such a microlevel, gendered focus will not only inform scholarship on globalization but also facilitate social justice movements around the globe.

Globalization results in the "widening, deepening, and speeding up of worldwide connectedness in all aspects of contemporary social life" (Held et al. 1999:2). Globalization speaks to the extent to which local events take on global significance across broadening geography and expanding chronology with increasingly dense networks and relationships beyond national borders. Consistent with Desai's microsocial emphasis, globalization presumes a replacement of local affinities and associations with global connections and networks, often disseminated and perhaps promoted by a widening system of global communications. Tomlinson (1999) describes this as a "rapidly developing and ever-densening network of interconnections and interdependences [that] characterize modern social life" (p. 2). Where Giddens sees an increasing collision between fundamentalism and cosmopolitanism, Tomlinson predicts the evolution of what he calls a global cosmopolitan society.

From this perspective, globalization involves the motion and absorption of goods and capital, politics and power, information and technologies worldwide. However, globalization also involves the transmission of pollution, crime, and other social problems across and beyond national, regional, and other spatial borders. Environmental hazards generated in one part of the world certainly show no respect for national sovereignty. Trafficking in drugs, guns, and human beings (as described in Blank's essay at the end of Chapter 4) is profitable precisely because material and human commodities are so easy to transport and market without regard for the same national borders. The persistence of widespread violence in some African, Asian, Central and South American, and Middle Eastern countries must be seen at least in part as grounded in transnational and increasingly worldwide systems of economic despair, political enmity, religious antagonisms, and cultural collisions in a global world.

In conclusion, Eitzen and Baca Zinn (2011) frame the implications of globalization as follows:

- The world is becoming "smaller" and we are becoming more interdependent.
- Globalization is a process involving immigration and travel, economies and consumption.
- The effects of globalization are not only economic but cultural, political, and social.
- The impacts of globalization are felt at the intimate level of the everyday activities of individuals, their families, institutions, and societies.

Eitzen and Baca Zinn (2011) also remind us that the experience of globalization varies. "It expands opportunities and enhances prosperity for some while leading others into poverty and hopelessness" (p. 2). In some societies, globalization is associated with an increased standard of living and a reduction in the gap between the poorest and the wealthiest families, greater access to education and health care, improvements in the status of women, and longer life expectancy. In other societies, globalization is associated with growth in income inequality, environmental degradation, and pressures to emigrate, leaving the most vulnerable family members behind (Wilson and Hennon 2008).

The "Globalization Debate"

The concept, processes, consequences, and social and familial implications of globalization are contested. Three positions on the significance of globalization in today's world are articulated by the skeptics, the hyperglobalists, and the transformationalists. Table 1.2 summarizes these positions.

Global skeptics debate the novelty of globalization as a force in historic social change. They note that economic interdependence, as well as international migration, trade, conquest, and other global phenomena, have existed in other periods, shaping the histories of such divergent locations as Buenos Aires and Bombay, Cairo and Chicago, Mogadishu and Moscow, Shanghai and Sydney.

An aptly titled article in *The Economist* presents the case that the level of integration across the world is actually very low. For example, only 3 percent of individuals live outside their country of birth and only 2 percent of students attend universities outside their home countries. On economic indicators, only 7 percent of rice is traded across borders, only 7 percent of directors of Standard & Poor 500 companies are foreigners, and exports account for only 20 percent of the global gross domestic product. Only 1 percent of American companies have any foreign operations. Furthermore, "some of the most vital arteries of globalization are badly clogged: air travel

Table 1.2   Three Positions in the "Globalization Debate"

Position	On Globalization	Representative Scholars
Skeptics	Globalization is a counterfeit concept that exaggerates the importance of international economics and obscures the importance of national governmental controls and regionalization.	Boyer and Drache, Hirst and Thompson, Huntington
Hyperglobalists	Escalating global capitalism increasingly affects other aspects of social life, creating a more borderless, transnational, and denationalized world. National economies and governments are subordinated and diffused by hybridization.	Appadurai, Greider, Hardt and Negri, Nederveen Pieterse, Ohmae
Transformationalists	The world is becoming interconnected to an unprecedented degree across not only economic and political but also cultural and other social systems. This global society is more uncertain, risky, and stratified.	Giddens, Ritzer, Rosenau

SOURCES: Adapted from Appadurai (1996), Boyer and Drache (1996), Castells (2004), Cochrane and Paine (2000), Giddens (2000), Greider (1997), Hardt and Negri (2000, 2004), Held et al. (1999), Hirst and Thompson (1992), Huntington (1996), Nederveen Pieterse (2004), Ohmae (1995), Ritzer (1993, 1995, 1996, 2004b, 2005b, 2007, 2010), and Rosenau (1997).

is restricted by bilateral treaties and ocean shipping is dominated by cartels" (p. 72).

Skeptics of globalization (e.g., Boyer and Drache 1996; Hirst and Thompson 1992) view globalization as a counterfeit concept that exaggerates the power of international economies while obscuring the control still exercised by regional and national governments. Skeptics see not a globally integrated system but increasing internationalization in the form of contacts among national economies. They see internationalization as accompanied by persistent inequality between more-developed and less-developed nations, as well as increasing regionalization that results in fragmented ethnic and cultural blocs, especially in opposition to Westernization (Castells 2004; Held et al. 1999).

Skeptics argue that not massive globalizing forces but the familiar— geographic proximity and cultural and economic ties, including common language, shared colonial past, and membership in a trading block— continue to shape social interaction and societal exchange. A skeptical approach to globalization and families suggests that families face challenges from myriad sources, internal and external to societies, with globalization being but one of those challenges.

To the contrary, hyperglobalists (e.g., Greider 1997; Ohmae 1995) contend that escalating global capitalism in economic marketplaces increasingly affects political, cultural, and other aspects of social life in profound ways. Hyperglobalists observe that systems of production and distribution, finance and trade are more transnational, borderless, and, in essence, denationalized than ever before in human history. Hyperglobalists see a dramatically globalizing economy, accompanied by widespread subordination of national economies and governments. They also see political, cultural, and other institutional systems as likewise globally diffused and hybridized into immense global systems (Cochrane and Pain 2000; Held et al. 1999).

Award-winning novelist and political activist Arundhati Roy (2003) speaks of globalization as "ripping through people's lives" (p. 70). To hyperglobalists, globalization is placing families and their members at increasing risk through migration, employment, media and culture, and especially war and other violence occurring at an accelerating rate across national borders.

The third party in the globalization debate, transformationalists (e.g., Giddens 2000; Rosenau 1997) recognize an increasingly interconnected, but more uncertain, world. Like hyperglobalists, global transformationalists see globalization as a historically unprecedented set of economic, political, and social forces shaping societies and the world through a wide range of cultural, demographic, ecological, military, technological, and other social patterns.

However, rather than confirming the advent of a single, unified world society, transformationalists point to increasing global stratification, as some societies and their members reap the benefits of globalization, while others become increasingly marginalized on the world stage (Held et al. 1999). Transformationalists view families as offering some resistance to the forces of globalization while sometimes benefiting in concrete ways from cultural, economic, and political changes that result from globalization.

Family Theories Around Globalization

Can we then speak of a theory of globalization? As discussed earlier, the concept of globalization has usually been approached from the perspective of economics, politics, or culture. These three dimensions do not encompass the entire theoretical scope of globalization. In explaining family opportunities and outcomes in the context of globalization, family scholars face a significant challenge in moving beyond economic, political, and culture-based theories that have dominated globalization studies to date. At the same time, family scholars can reexamine and sometimes repackage theories that have informed family sociology and family studies to better explain the effects of globalization on families.

Family studies and family sociology have made great strides in theoretical development in the four decades since publication of Christensen's *Handbook of Marriage and the Family* in 1964. That elegant, classic volume included review essays on only four theoretical schools: the institutional approach (Sirjamaki 1964), the structural-functional approach (Pitts 1964), the inter-actional and situational approach (Stryker 1964), and the developmental approach (Hill and Rodgers 1964).

A half-century later, Karraker and Grochowski's (2012) *Families With Futures* includes eight theoretical perspectives:

- Exchange or rational choice theory
- Symbolic interaction theory
- Family life course development theory
- Family systems theory
- Family ecology theory
- Structural functional theory
- Conflict theory
- Feminist theory

Even more family theories might be added to that list, either as distinct in their own right or as important extensions of or variations on other family theories. For example, Ingoldsby, Smith, and Miller (2004) and White and Klein (2007) consider life course theory a strand of family developmental theory. Others (e.g., Allen 1989) argue that life course is a distinct theory. The *Sourcebook of Family Theory and Research*, edited by Bengtson et al. (2005), and White's (2005) *Advancing Family Theories* provide excellent overviews of the field. The *Journal of Family Theory and Review* is a best source for the most current work in family theory.

The study of globalization and families would benefit from the kind of interdisciplinary empirical and theoretical scholarship advocated by Karraker and Grochowski (2012) and Scott et al. (2004). Already, some scholars (e.g., Giele 2004; Giele and Holst 2004) are using life course and family systems theories, as well as exchange and symbolic interaction theory, to understand the effects of new global divisions of labor between men and women on patterns in family life across societies. Structural functional theory still offers an opportunity to consider the manifest and latent functions and dysfunctions embodied in now-global economic, political, cultural, and other changes shaping the family. Conflict theory exposes the systems of exploitation and oppression reflected in social arrangements for men, women, and children in families both within and between societies. By including the world system in understanding the family as located in human-built, social–cultural, and natural physical–biological environments, family ecology theory (e.g., Bubloz and Sontag 1993) can detect opportunities, as well as constraints, for families operating in global societies. By extension, an ecological approach implies that global policymakers should consider the effect on families of supranational legislation and other social initiatives, perhaps even composing global family impact statements.

Each of these middle-range theories (see Merton 1968) may prove useful for analyzing certain aspects of families in global context. Also, family scholars are exploiting theories beyond those on which family scholars usually draw. For example, Ward (1990) has examined the "global assembly lines" that disproportionately exploit women (and compromise their families) through the lens of world systems theory. Ward describes the "assembly lines" as occurring in semiperiphery or periphery countries, while research, management, and profit are controlled by core or more-developed countries. Postmodernism and feminist theory (both of which are described later in this chapter) may offer even greater promise for articulating the consequences of globalization, including risk, across family systems and through intersections of class, gender, race/ethnicity, immigration status, and other dimensions of social opportunity.

Family theory that does not take into account globalization theory falls short of the potential to explain the challenges and opportunities experienced by families in an increasingly global world. To utilize globalization theory fully, family theorists must push the "territorial frontiers" that presume that a family's biography and culture is bound by national society. Family scholars must forgo the assumption that "nation" necessarily equals "society" (Beck and Beck-Gernsheim 2004:501). Family sociologists must acknowledge that families may move among "local and international, indigenous and foreign" networks (p. 501).

Further, any examination of the effect of globalization on families should be sensitive to the potential for glocalization, the "interpenetration of the global and the local resulting in unique outcomes" (Ritzer 2007:268). Dobratz, Waldner, and Buzzell (2012) define glocalization as "how human beings reconstitute and redefine a global phenomenon and give it local flavor" (p. 355). The concept of glocalization recognizes the significant, creative potential of individuals and local groups not only to resist the homogenizing forces of globalization but also to fashion an increasingly pluralistic world (Robertson 1995). Chapter 3 includes a discussion of ways in which some families, including parents and their children, "push back" against globalization, and, thus, epitomize glocalization.

Glocalization also involves increases in ethnic group and other more local cultural solidarities that transcend national borders. Edgar (2004) has referred to these project-identity social movements as a new tribalism. Islamic fundamentalism and the ethnic/national rebellions in the former Soviet Union and the Balkans are just such movements. Other such identity movements are aimed at building a certain civic ethic. See, for example, Joseph's (2002) work on the global/glocal intersections of politics, economics, and other aspects of queer life. Still other identity movements (e.g., the cohousing movement) are smaller and seem to offer a sort of functional equivalent for individuals seeking more family-like connections to others. Thus, families and their members are linked not only to national and transnational systems but also to more local and glocal identity systems.

Risk in a Global Postmodern World

The concept of risk illuminates the challenges posed by globalization for families in a postmodern world. In postmodern theory, risk refers to uncertainty and insecurity in economic, political, and other spheres of life. Risk also connotes a heightened level of personal responsibility for individual achievement, personal outcomes, and quality of life as one experiences life less and less enmeshed in localized, communal family, neighborhood, and community, or even in the predictable features of class, gender, ethnicity or race, religion, tribe or nation. Quintessentially, such risk is the story of globalization.

Beck describes globality in precisely such a sense: national, regional, and other spatial boundaries are increasingly illusory. Through globalization, national boundaries are interwoven and destabilized by transnational actors in financial, government, cultural, religious, and other institutions. From this perspective, denationalization (the decline of the nation-state) and the development of transnational organizations and even transnational states such as the European Union can be seen as part of a "second modernity" (Beck 2000). With this increasing (post)modernity comes a loss of tradition and the certainty that accompanies the familiar. Globalization implies that more individually determined senses of self and identity may be chosen and created without reference to customary relationships, including families. In such a postmodern, self-reflexive social order, everything, even sense of self and relationships, is subject to constant revision and refabrication as new information and new social forms are constantly being received and evaluated (Giddens 1991). Lawler, Thye, and Yoon (2011) write of this in terms of the reduction in individuals' commitments that accompanies globalization.

Thus, globalization heightens social risk by placing the individual in jeopardy outside the formerly comfortable boundaries of nation, society, culture, kinship, and family. For example, in the case of increasingly global job markets, workers and their families face greater uncertainty as jobs are outsourced and families dislocated, with some members migrating for employment while others remain behind. Such associated risks come not once but over and over again, many times in a lifetime.

No region or nation, regardless of economic or political advantage, is totally immune from the risks associated with postmodern life. Witness, for example, the events associated with the bombings of the Pentagon and the World Trade Center in the United States on September 11, 2001, and the bombings in the mass transit systems in London on July 7, 2005, as well as the ongoing tragic fallout in the southeastern United States resulting from Hurricane Katrina in the summer of 2005 and the earthquake and resulting tsunami that led to the catastrophic nuclear meltdown in Japan in the spring of 2011. Still, the positive and negative effects of globalization are unequally distributed. For some families, globalization can enhance mobility and freedom to create security, meaning, and opportunity. Bauman (1998) writes of privileged elites who are able to move easily across global borders and, likewise, those who are not able to do so. He differentiates between tourists (those who move about the globe because they can and want to do so) and vagabonds (those who move about the globe because they find their location hostile or intolerable).

Most certainly, poverty and other inequalities attract uneven quantities of risk. The most severe consequences of risk disproportionately fall to poor nations, continents, and the southern hemisphere. Not only does globalization not eliminate scarcity and want, but the pervasiveness of global media (as discussed in Chapter 3) that can transmit generous images of affluence serves to worsen the sense of absolute or relative deprivation of the world's most needy (George 1999). The risks that accompany globalization exacerbate class and other divisions in society (Beck 1992), and the risks associated with global inequalities apply to individuals as well as nations, continents, and hemispheres (Ritzer 2004a). Families experience risks and disadvantages associated with large-scale, global social change in disproportionate measures to their privilege and material and other resources.

A theme of "runaway risk" and the accompanying anxiety and fear created by globalization runs through postmodernism (e.g., Giddens 2000). Some postmodernists (e.g., Beck 1992) see risk as a fundamental, defining characteristic of modern society, but the application of risk to family life is only a recent development. For example, Furlong and Cartmel (1997) and Nayak (2003) have applied the concept of risk to adolescence in working-class families in Great Britain and other Western societies. Don Browning (2003), Professor Emeritus of Divinity, and Alexander Campbell, Professor of Religious Ethics and the Social Sciences at the University of Chicago, write of postmodern marriages and families at serious risk in a global world. These scholars emphasize that the positive changes found in modernizing societies around the world (e.g., higher family income, better health, longer life expectancy) are unevenly distributed. They also see some of the changes moving across the global landscape (expanding educational and employment roles for women, smaller families, more egalitarian gender roles in marriage, less involvement of extended kin) as creating crises around issues such as providing care to children, elders, and other family members.

Such postmodern families represent "a deconstruction or transformation of at least one aspect of the traditional family" (Silverstein and Auerbach 2005:34). A family no longer requires two parents, male and female, sharing a household with their biological offspring. An accurate construction of the postmodern family must include single mothers by choice, lesbigay couples, families constructed using new reproductive technologies (e.g., in vitro fertilization, surrogate mothers, sperm donors), and transnational families working and living across borders, such as those described in Chapter 5. The uncertainties associated with these new diversities of family form and function—adaptive as they may be—represent yet another potential source of risk and anxiety for 21st century families, especially when they are not acknowledged or affirmed by the dominant society. Risk is heightened by the absence or withdrawal of the state as a provider of social safety nets. Such postmodern families challenge traditional gender, sexual, and other ideologies and can benefit from feminist analysis.

Globalization Through a Feminist Lens

Anthropologists Gunewardena and Kingsolver (2007) argue that women (and, we would add, their families) have been marginalized in global analyses.

> The gender of globalization has been obscured by "neutral" analytical lenses that overlook the powerful incongruity between women's key roles in the global labor force and their social and economic marginalization, as well as their persistent efforts to navigate the processes that produce this incongruity. (P. 3)

Certainly, globalization and the risks associated with postmodern life on a worldwide scale are not gender neutral. Marchand and Runyan (2000), Naples and Desai (2002), and Sarker and De (2002) suggest that resistance to globalization is often profoundly gendered, as women and their families disproportionately bear the consequences of demographic transitions, worldwide culture shifts, international violence, and transnational employment. A gender lens offers a distinctive opportunity to understand global restructuring, encompassing the effects of globalization on the lives of women and their families and the place of gendered ideologies in globalization.

The transnational commoditization of care work and mate selection and the global networks that characterize not only reproductive labor but also such intimacies as sexual exchanges are "prime manifestation[s] of the complex gendered dynamics of contemporary globalization" (Hawkesworth 2006:2). Safa (2002) reveals how patriarchy continues to structure inequality in the global labor force, using the example of women in the Dominican Republic who continue to toil under patriarchy and a male-breadwinner model "reinvigorated" by globalization. These women encounter pernicious sexism and face occupational discrimination and the unwillingness of labor unions and other social organizations to consider critical women's and family concerns, such as maternity leave.

In a concise but comprehensive articulation of contemporary feminist theories, Lengermann and Niebrugge (2010a) frame basic theoretical questions, describe contemporary feminist theories, and offer insights into where feminist theories can take sociological theory. To begin, they define feminist theory as "a generalized, wide-ranging system of ideas about social and human experience developed from a woman-centered perspective" (p. 185). Feminist theory takes women's experience as the starting point for sociological study and attempts to view society from the point of view of women.

Lengermann and Niebrugge's (2010a) four varieties of feminist theory are gender difference, gender inequality, gender oppression, and structural oppression (see Table 1.3).

Table 1.3   Four Varieties of Feminist Theory

Feminist Theory	What About the Women?	What Causes This Situation? (distinctions within theory)
Gender difference	Women's position in and experience of most social life *differs* from men's experience.	Cultural Institutional Interactional Phenomenological
Gender inequality	Women's position in social life is both different from and *unequal* to men's position.	Liberal feminism Rational choice
Gender oppression	Women are not just different from or unequal to men but also *oppressed*, i.e., constrained, subordinated, shaped, used, and abused by men.	Psychoanalytic feminism Radical feminism
Structural oppression	Women's experiences of difference, inequality, and oppression vary by social *location* within capitalism, patriarchy, and racism.	Socialist feminism Intersectionality

SOURCE: Lengermann and Niebrugge (2010b). Adapted with permission from G. Ritzer, *Contemporary Sociological Theory and Its Classical Roots: The Basics.* 3rd ed. New York: McGraw-Hill, 2010.

Each of these varieties holds promise for the understanding of the effects of globalization on families. For example, Iwao's (2001) work on the "battle of the sexes" among young Japanese suggests that, in spite of dramatic modernization in that nation, men and women continue to experience modern life in profoundly different ways—perhaps because of their respectively different phenomenological locations, as suggested by gender difference theories. Gender inequality theories, such as that by feminist economists Barker and Feiner (2004), are already enabling us to understand the persistence of gender inequality in the transnational workforce.

Most gender oppression theorists would say societies fall far short of Jackson's (2001) contention that "men's social dominance was doomed from the beginning. Gender inequality could not adapt successfully to modern economic and political institutions" (p. 81). More typically, scholars such as Bose (2006b) and Ollenburger and Moore (1998) draw on feminist theories of structural oppression to lay bare the intersections of patriarchy, capitalism, and colonization while recognizing that gender intersects with class, race, ethnicity, immigration status, and sexual orientation. Feminist theorists working in the area of globalization and family can also fruitfully extend and expand Collins's (1990) classic formulation of black feminist thought—as representing the intersectionality of race, class, and gender, and, more recently, sexual orientation—to consider global issues of colonialism, immigration, and nationality. Some scholars (e.g., Eisenstein, 2004, author of *Against Empire: Feminisms, Racism, and the West*) are beginning to accept the challenge.

Lengermann and Niebrugge (2010b) argue that postmodernism and feminism have much in common. Both postmodernism and feminism are concerned with whose formulations of knowledge matters. Both postmodernism and feminism aim to use the method of deconstruction to unpack the place of gender in postmodern society. Both also are concerned with resisting the inclination for theory to become a means of categorizing and, therefore, oppressing disenfranchised members of society. At the same time, Lengermann and Niebrugge are suspicious of postmodernism's fixed place in the privileged academy, as opposed to venues that would facilitate inclusion and liberation of marginalized groups. Likewise, postmodernism's emphasis on individualization and de-emphasis on broadly conceived social–structural constraints rankles feminist concerns for identifying systemic sources of inequalities.

As the title of Turpin and Lorentzen's (1996) book *The Gendered New World Order* suggests, globalization may be arranging the planet in novel ways, but gender remains a primary determinant of those arrangements. Feminist theory is increasingly important in family studies (Baber and Allen 1992), and some scholars (e.g., Haney and Pollard 2003) are revising existing family theories around feminist frameworks in order to better understand the effects of globalization on families.

In *Global Families*, I apply concepts from globalization theory (globalization and glocalization), postmodernism (risk), and feminism (gender difference, inequality, oppression, and intersecting structures) to explain the complex systems through which globalization affects families. Like Walby (2009), I see feminist theory, especially when combined with understanding of the intersections among gender, race, class, natality, and sexualities, as a promising way to explore the social–structural sources of inequalities most pertinent to the quality of family life in a postmodern, global era. In asking, "Where are the women?" feminist theory has much to offer the global analysis of family in examination of areas associated with both public and private spheres.

Eitzen and Baca Zinn (2011) argue that "some of the most devastating effects of globalization fall on women" (p. 185) and that a gender lens "reveals that inequalities between women and men serve as building blocks of the global order" (p. 186). However, those same inequalities may be simultaneously restructured by globalization, suggesting that feminist perspectives can inspire those who wish to transform society. For example, in seeking ways to address the global scourge HIV/AIDS, Bill Gates, chair of Microsoft Corporation and cochair of the $62 billion Bill and Melinda Gates Foundation, said at the opening of the 16th International AIDS Conference in Toronto: "We need to put the power to prevent HIV in the hands of women" (Picard 2006:A1). Gates recognizes that needed social change in lowering HIV/AIDS rates will not come about without empowering women in their relationships, families, and society.

Global Families: Plan of the Book

Global Families answers a call extended by sociologist Ian Robertson (1990) more than two decades ago: to "redirect theory and research toward explicit recognition of globalization" (p. 15). Family scholars must avoid having "'globalization' . . . become an intellectual 'play zone'—a site for the expression of residual social-theoretical interests, interpretative indulgence, or the display of world-ideological preferences" (p. 16). That challenge is never far from my mind as I synthesize scholarship around such intellectually and socially charged issues as HIV/AIDS, globalized media, sex trafficking, global care chains, and supranational policies aimed at the family.

Continuing to avoid globalization as an organizing principle in the study of family would be a grievous error. Globalization has consequences not only for societies but also very significantly for human development and families. Such analysis requires consideration of demographics, culture, violence, and employment, as well as the role of national, regional, and international political bodies in shaping family-centered issues worldwide. I have organized the chapters that follow around these five themes critical to the study of global family life.

Chapter 2, "Global Change and Demographic Shifts: Family Characteristics and Societal Transformation," places global families against the backdrop of dramatic changes in population characteristics. Declining fertility, variable mortality, and especially sweeping migration are shaping the structure and function of contemporary families in fundamental ways. A particular case— that of AIDS orphans even in the face of now-declining worldwide HIV/AIDS infection rates—illustrates the broad effect on family life of global demographic shifts.

Chapter 3, "Families and Worldwide Culture Systems: Media, Technology, and Consumption," explores the effect of globalization on the cultures in which families are embedded. The chapter examines the controversy surrounding globalization and cultural homogeneity, as well as the effect of mass media—including television and computer-assisted technologies—and consumerism on families. The chapter concludes with an examination of globalization and family values.

The effects of globalization on families too often occur in the context of international violence against families and their members. Chapter 4, "International Violence: Family Legacies of Oppression and War," reveals the extent to which colonialism and armed conflict shape families and family life in extreme ways. The chapter reveals potentials for not only risk but also resiliency in the face of international violence. Sexual domination, in the form of rape, sexual slavery, and sex trafficking, is offered as a system through which families are reshaped by global economies in a criminal context.

Chapter 5, "Transnational Employment: Work–Family Linkages Across Borders," summarizes the literature on families and international labor force participation, with a particular focus on domestic-labor migrants and the effect of transnational employment on family care work. The concept of global care chains is used as an example of the complex means through which global labor and family are woven together.

The concluding chapter, "Positioning Families in Global Landscapes: Families, Policies, and Futures," notes the persistence of global disparities among families and the issue of human rights as family rights. Almost three decades after the International Year of the Family, social scientists are positioned to view social policies regarding the family from a global perspective. Returning to earlier themes by way of critical appraisal, *Global Families* concludes by asking if we are entering a postfamily global society—a society in which globalization severely compromises the ability of the institution and individual families to fulfill their obligations to society and their members.

Finally, each chapter closes with an essay authored by an authority in the field.

Chapter 1: "Globalization and Family Down Under," by Janet R. Grochowski, PhD, Marie and Robert Jackson Professor of Education, College of Saint Benedict/Saint John's University

Chapter 2: "Immigrant Women, New Neighbors, Global Families," by Margaret L. Kvasnicka, a Sister of St. Joseph and former director of Sarah's . . . an Oasis for Women

Chapter 3: "Contested Norms and Values in Transnational Families," by Cawo M. Abdi, PhD, Assistant Professor of Sociology, University of Minnesota, and Research Fellow, University of Pretoria

Chapter 4: "Sex Trafficking: A 'Family Business,'" by Jennifer Blank, MA, Criminologist

Chapter 5: "A Migrant Mother's Story: Paula Rodriguez," by Joanna Dreby, PhD, Assistant Professor of Sociology, Kent State University

Chapter 6: "The Global Human Rights of Families," by Marsha A. Freeman, PhD, Director of the International Women's Rights Action Watch and Senior Fellow in the Law School Institutes, University of Minnesota

These essays serve as cases to illustrate and extend key issues raised in *Global Families*.

Summary

Families increasingly operate in global milieu. In spite of a long tradition of cross-cultural and international scholarship, family studies have yet to realize an authentically global perspective on families. *Global Families* calls for inclusion of globalization as a critical tool for analyzing families and the family institution in the 21st century.

Globalization is the development of economic, political, cultural, and other relationships beyond national and regional borders. The social consequences of globalization are evident at macro and micro levels. Yet, globalization is a contested concept. Skeptics see globalization as a false concept that exaggerates and obscures the power of international economies controlled by regional and national governments. Hyperglobalists see increasingly borderless, global economies accompanied by diffusion and hybridization of political, cultural, and other institutional systems. Transformationalists see globalization as a historically unprecedented set of economic, political, and social forces transforming societies and the world through a range of cultural, demographic, ecological, military, and technological patterns and increasing worldwide stratification.

While an increasing number of theories drawn from family studies is being used to examine the family globally, any global analysis must resist the tendency toward Western bias and take into account worldwide economic, political, cultural, and other institutional influences. In addition to theories traditionally employed in family sociology and family studies— exchange or rational choice theory, symbolic interaction theory, family life course development theory, family systems theory, family ecology theory, structural functional theory, conflict theory—postmodernism, with an emphasis on risk analysis, and feminism are among the most promising complements for the analysis of globalization and families.

In the five chapters that follow, *Global Families* reveals the complex effects of demographic transitions, worldwide culture, international violence, and transnational labor on families. *Global Families* also considers the effects of supranational organizations, such as the United Nations, as well as other national and international political bodies on families in a global world.

GLOBALIZATION AND FAMILY DOWN UNDER

By Janet R. Grochowski, PhD

Australia has the distinction of being both a society historically grounded in global processes and one that today embraces globalization. The original human inhabitants of this island continent arrived 30,000 to 50,000 years ago, but the earliest recorded European mariners did not reach "Terra Australis Incognito" (unknown southern land) until 1606. About 54 European merchant ships visited this new land prior to 1770, when Captain James Cook claimed the entire east coast of Australia for England, naming it New South Wales. In 1788 an English colony was established when 11 ships carried 1,350 English settlers to the territory. Shortly thereafter, the first penal colony was established in Sydney, starting a flow of convicts from the United Kingdom to Australia that did not end until 1968 (Australian Government 2008).

The penal colonies were populated primarily by convicts, marines, and families of the marines, creating a serious gender imbalance. Efforts were made in the 1820s and 1830s to address the shortage of single women, but subsequent gold rushes rekindled the imbalance. Today the current sex ratio is 1.03 males to 1.0 females for Australians 15 to 64 years of age (U.S. Central Intelligence Agency 2011).

The fate of the first immigrants, Aboriginals, also left lasting imprints. While 1818 is marked today as the official date of the founding of Australia as a British colony, for many Aboriginals that date symbolizes not celebration but grief. Contact with British immigrants often resulted in economic marginalization, a loss of political autonomy, and death by disease for the Aboriginals. By the 1940s, most Aboriginals were "missionized" and assimilated into rural Australian society as low-paid laborers with limited rights.

Many Aboriginal children were taken from their natural parents and given to foster parents (Moses 2004). As recently as July 2000, Australia faced harsh criticism over its past and current discriminatory treatment of Aboriginals (Doole 2000).

With the establishment of The Commonwealth in 1901, Australia became an increasingly desirable destination for voluntary immigrants, especially those flooding out of continental Europe after World Wars I and II. Between 1948 and 1975, 2 million European immigrants chose Australia as their new home—a home that, while welcoming a European cultural mix, resisted non-white immigration. The 1972 election of the Labor Party ended the White Australia Policy, while adoption of a nondiscriminatory immigration policy in 1989 helped usher in the National Agenda for a Multicultural Australia (Inglis 2004). Today a growing proportion of Australia's more than 20 million people are from Asia. In fact, Asian-born immigrants make up 24 percent of the foreign-born population in Australia (Inglis 2004:2). Yet, racism and xenophobia surface even today in corners of Australian society.

In 2002 a United Nations Commission on Human Rights report on racism in Australia offered 10 recommendations to enhance Australia's multiculturalism policy. These recommendations focused on further reducing discrimination toward Aboriginals and stressed that the Australian government should review its policy of multiculturalism (Glele-Ahanhanzo 2002). Since that time, Australia has reduced discrimination and enhanced multiculturalism. While the Declaration and Program of Action signals progress, work remains to ensure that all Australians enjoy the full benefits of living in a multicultural society.

> There are a lot of positives to build on, but the real test will be whether Australia's positive engagement with the UPR process translates into action on the ground. If the Government takes its human rights obligations seriously, it needs to set a concrete implementation plan with clear responsibilities, time-frames and targets. (Schokman, quoted in Human Rights Law Centre 2011:1)

While Australian society still struggles with discrimination, this land of immigrants increasingly recognizes a need to embrace diversity, as well as a distinctive Australian flare for life. Australian culture today embodies attitudes and behaviors that link economics, politics, cultures, and families to the global community beyond. These globally receptive attitudes are reflected in the Australian Survey of Social Attitudes (AuSSA), a national survey first conducted in 2003 by the Centre for Social Research at the Australian National University (Wilson et al. 2005).

Globalization is complex but often wrongly reduced to a one-dimensional process. Some analysts (e.g., Marsh, Meagher, and Wilson 2005) suggest that

Australians are closed toward globalization. Still others argue that this assessment overgeneralizes and neglects to consider the complex realities of Australian attitudes toward globalization. Those scholars propose a more compelling understanding of globalization and social responses, based on a four-fold classification of globalization (James 2006; Nairn and James 2005).

The first component of this classification is embodied globalization, which tracks the immigration patterns of people. Australians maintain firm opposition to human trafficking. Beyond that, between 1996 and 2003, Australians expressed an increased positive attitude toward immigration. "In 2003, 69 percent of respondents thought that 'immigrants are generally good for the economy' and 74 percent believed that 'immigrants make Australia open to new ideas and cultures'" (James 2006:3). James suggests that future research needs to ask Australians about their attitudes toward tourism and the movement of family, friends, and themselves around the world. This shift in attitudes toward embodied globalization surfaces in Australian families whose members travel extensively. The immigration experience itself has shifted profoundly. "A significant proportion of immigra[nts]—particularly skilled immigrants—is no longer looking for permanent residence: they see themselves as international citizens, operating in a global labour market" (Markus, Jupp, and McDonald 2009:4)

The second component of this classification is object-extended globalization, which centers on the movement of objects, including traded commodities, around the world. With expanding trade, James (2006) suggests that Australians desire more global choices while wishing to protect their economy and environment. As Australian families negotiate the benefits and costs of engaging in the global marketplace, they are both receptive to and cautious about global consumption. The third component, agency-extended globalization, reflects global shifts in locations of companies and corporations. Australian families recognize the wisdom of reclaiming control of their natural resources and production in-country, rather than shipping off so much of their raw mineral wealth.

The fourth component, disembodied-extended globalization, involves the worldwide reach of information and communication technologies typical of global networks of computers and other digital devices. Access to the World Wide Web is highly valued in Australian families; 70 percent of the respondents to the AuSSA reported having Internet access (Denemark 2005). The Internet and instant wireless communications make families living in the outback less remote and connect Australians to families and friends on a global scale. While telecommunications are embraced enthusiastically, technology remains the least regulated of the four forms of globalization.

The AuSSA also reveals Australians' increasingly pluralistic attitudes toward what constitutes a family. For many Australians, having a child or children appears more important in defining family than the religious or even civil status of marriage. Ninety-two percent of 18- to 34-year-old Australian adults viewed single-parent households as families. Sixty-two percent of this same demographic agree that gay and lesbian couples with children are also families (Evans and Gray 2005:19). These findings have important repercussions for Australian educational, governmental, and social agencies, including the development and delivery of Australian family policy and services.

While embracing family diversity in the face of globalization, Australia has advanced national initiatives aimed at building local communities and strengthening families (Scott 2000). Many Australians do not see families as islands unto themselves but, rather, as elements in larger ecological systems composed of families, communities, and the global environment.

The winds of globalization demand that societies such as that in Australia continue to reflect on multicultural responsibilities and project truly global communities while embracing change, diversity, and challenge. Such an understanding of globalization provides a richer analysis of the impacts of globalization on societies and families. Australian families hold balanced and increasingly positive appreciation of living in a global world, even encouraging their children to be global learners. Such emerging globally inclined attitudes are consistent with innovative structures of families in a diversifying multicultural community.

Janet R. Grochowski, PhD, serves as Marie and Robert Jackson Professor of Education and Department Chair at the College of Saint Benedict and Saint John's University in St. Joseph, Minnesota. She also is Professor Emerita at the University of St. Thomas, where she was employed for more than 25 years. Her international and multicultural research includes studies of Australian families' resilience, education, and health.

CRITICAL THINKING QUESTIONS:

1. How does a global perspective on families differ from a cross-cultural or comparative perspective on families?

2. What about globalization may place families at risk? What about globalization may enhance the quality of family life?

3. How can postmodernism or a feminist lens augment a global approach to families?

4. Grochowski discusses Australian family in a global context. In a similar fashion, how would you place families in another society in such a global context?

2

Global Change and Demographic Shifts

Family Characteristics and Societal Transformation

The year 2011 marked 30 years since the onset of the global AIDS epidemic. During that time, more than 60 million people have become infected with human immunodeficiency virus (HIV, the virus that causes acquired immune deficiency syndrome, AIDS) and AIDS has claimed more than 25 million lives. Every day, more than 7,000 people, including 1,000 children, are newly infected. Yet the global incidence of HIV is declining and access to treatment is expanding. Furthermore, social movements have gained traction to secure the respect and rights of those infected and others affected by the disease (United Nations 2011). Still, the World Health Organization (2011d) estimated that the number of AIDS orphans—children under 15 years of age who have lost a mother or both parents to HIV/AIDS—would reach 41 million by the year 2010.

The HIV/AIDS pandemic illustrates the effects of an overwhelming health crisis on families in societies across the globe but especially in less-developed parts of the world. Many of the people infected with the virus are in their most productive years, often having just begun new families. The burden of care for family members infected with HIV/AIDS and the increasing number of children orphaned by HIV/AIDS stresses families and societies. At times of uncertain or dwindling resources, extended families and the communities in which those suffering with HIV/AIDS live may be reluctant or unable to commit scarce resources to feed, shelter, or educate orphans. Adult death from AIDS within a household leads to loss of income, which in turn leads to children dropping out of school to look for work or to care for other family members (World Health Organization 2011d). Yet, as I will discuss in this chapter, HIV/AIDS is not the only health crisis facing sub-Saharan Africa. Malaria and other insect-borne diseases, as well as diabetes and other diseases associated with obesity and inactivity, are becoming epidemic across the globe.

The impact of globalization on families may originate in economic, political, cultural, technological, or other spheres. Perhaps in no other area of family life, however, are the effects of globalization more evident than in changes in population characteristics. Morbidity and mortality, fertility, and migration serve as powerful driving forces through which global economic, political, and other patterns influence marriage, parenting (including adoption), and other family structures (including marriage), often in very gendered ways. Still, the paucity of demographic data in some areas, such as concerning the death, birth, and migration patterns of lesbian, gay, bisexual, transgender, or questioning (LGBTQ) individuals, still limits our understanding of the effects of demographic forces on the full range of diverse family forms in a global society.

I begin Chapter 2 with a brief presentation on the significance of demographic transition and the place of population dynamics in families' lives, followed by a summary of what we know about the global morbidity and mortality, fertility, and migration of families today. I apply a gender lens to migration and examine the phenomena of migration for marriage and transnational adoption. I close the chapter with a discussion of the ways in which demographics in general and migration in particular are contested, particularly across generations, as well as the ways in which our full understanding of global immigration is hampered by a limited definition of family. Finally, an essay by Margaret L. Kvasnicka—a Sister of St. Joseph Carondelet, St. Paul Province, and former director of a refuge for immigrant and refugee women in St. Paul, Minnesota—demonstrates the potential for personal and family resiliency even under the most trying circumstances.

Demographic Transition and Family Dynamics

Demographers examine changing population characteristics through the intersections among death rates, birth rates, and migration rates. The net sum of changes in those three rates provides an estimation of a population's growth rate. While individual and family actions and outcomes compose the data that result in population growth and decline, demographic transitions both reflect and shape families' competition for such scarce resources as food, shelter, and employment, as well as the supply of eligible marriage partners and family members available to care for dependent members.

Briefly, the theory of demographic transition explains how premodern societies with high mortality rates and high fertility rates shift to modern societies with low fertility and low mortality rates. In early stages of demographic transition, death rates decline due to control over infectious diseases, as well as improved standards of living around nutrition, sanitation, and childbirth. Demographic transition holds that, as societies modernize, cultural patterns involving labor shift and women and their partners acquire both the desire and the means to control human reproduction effectively. Children become more expensive in terms of both direct and indirect costs. (Thus, the rational choice is to limit family size.) Hence, cultural changes weaken the value of larger family sizes but increase the value placed on each child. The ensuing declines in fertility rates and mortality rates produce slower population growth (Kirk 1996).

As depicted in Table 2.1, total world population increased dramatically in the last quarter of the 20th century, from 2.8 billion to 6.1 billion. Although the world population growth rate has slowed, the total world population is still projected to reach 10.1 billion by the year 2100. The most dramatic increases in population growth over the 21st century are projected to occur in the less-developed region of the world, which will grow from almost 5 billion in 2000 to almost 8.8 billion in 2100. The continent of Africa is projected to grow from 811 million in 2000 to almost 3.6 billion in 2100—an increase of more than 340 percent! While population in the more-developed region of the world is also projected to continue to increase slightly throughout the 21st century (from 1.2 to 1.3 billion), the population of Europe is projected to decline, from 727 million to 675 million.

Morbidity and Mortality

As a society moves through the stages of demographic transition, the rates of infection and death from such factors as disease and childbirth decline. Significant declines in morbidity (the incidence of disease) and mortality (the incidence of death) provide families with greater certainty that adults, as well as the next generation, will be around to provide economic support, protection, socialization, and care for family members.

Table 2.1 World Population by Continent and Region, 1950–2010

Year	1950	1975	2000	2025	2050	2100
				Thousands		
World total	2,772,882	4,076,419	6,122,770	8,002,978	9,306,128	10,124,926
Continent						
Africa	229,895	420,318	811,101	1,417,057	2,191,599	3,574,141
Asia	1,403,389	2,393,056	3,719,044	4,730,130	5,142,220	4,596,224
Europe	547,287	676,123	726,777	743,890	719,257	674,796
Latin America and the Caribbean	167,368	323,074	521,429	678,778	750,956	687,517
Northern America	171,615	242,360	313,289	388,472	446,862	526,428
Oceania	12,675	21,489	31,130	44,651	55,233	65,819
Region						
More developed	811,187	1,046,264	1,188,809	1,286,739	1,311,731	1,334,786
Less developed	1,721,042	3,030,155	4,933,961	6,716,239	7,994,397	8,790,140

SOURCE: Compiled from U.N. Department of Economic and Social Affairs (UNDESA 2011).

According to the World Health Organization (2011c), cardiovascular disease is the leading cause of death across the globe. However, as revealed in Table 2.2, the "top 10" causes of death vary enormously between low-income and high-income countries. In low-income countries, respiratory infections and diarrheal diseases account for one out of every four deaths. In high-income countries, heart disease and stroke account for one out of every four deaths. HIV/AIDS, malaria, tuberculosis, prematurity and low birth weight, birth asphyxia and birth trauma, and neonatal infections do not even appear on the "top 10" list for high-income countries. Likewise, cancers, dementias, chronic pulmonary disease, diabetes, and hypertension do not appear on the "top 10" list for low-income countries.

Clearly, then, morbidity and mortality have very different faces in poor and wealthy nations. In high-income nations, death is more likely to be by diseases characteristic of affluent lifestyles. In the less-developed world, infectious diseases (those caused by bacteria, viruses, parasites, or fungi) remain one of the prime causes of death, especially of children. A search of the World Health Organization (2011b) website reveals a compendium of infectious diseases virtually unheard of in the Western world—cholera, dengue fever, leprosy, malaria, polio, sleeping sickness, yellow fever, to name but a few—but clear and present dangers in other parts of the world.

For example, trachoma, once endemic in most parts of the world, today affects about 84 million—mainly in the most remote, poorest rural areas of Africa, Asia, Australia, Central and South America, and the Middle East. In those areas, the active disease is most common in young children, who experience rates as high as 60 to 90 percent. Because they spend more time in close contact with children, women are at much greater risk of developing blindness as a result of the disease than are adult men (World Health Organization 2011f).

One of the most striking demographic differences between more- and less-developed nations is infant mortality, often associated with premature birth and low birth rate, birth asphyxia and birth trauma, and neonatal infections. The infant mortality rate refers to the probability of dying between birth and exact age 1, expressed as deaths per 1,000 births. According to UNDESA (2011), the infant mortality rate around the world ranges from 6 in the more-developed regions to 50 in the less-developed regions. Countries with the lowest rate (2) include Iceland, Luxembourg, and Singapore. In Afghanistan, a shocking 136 out of every 1,000 infants— almost 14 percent—die before reaching their first birthday. At 7 deaths per

Table 2.2   Top 10 Causes of Death in Low-Income and High-Income
Nations, 2008

CAUSE OF DEATH	Rank	Millions	Percentage
Low-income countries			
Lower respiratory infections	1	1.05	11.30
Diarrheal diseases	2	0.76	8.20
HIV/AIDS	3	0.72	7.80
Ischemic heart disease	4	0.57	6.10
Malaria	5	0.48	5.20
Stroke and other cerebrovascular disease	6	0.45	4.90
Tuberculosis	7	0.40	4.30
Prematurity and low birth weight	8	0.30	3.20
Birth asphyxia and birth trauma	9	0.27	2.90
Neonatal infections	10	0.24	2.60
High-income countries			
Ischemic heart disease	1	1.42	15.60
Stroke and other cerebrovascular disease	2	0.79	8.70
Trachea, bronchus, lung cancers	3	0.54	5.90
Alzheimer and other dementias	4	0.37	4.10
Lower respiratory infections	5	0.35	3.80
Chronic obstructive pulmonary disease	6	0.32	3.50
Colon and rectum cancers	7	0.30	3.30
Diabetes mellitus	8	0.24	2.60
Hypertensive heart disease	9	0.21	2.30
Breast cancer	10	0.70	1.90

SOURCE: World Health Organization (2011c).

1,000 births, the United States has a relatively low infant mortality rate (UNDESA 2011) but wide variations within its populations, with children born to the poorest mothers having considerably higher mortality rates than those born to more affluent mothers, due to differences in quality of and access to prenatal, childbirth, and maternal health care.

A rising public health concern, one historically associated with more-developed societies, is the number of people worldwide who suffer from diseases that can accompany social development as nations become wealthier (and more obese and less active). Almost 10 percent of the world's adults have diabetes. The number of adults living with diabetes has more than doubled since 1980—347 million up from 153 million. Diabetes increases a person's risk of blindness, heart attack, kidney failure, and other problems. As the incidence of diabetes rises, societies' health care systems will be severely taxed (Brown 2011). Another growing public health concern across the less-developed world involves the issue of road safety. By 2030 the World Health Organization expects road accidents to be the fifth leading cause of death worldwide ("Fighting Road Kill" 2011). The costs of higher medical expenses and physical disabilities from illnesses and accidents will inevitably be borne by families.

I opened this chapter with a synopsis of the crisis facing families as a result of the HIV/AIDS pandemic. In spite of the considerable success of global efforts to reduce transmission of and alleviate suffering from the disease, HIV/AIDS remains the leading fatal infectious disease. As with so many other global concerns, the southern hemisphere bears a grossly disproportionate share of the pandemic. More than 2 million children are living with HIV/AIDS—most of them in sub-Saharan Africa—having contracted the disease from their mothers during pregnancy, labor, delivery, or breast feeding (World Health Organization 2011a).

That quintessential feature of globalization, geographic mobility (even short-term movement, as in the case of men involved in long-haul trucking), is a significant risk factor in the transmission of HIV. Population movement increases dissemination of the virus while setting in motion risky sexual behaviors such as frequent casual sexual relations with multiple partners among individuals (mostly men but also women) who move frequently from place to place for reasons related to employment, war, and other actions (Legarde et al. 2003).

In most societies, women's lower social and sexual status places them at particular risk of HIV infection by their male partners. A series of factors characteristic of patriarchal social systems further increase the frequency of women's exposure and decrease women's ability to reduce the likelihood of transmission. These factors include

- men's entitlement to sexual access to women,
- women's limited power to negotiate safe sex practices,
- coerced or violent sexual contact, and
- polygyny (one man with multiple wives).

To reduce their perception of the risk of HIV infection, African and Asian men—but also European and other men—may seek young girls as sexual partners, presuming them to be infection free. However, the practice does little to reduce men's actual level of exposure, because young girls are prostituted and sold as "virgins" multiple times. Such practices result in higher demands for young girls in the sex trade and, consequently, in more girls being infected at earlier ages. According to the World Health Organization (2011d), on average females contract HIV at ages 5 to 10 years younger than do males. Slightly more than half (52 percent) of all cases of HIV infection borne by adults are found among women (World Health Organization 2009). Moral constructions of sex as "healthy" (heterosexual "love matches") or "risky" (homosexual) complicate AIDS prevention for both men and women (Esacove 2010).

Such sexism in cultures is often reflected in programs and policy, with the results borne not only by women but also by their families. When adults become ill, their ability to provide for their families is compromised. Family systems are strained as the balance between well and infected members shifts. As the traditional caretakers for their families, when unmarried women, wives, and mothers become ill they are often bereft of someone to care for them. When women become ill and die, they leave entire households and family systems without a primary caregiver. Extended family systems are taxed as parents die, leaving behind orphaned children. Children may be forced from school in order to seek employment or to care for other family members (World Health Organization 2011d). Further, in male-dominated societies, the death of husbands and fathers leaves children, women, the elderly, and other surviving vulnerable family members more exposed to sexual and economic exploitation.

Of course, some children and youths left to head households as a result of HIV/AIDS manage to maintain functional ties to family and other sources of support. In a study of support and conflict networks of 27 children and youth heads of household in northern Namibia, Ruiz-Casares (2010) found both a strong presence of and satisfaction with extended kin (cousins, aunts, and uncles) as supporters, especially when the young heads of household needed to discuss important matters, required practical assistance with food or clothing, or wanted to receive positive feedback. She also found that those young heads of household drew support from same-age peers, especially for advice and companionship. This suggests that programs aimed at providing assistance to youth heading HIV/AIDS households should build on the full range of networks available, both adult and peer.

Browning has described AIDS in Africa as a study in how globalization threatens marriage and the family. Browning begins with Kilbride and Kilbride's (1990) analysis of how modernization and globalization have compromised "Africanity," the high value in East African societies placed on procreation, children, and parenting as a way of "realizing the divine in human life" (Browning 2003:181). While traditional values often endorsed polygyny—a double sexual standard—and higher status for men, Africanity was a culture embedded in mutual care that stretched across the local community. Browning believes that the increased emphasis on male participation in a wage market (often involving long periods of time away from wives) and the continued discrimination against women in the same system, as well as the geographic mobility and urbanization that has accompanied modernization, has weakened extended family ties, bringing "the East African family system to the verge of chaos" (p. 181).

Browning's argument is persuasive. Economic and social systems such as those found in globalizing Africa are ripe for the widespread transmission of HIV/AIDS. HIV/AIDS decimates families by fostering child abandonment and fatherlessness, contributing to a rising prevalence of children raising themselves on the street, and increasing the overdependence on grandparents as surrogate parents. The pandemic not only threatens individual families and entire social systems but potentially destabilizes the entire world as family disintegration, poverty, and other deprivations erode the very fabric of society, making society vulnerable to internal and external violence and oppression.

In the words of then U.S. Secretary of State Colin Powell, speaking in recognition of World AIDS Day in 2003: "Each death represents a personal tragedy—the loss of a mother, father, sister, brother, son, daughter, loved one. Each death also is an irreparable loss to our international community" (U.S. Bureau of International Information Programs 2003).

Left to ravage, the disease decimates a society's most productive members. It sickens those between the ages of 15 and 24, those who take care of the very young and the very old. It destroys those who teach and trade, support their families, and otherwise contribute to their nation's development. AIDS saps global growth. Unchecked, AIDS can lay waste to whole countries and destabilize entire regions of the world.

Biological and social risks of AIDS are inextricably woven together (Gdadebo, Rayman-Read, and Heymann 2003), and the magnitude of the pandemic and its effects on individuals, families, societies, and whole regions is almost unfathomable. However, innovative research programs and intervention strategies offer considerable hope. For example, a recent partnership between the Harvard University School of Public Health and the government of Botswana aims to better understand workplace, home, and community experiences that affect those infected with HIV or those caring for others who are living with HIV/AIDS. The program administers social and medical interventions in the workplace, where most adults spend their time. Such research-guided programs could dramatically improve the quality of family life, including the care and survival of not just those living with HIV/AIDS but also those orphaned by AIDS and caring for those with health and other problems associated with the virus (Project on Global Working Families 2006).

Eradication and treatment of HIV/AIDS is a key initiative of the United Nations and the World Health Organization. A record number of people are receiving HIV antiretroviral therapy in low- and middle-income nations. This progress represents the largest ever annual increase in the number of people accessing HIV treatment—6.6 million in 2010 compared with 1.4 million in previous years—but the majority of individuals infected in those countries still live without treatment. The World Health Organization is committed to "closing the remaining gap through more effective HIV programmes." The organization hopes to do so by innovatively linking HIV diagnosis and treatment with other health services, such as maternal and child health, tuberculosis, drug dependence, and primary care (World Health Organization 2011e). Not surprisingly, the presence of nongovernmental organizations (NGOs) concerned with health and women's rights are associated with lower levels of HIV prevalence for women, at least in democratic nations (Shircliff and Shandra 2011). Their presence is likely also associated with lower levels of other infectious diseases, malnutrition, and other morbidities.

Compromised morbidity and mortality have several direct effects on families in society. Orphans are often forced from education into employment or to live in dangerous circumstances. A higher dependency ratio places strains on the healthy and able to care for the disabled or the infirm. A culture of uncertainty may impede a society's investments in the future. Higher health care costs must be borne by society and often by families themselves. Finally, families and their members are stricken by the grief over loss or disability of a loved one.

Declining Fertility

Morbidity and mortality are critical parts of the engine that drives demographic transition. Fertility is another. As societies move through the first to the second stage of demographic transition, human fertility levels remain high long past the time death rates begin to fall. Of course, religious and other cultural supports for high fertility can persist beyond the time when infant mortality begins to fall and life expectancy begins to rise (and parents begin to trust that their children may survive them and that the parents may live to see their children grown).

Across the globe, the total fertility rate (the mean number of children born to women of childbearing age) has been on a steady decline. As indicated in Table 2.3, the fertility rate dropped steadily around the world, from just under 5 in the middle of the 20th century to 2.62 (just over the rate needed for population replacement) at the turn of the century. In fact, by the end of the 20th century, some Western European nations (e.g., Italy, with a rate of 1.22 for the period 1995–2000) found themselves with fertility rates well below human replacement level, thus creating grave problems for labor supply and economic consumption (UNDESA 2011). With such precipitously declining fertility rates, more-developed, postmodern economies such as Italy's find themselves with greater need for immigrant workers and their families, who historically have higher fertility rates.

Statistical averages regarding national fertility rates can mask variations within countries, such as higher fertility rates in urban areas of India, while rates remain high in rural areas in the same country (Singh 2004). Still, the United Nations predicts a slight increase in fertility rates in the world overall and in some areas (i.e., Asia, Europe, and Latin America and the Caribbean) by the end of the 21st century. Furthermore, gaps in fertility rates across continents and even between more- and less-developed regions will have all but converged by the year 2100.

By the last decades of the 20th century, mean household size had fallen to 2.8 in more-developed regions of the world, while mean household size fell dramatically even in less-developed regions—to 3.7 in East Asia, 4.1 in the Caribbean, 4.9 in Southeast Asia, and 5.7 in North Africa. Across the world, families are shifting from large, extended units to smaller, nuclear units and single-person households (U.N. Programme on the Family 2003).

Declining worldwide fertility is both a cause and a consequence of major changes in values and norms regarding women's roles, as well as national and international population control efforts. Declining fertility rates, as well as increasing age at first marriage, increasing divorce rates, and increasing

Table 2.3 Total Fertility Rate by Region and Selected Countries

Period	1950–1955	1975–1980	2000–2005	2025–2030	2050–2055	1995–2100
World total	4.95	3.84	2.62	2.29	2.15	2.03
Continent						
Africa	6.60	6.57	4.94	3.59	2.77	2.13
Asia	5.82	4.05	2.41	1.99	1.87	1.93
Europe	2.65	1.98	1.43	1.76	1.93	2.06
Latin America and the Caribbean	5.86	4.47	2.53	1.89	1.79	1.93
Northern America	3.33	1.80	1.99	2.06	2.08	2.09
Oceania	3.81	2.74	2.41	2.36	2.18	2.02
Region						
More developed	2.81	1.93	1.57	1.85	1.99	2.07
Less developed	6.54	6.58	4.85	3.34	2.65	2.13

SOURCE: Compiled from UNDESA (2011).

longevity, coupled with general patterns of aging, are correlated with substantial shifts in family structure and quickly shifting demographics across the world. For example, the reduced population growth over the past quarter century in certain European countries with low and declining birth rates is a cause of major concern, as those nations find themselves with too few workers and too few consumers to sustain their economies.

But to what extent can demographic transitions be said to be impacted by globalization? Global fertility transitions can be viewed from demographic but also historical, sociological, psychological, economic, gender, and policy perspectives—all of which *Global Families* argues are more or less shaped by globalization (Bulato 2001). Demographic theories associate declining fertility rates with declining mortality rates. Historical theories emphasize socio-economic development and the availability of effective contraception, as well as ideologies regarding population explosion. Sociological theories use mortality reduction, declines in the demand for children, and increases in the ability to regulate fertility. Psychological theories stress the individual's readiness, willingness, and ability to moderate fertility. Economic theories rely on micro-economic factors originating in the family along with human capital theory, including the cost of raising children and opportunity costs, particularly regarding maternal employment. Gender perspectives consider the indirect influences of family and gender systems, such as women's autonomy in more or less rigidly stratified societies. Finally, policy perspectives seek to reveal the place of population policy, including family-planning programs, regarding access to contraception and attitudes favorable to contraceptive use.

Rather than a single theory, a combination of theoretical approaches provides the best fit in terms of explaining global shifts in fertility. A study conducted by the Organisation for Economic Co-operation and Development (d'Addio and d'Ercole 2005) confirmed that cross-country variations in fertility rates are related to both macrosocial drivers (such as labor markets, social and fiscal policies) and microsocial drivers (including individual characteristics and patterns of interaction). For example, demographic transition can be mediated by historical events such as wars, which can in turn yield dramatic imbalances in the gender ratio (at least in the short run). Families may produce a bumper crop of babies in anticipation of or immediately following periods of extended separation due to migrant employment, military deployment, or other circumstances. Or, as discussed earlier, the extent of the lag between declining death rates and declining fertility rates can be shaped by psychological factors, including perceptions of the risk of infant mortality or adult death from disease or violence.

Dramatic, long-term changes in population rates are usually associated with social development, including the indirect effects of changes in women's educational and employment opportunities. Otherwise, spectacular reductions in fertility rates have been achieved in relatively short periods of time by coordinated, often aggressive, family-planning policies. Some government interventions, such as China's one-child policy, have had demonstrable effects not only on fertility rates but also on sex ratios (Sheng 2004; Yi 2002). That country's population policies have been accompanied by increases in the selective abortion of female fetuses and in female infanticide, demonstrating that changes in the mean preferred number of children can be complicated by traditional gender structures, including male preference. In China, the sex ratio (the number of males born per 100 females) reached 121 by 2000.

Other countries—such as India, with only 933 females to every 1,000 males in the total population—are moving in the same demographic direction. Although the crisis is even more acute in urban areas (with 900 females per 1,000 males) than in rural areas (with 946 females per 1,000 males; Office of the Registrar General and Census Commissioner, India 2010–2011), the consequences of the gender imbalances produced by such demographic imbalances are only now beginning to be felt, especially in urban areas, as the one-child generation enters adulthood and becomes eligible for marriage.

Effects of sweeping social policies surrounding fertility have also been observed in more-developed countries. Births in Germany dropped 4 percent from 2004 to 2005, to 690,000—the lowest number since World War II ("Germany Beefs Up Benefits" 2007). However, effective January 1, 2007, Germany's *Elterngeld* program allows a worker who leaves employment after the birth of a child to receive up to two thirds of her or his net wage, up to $2,375 per month for a year following the birth. Similar incentives in other countries, such as those found in France (Moore 2006), may be impacting fertility rates across Western Europe, if only moderately.

The attainment of equilibrium in fertility and mortality is complex and rarely involves couples' explicit calculations of death and birth rates. As societies develop, children contribute less economically. Children in more-developed societies spend less time in work and more time in education. Essentially, children in more-developed societies are more directly costly than children in less-developed societies. Children in more-developed societies are also more indirectly costly, as they compromise adults' economic and other opportunities, including maternal employment and earnings and family savings.

During periods of economic development, societies shift from expectations that families will be larger, multigenerational households emphasizing communal values to expectations for smaller, conjugal households emphasizing individualistic values. High fertility is often supported by religious institutions and close community associations. As societies modernize, both state-sanctioned norms and more informal social controls encourage individual decision making regarding fertility and, consequently, smaller family size. At the same time, diffusion of information and values serves to provide individuals and couples with access to cultural ideas and practices that shape fertility patterns.

Population decline intersects with a range of social changes, including

- mortality reduction, counting maternal and infant mortality;
- reduced economic contributions from children;
- opportunity costs of bearing children;
- family transformation;
- vanishing cultural supports for childbearing;
- marriage delay;
- cultural diffusion surrounding fertility practices; and
- improved access to effective fertility regulation (Bulato 2001).

Fertility shifts have been dramatically affected by the last of these factors: the availability and distribution of effective contraceptive technology. With social development comes improved technology and access to effective, safe fertility regulation, including contraception and abortion. Today, the percentage of married women using some form of modern contraception is highest in more-developed societies (e.g., 78 percent in Germany, 79 percent in Switzerland) and lowest in less-developed societies (e.g., 1 percent in Burundi, Chad, and Mauritania; Seager 2003:104–11).

The factors implied in the eight explanations do not operate in mutually exclusive ways, however. For example, government family-planning programs are often associated with societal development (Bulato 2001). Also, sociohistorical crises can interrupt the usual demographic patterns, at least on a temporary basis. Caldwell (2004) found this to be the case during both the English civil war of the 17th century and the fall of communism in Eastern Europe in the late 20th century. At times such as those, deferred marriage and declining marital fertility may also reflect uncertainty about the future during new socioeconomic and legal times.

Coale (1973) argued that three factors must be present in order for fertility rates to decline in a society. First, fertility must be within the realm of possible rational choice. Second, reduced fertility must be perceived as an advantage for the individual (or couple or society). Third, effective techniques—contraception and/or abortion—must be available for fertility control. Likewise, delayed marriage in more-developed societies reduces the potential years of partnered fertility, particularly in societies in which nonmarital fertility is negatively sanctioned.

The case of Italy demonstrates how demographic factors come together to shape population growth. As described in Table 2.4, both the total fertility rate and the crude death rate in Italy changed little during the last half of the 20th century. Yet, due to dramatic increases in the migration rate, the population in Italy grew by more than 10,000 between 1950 and 2000. Population growth in Italy is due not to shifts in the birth or death rates but, rather, to the influx of migrants—legal as well as illegal—into that country.

Table 2.4   Factors in Population Growth for Italy, 1950–2100

Period	1950–1955	1975–1980	2000–2005	2025–2030	2050–2055	2095–2100
Total fertility rate	2.36	2.29	2.47	2.52	2.35	1.94
Crude death rate	9.9	9.9	9.7	11.6	14.1	11.0
Net migration rate	−0.9	0.6	6.4	2.2	2.0	1.6
Population growth rate	0.75	0.41	0.58	−0.09	−0.28	0.12
Population (thousands)[1]	46,367	55,096	56,986	61,114	59,158	55,619

1. Population is for the year beginning the period (e.g., 1950).

SOURCE: Compiled from UNDESA (2011).

As the country moves further through the 21st century, Italian families share many characteristics with families in other societies with a declining rate of population growth:

- Increasing age at first marriage
- Increasing percentage of cohabiting unmarried couples
- Increasing separation and divorce rates
- Increasing percentage of single-parent families
- Increasing percentage of blended families
- Declining birth rates
- Increasing birth rates outside of marriage

Other changes in structural arrangements of families in countries such as Italy reflect religious, national, and cultural differences, as well as economic constraints. For example, Italy's divorce rate of 12.5 percent (8 divorces for every 100 marriages) lags far behind the 44 percent divorce rate of Sweden and England. Also, while young adults in Italy are delaying marriage, they are often doing so while continuing to live in the same household with their family of origin, rather than alone or in cohabiting arrangements. In other words, Italians continue to value attachments to their families of origin, even as they may be less likely to form new families of their own (Comunian 2005:227).

Decreasing family size in countries such as Italy shapes marital dynamics, including decline in polygyny and arranged marriage and increase in frequency of cohabitation and forms of nonmarital pairing (Adams 2004). Both macrosocial forces (e.g., economic and legal changes and improved educational and employment opportunities for women) and what Jelin (2004:405) calls "sociocultural factors linked to individuation" (e.g., modern values such as personal autonomy and free choice of marriage partners based on romantic love) influence marriage, divorce, and remarriage patterns during periods of declining fertility. In fact, the very meaning of marriage as a "divine match," a holy sacramental union, appears to wane with macrosocial changes in societal development and fertility (Singh 2004). As a consequence, families in many parts of the world, even the least-developed societies, are shifting from being stable households of economic producers to more fragile collections of individuals economically bound primarily as consumers (Adams 2004; Vincent 2000).

While some (e.g., Comunian 2005:226) choose to describe these changes in Italian society as "institutional crisis," many of the changes are rooted in gender liberation, specifically the greater equality between men's and women's roles, as well as increasing legal protection of the rights of women and children. Eventually, lower fertility contributes to "grayer" demographics. Declining fertility rates, coupled with increasing life expectancy, have increased the proportion of older persons (60 years and older) within overall populations and decreased the support ratio (the number of working people relative to the number of retired people). By the year 2050, the number of older persons worldwide will more than triple, from 606 million to 2 billion. In more-developed regions, the population of those older than 60 is predicted to increase from 20 percent to 33 percent; in less-developed regions, the population of those older than 60 is predicted to increase from 8 percent to 20 percent (U.N. Programme on the Family 2003). The effects of demographic aging ripple across all institutions of society but are particularly noticeable in families. As a population ages, families face challenges to intergenerational solidarity and caregiving as well as housing, social security systems, and health costs.

China is another society undergoing such a demographic shift. By 2030 the number of Chinese over age 60 will double from today's 178 million. In just one decade, the proportion of China's population over the age of 60 will increase from one out of eight in 2010 to one out of five in 2020. China's dependency ratio (the number of people of nonworking age, both young and old, as a proportion of those of working age) will reach an all-time low by 2015. This is likely to slow economic growth and fuel an increase in industrial wages as the supply of rural labor declines. As a result, China will see falling demand for schools but a rising demand for retirement homes. Those smaller families created not only by China's one-child policy but also by the fact that children are expensive in China will need assistance in providing care for their elders ("Getting On" 2011).

Population Control as an International Policy Concern

Ideological concerns regarding population are a key part of understanding fertility transition in global perspective. Caldwell (2001) discusses how, beginning in the 1940s, simultaneously but in contrast to deeply rooted pronatalist traditions, Western ideologies grew around beliefs "that the deliberate control of fertility in poor, high-growth countries was desirable, even the path of virtue" (p. 102). By the middle of the 20th century *The New York Times* and other news outlets had published editorials endorsing worldwide population control, the World Council of Churches had adopted a policy position favoring the same, and the American Public Health Association formally advocated the inclusion of family-planning services as part of health services. By the late 1960s *The Population Bomb* (Ehrlich 1968) had encapsulated the belief that fertility decisions and outcomes were of consequence not only to individuals and their families but also to nations and the entire planet.

As in the case of Italy, governments in more-developed societies are more likely to view their fertility rates as being too low. Governments in the global South are more likely to view their fertility rates as too high (Seager 2003). In more-developed parts of the world, population control ideology has provided couples, and especially women, with a belief system to support delaying childbearing, limiting family size, and even, for a few, deferring marriage or childbearing altogether. Economic prosperity as well as other social movements (e.g., the civil rights movement, women's movements) provided corollary inducements for such dramatic social changes as extending the time spent in formal schooling, women's employment, and delayed marriage.

Rosero-Bixby (2001) argues that government-led family-planning programs play an important part in fertility decline. Those programs can stimulate consideration of previously taboo subjects (such as birth control) and can create a critical mass in the population. In turn, these processes can increase demand for family-planning services and technology and, eventually, stimulate supply of those services and technology. Rosero-Bixby distinguishes between two rationales shaping global family-planning programs—one macrolevel rationale and another microlevel rationale consistent with social activism, such as that led by Margaret Sanger in the early 20th century in the United States.

The macrolevel rationale may be favored by centralized government officials in their efforts to stem the rate of population growth and associated economic and social problems related to environmental degradation, economic development, social unrest, and rural-to-urban migration. The microlevel rationale may be favored by health practitioners and social workers concerned about women's reproductive health, sexuality, and rights, often across national borders. By the 1994 International Conference on Population and development, family planning policy shifted demonstrably from macro- to microlevel rationale. This shift has had implications for political and social support, funding, effectiveness, and persistence of global initiatives directed at population control.

These national population ideologies can shape access to reproductive health systems, not only domestically but also abroad. At the turn of the century, major donors for overseas population programs gave more than 10 million U.S. dollars annually to overseas population programs, primarily in Southern countries. Most of this funding (63 percent) was in the form of direct assistance from more-developed countries, with another 20 percent in the form of loans from the World Bank. A smaller, but still significant amount of funding (11 percent) came from private foundations and NGOs. Six of the seven biggest donors among private foundations and NGOs were from the United States. Those donors include the Bill and Melinda Gates Foundation, the Ford Foundation, the Packard Foundation, the Population Council, the MacArthur Foundation, and the Rockefeller Foundation. Marie Stopes International, a foundation based in the United Kingdom, was the second-biggest donor among private foundations and NGOs (Seager 2003:42–3).

Since that time, however, opposition to public funding for population control has gained traction among Americans. Such opposition is often rooted in religious beliefs, especially among those opposing abortion. Opponents oppose funding for domestic programs such as Title X of the Public Health Service Act, as well as development programs through the U.S.

Agency for International Development. Some organizations have supported a full ban on funding for the U.N. Population Fund (UNFPA), arguing that funding population programs that include contraception and abortion harms women and children in poor countries (see, e.g., Population Research Institute 1999). However, regarding President Obama's intention to restore U.S. funding for the UNFPA, Nicholas Kristoff (2009), Pulitzer Prize–winning coauthor of *Half the Sky* (Kristoff and WuDunn 2009) wrote:

> One of the scandals of the early 21st century is that 122 million women around the world want contraception and can't get it. Whatever one thinks of abortion, it's tragic that up to 40 percent of all pregnancies globally are unplanned or unwanted—and that almost half of those result in induced abortions. By some measures, more than one quarter of all maternal deaths could be avoided if there were no unplanned or unwanted pregnancies. (p. 134)

As a result of improved contraceptive technology and increased access to safe abortion, virtually certain birth control with little or no risk has been available to most women in Western societies. Beginning in the 1960s, the birth control pill and intrauterine contraceptive devices, as well as sterilization (of males and females) for family planning and safer, easier suction abortion techniques, made birth control increasingly widely available and practiced in the most-developed countries (Caldwell 2001). Birth control methods with higher user and technical failure rates, methods with more side effects, methods involving coital partner cooperation, and methods available only through medical sources have lower rates of adoption, continuation, and success in preventing pregnancy than do other methods.

Research has repeatedly confirmed that individuals in the least-developed societies are less likely than individuals in the most-developed societies to practice effective birth control—and are unlikely even to contemplate restricting family size—because they do not have access to family-planning services. In the least-developed nations of the world, methods of contraception are often unavailable and abortion is rare and not used to limit family size (Balfour et al. 1950; Caldwell 2001).

While unplanned children are certainly not the same as unwanted children, when women are unable to control the number and timing of their births, their children and their families bear substantial direct and indirect costs. Quantity and quality of physical and social resources, as well as parental time and energy, may be strained. Further, a woman's childbearing patterns, including the number and spacing of children, are directly related to her ability to maintain employment and pursue economic advancement and independence, as well as her own and her children's health and well-being.

Fertility in a Global, Postmodern World

In some ways, fertility preferences in a global, postmodern world can be perplexing. Bachrach (2001) suggests that certain values, attitudes, and orientations associated with the postmodern individual are likewise associated with changes in fertility preferences. She identifies these ideals as self-realization, personal freedom (in lifestyle and relationships), quality of life valued over material well-being, questioning traditional authority, and tolerating and respecting diversity. Further, she connects these traits with a declining reliance on institutions that support high fertility. The postmodern individual relies less on traditional, authoritarian religious systems and communal, patriarchal family systems. Thus, a postmodern culture emphasizing self-actualization may act to decrease fertility. Individuals may prefer to postpone or avoid childbearing altogether to pursue personal objectives related to work and leisure (Bachrach 2001).

However, in societies such as those of Finland and Sweden where a high percentage of the population espouses postmodern views, preferred fertility rates continue to surpass actual fertility rates. Fertility preferences may be slow to change, or childbearing and childrearing may be a source of personal fulfillment in a postmodern world (Bachrach 2001). These postmodern value orientations may well be global phenomenon, associated with transnational contact via educational programs, mass media, international social policies, or other venues.

Fertility control illustrates the relevance of privilege, whether class or race based, within a society or across societies. Ironically, in the United States and in some other Western societies, a population "double standard" exists. While women of economic, racial, and other privilege may be celebrated for their fertility and for taking heroic means to resolve infertility, poor women, women of color, and immigrant women, especially those receiving some form of public assistance, are stereotyped (e.g., as "welfare queens") and denigrated for having children.

Surrogacy presents another twist on the intersections among race, class, and gender privilege and presents what is perhaps the ultimate form of global outsourcing. Over the past three decades, infertile upper-middle-class families have turned to assisted reproductive technologies and surrogate mothers, sometimes crossing national boundaries. Reproductive outsourcing is a rapidly expanding business in countries such as India.

> Clinics that provide surrogate mothers for foreigners say they have recently been inundated with requests from the United States and Europe, as word spreads of India's mix of skilled medical professionals, relatively liberal laws and low prices. (Gentleman 2008)

In *Outsourcing the Womb,* Twine (2011) provides a comparative overview of the global surrogacy market, focusing on Egypt, India, Israel, and the United States, while asking questions of what she calls reproductive justice. Opponents to this "global exchange of money for babies" fear that it threatens international adoptions, is "fraught with ethical and legal uncertainties," and risks exploitation of poor women (Marsh 2008).

Sweeping Migration

In addition to mortality and fertility, demographic transition depends on migration (movement across borders), both emigration (movement from a sending country) and immigration (movement into a receiving country). Although earlier periods (e.g., 19th century migration from Europe to the United States) have witnessed great waves of immigration, movement across national borders is truly more globalized. More countries are affected by migration, and migrants' origins are more diverse, resulting in an increase in the number of multiethnic and multicultural societies around the globe (Mascia-Lees 2010). This greater scale, however, as well as migration's intersections with global economics, politics, and culture and factors such as the feminization of migration and irregular (i.e., illegal, undocumented, unauthorized) migration mean the consequences of migration have never been greater (Koser 2009).

Today, 3 percent (175 million) of the world's population live outside their country of birth, and the United Nations estimates that 20 million people worldwide are refugees. Migration has always been a potent force in human history. Migration and refugee status are linked not only to economic aspirations but also to discrimination, violence, and even natural disasters across the globe. Cultural, ethnic, racial, and religious differences and lack of integration into the host country place significant stress on relationships among parents, children, elders, and other family members. Migration, both internal and seasonal, by men contributes to higher numbers of female-headed households worldwide. Meanwhile, sex trafficking and sexual exploitation of women and children and associated international crime continues to increase (U.N. Programme on the Family 2003).

Like morbidity and mortality, as well as fertility, transnational migration plays a key part in determining the demographic complexion of a society. The migration rate is the difference between the number of immigrants and the number of emigrants, expressed as net number of migrants per 1,000 population. Table 2.5 shows that the net effect of migration has favored immigration into more-developed regions (North America but also Europe and Oceania) and emigration from less-developed regions (Africa but also Latin American and the Caribbean and Asia). As in the case of fertility rates, net migration rates for continents and regions are predicted to converge in the last half of the 21st century.

Table 2.5   Net Migration Rates, 1950–2100

Period	1950–1955	1975–1980	2000–2005	2025–2030	2050–2055	2095–2100
Continent						
Africa	–0.5	–0.6	–0.7	–0.3	–0.2	0.0
Asia	0.0	–0.2	–0.4	–0.2	–0.2	0.0
Europe	0.7	0.6	2.6	1.3	0.8	0.1
Latin America and the Caribbean	0.1	–1.3	–2.2	–0.7	–0.4	0.0
Northern America	2.0	3.2	4.5	2.8	2.1	0.0
Oceania	7.2	0.8	4.3	2.2	0.9	0.0
Region						
More developed	0.1	1.1	2.9	1.7	1.2	0.1
Less developed	0.0	–0.4	–0.7	–0.3	–0.2	0.0

SOURCE: Compiled from UNDESA (2011).

Families on the Move

In the past, immigration has been a one-way path of no return. Immigrants departed the home country with little or no expectation of ever returning to the society and loved ones left behind. When almost one out of every seven Irish-born people emigrated from that country, Peter McCorry (1984), Irish nationalist and weekly newspaper editor for the Irish community in New York City in the late 1860s and early 1870s, wrote in 1870:

They had passed the bitter ordeal of leave-taking with friends and relations; they had looked for the last time on the graves of parents and children, gazed tenderly and affectionately on the well-remembered spots of their childhood, with feelings which no pen has ever yet or ever shall be able to describe. Some had left fathers and mothers, and sisters and brothers; some had left wives and young families, dependent on the mercies of a cold and callous world, who sustained themselves with the thought that, with God's help, before long, they would be able to send the first remittance to cheer the desolate homes they had left forever. (P. 154)

Miyoshi (1993) described the experience of migrants who, upon arriving in the new country, are "cut off from their own homes . . . [and who] disappear into huge urban slums without the protection of a traditional . . . mutual dependence system" (p. 748).

"Family in Refugee Camp, Jalozai, Afghanistan"

Photograph by A. Banta. Reprinted by permission of the U.N. High Commission on Refugees.

Organizations such as the International Organization for Migration (2011), an intergovernmental organization founded in 1951, are "committed to the principle that human and orderly migration benefits migrants and society." Today, family reunification is a primary goal of the immigration policies of most nations. As demonstrated in Table 2.6, by far the most frequent class of immigrants admitted to the United States is immediate relatives

Table 2.6   Immigrants Admitted by Class of Admission, 1990–2009

CLASS OF ADMISSION	1990[3]		2000[4]		2009[4]	
	N	Percentage	N	Percentage	N	Percentage
Family-sponsored preferences	214,355	22.7	235,092	28.0	211,859	18.7
Employment-based preferences	155,330	16.4	106,642	12.7	144,034	12.7
Immediate relatives of U.S. citizens	406,074	43.0	346,350	41.2	535,554	47.4
Refugees and asylum seekers	71,230	7.5	62,928	7.5	177,368	15.7
IRCA[1]	128	0.0	n/a	n/a	n/a	n/a
Other immigrants[2]	99,025	10.5	89,990	10.7	62,003	5.5
Total immigrants	946,142	100.1	841,002	100.0	1,130,818	100.0

NOTES: 1. The Immigration Reform and Control Act (IRCA) of 1986 virtually completed this amnesty process before 2000. 2. "Other" includes immigrants admitted under laws intended to diversify immigration, parolees, and those who qualify under the Nicaraguan Adjustment and Central American Relief Act and the Haitian Refugee Immigration Act.

SOURCES: 3. Adapted from U.S. Bureau of the Census (2006). 4. Adapted from U.S. Bureau of the Census (2011).

of U.S. citizens. In fact, two out of every three immigrants admitted into the United States in 2009 were children, spouses, siblings, or grandparents, or family-sponsored individuals being reunited with kin.

An estimated 2 million people—husbands, wives, children, and siblings of legal, permanent residents of the United States—qualify for admission but remain on waiting lists to become legal, permanent residents. A backlog in processing applications, plus the immigrant visa quotas set by the U.S. Congress, ensure that only a small number of family members are admitted to legal, permanent residence status each year (Hopfensperger 2006:A1). According to State Department statistics, the lag time is as much as 22 years for siblings from the Philippines who applied in 1984 (p. A21). Such delays create significant hardships for families, who are unable to reunite and who, therefore, may be forced to live alone or as single parents while waiting for family reunification.

Although policies of first preference in granting visas for family-sponsored immigration favor unmarried daughters and sons of current U.S. citizens, marriage to an American citizen has long been a model for immigration into the United States. Time-series analysis has revealed that an increase in marriages to U.S. citizens often accompanies a change in the law guiding qualifications for immigrant visas (Jasso 1997).

While an American citizen can apply for a visa to bring a spouse or fiancé(e) into the United States, marriage to an American citizen is no longer the guarantee of citizenship that it once may have been. Further, immigration procured through marriage to a citizen of the receiving country has potentially troubling consequences for the families thus established. Immigration-motivated marriages may be more fragile and less stable than marriages contracted under other circumstances.

The case of nurses from the Philippines who immigrated to the United States ahead of their families illustrates the uncertainties of the immigration system. To meet the growing demand for foreign nurses in the United States, particularly in the elder care sector, the Immigration and Naturalization Service created a special pool of 50,000 visas restricted to foreign nurses and their families. The last of those special visas was issued in December 2006. Such a system has been criticized for creating a "brain drain" in the Philippines and other countries that send skilled workers to developed societies such as the United States, but the termination of that special immigration program left nurses who immigrated ahead of their families with no assurance that they would be reunited in the near future, if ever (Hopfensperger 2006).

Migration and Family Processes

A review of the last decade of research on immigrant families in the United States revealed two dominant perspectives: assimilation and acculturation. Family scholars who emphasize assimilation perspectives focus on family formation, finding over time and across generations greater similarity between the immigrants and the receiving country on such factors as intermarriage, fertility, and other behaviors such as child naming.

Families are critical in negotiating assimilation for their members. Occupational segregation and concentration in urban ghettos, as well as the settlement house and immigrant language, education, and civic programs, played critical roles in the "Americanization" of new immigrants to the

United States. Yet assimilation presents the immigrant with struggles over retaining or losing one's cultural identity to the dominant culture (Ewing 2011). Even under the best of circumstances, immigration and assimilation may severely disrupt family order as the family negotiates differences between the adopted society and the home society. This can lead some couples to seek professional help in dealing with the social class, culture, and especially gender contradictions caused by the immigrant experience (Inclan 2003). Not surprisingly then, immigrant families are overrepresented as clients in the social service system (Roopnarine and Shin 2003).

A pure assimilation approach to immigration studies has fallen into disfavor among immigration scholars. A more recent "segmented assimilation" approach (see Portes and Zhou 1993) emphasizes the variations in adaptation and among different types of immigrants (i.e., highly skilled professionals, executives, and managers; undocumented and low-skilled workers; refugees and asylum seekers). A segmented assimilation approach emphasizes the divergent resources and consequent risks these different immigrants and their families bring with them into the host country. These resources are financial and human capital, such as social class from the home country; political capital, such as legal status upon entry into the destination country; and social capital, such as social networks, family structure, and family cohesion (Landale 1997; Rumbaut 1997). From this perspective, the most advantaged immigrants may arrive in the host country with an abundance of resources and quite well suited to family life in the new society.

Hutter (1986–1987) argued that the ultimate ability of an immigrant group to establish itself in the host country has been highly dependent on the group's ability to reestablish and normalize family life in the host country. In contrast to groups that have assimilated, Hutter has described the resettlement of groups such as the Hutterites from rural Russia to relatively isolated rural communities in the United States in the late 19th century. Due to their isolation, Hutterites were thus better able to maintain idiosyncratic patterns of family life, including early marriage, strict expectations of endogamy (marriage within extended kinship groups), very high fertility, and virtually universal remarriage after widowhood in the context of a cooperative, patriarchal social structure.

Scholars who emphasize acculturation perspectives focus more on intrafamily relationships, finding changes among immigrants and their families on attitudes and values, including intergenerational tensions around areas such as ethnic identity, second-language acquisition, and parental control (Glick 2010). Once an international couple marries, acculturation may be selective, as in the case of North African women in France. In that case, first-generation women from the Maghreb (Algeria, Morocco, Tunisia) living in

France made "cultural choices" around such issues as wearing the headscarf (prohibited by the French government). Some women wear the headscarf as a sign of religious freedom and their Muslim identity. Other women defer wearing the headscarf, although they might prefer to do so, because of the advantage that decision offers for employment (Killian 2006).

Other scholars have emphasized the extent to which social structure shapes opportunities for and consequences of both assimilation and acculturation. For example, around the time of World War II, intermarriage between Americans of Japanese heritage and white Americans decreased along with increased exclusion of Japanese from American society (Ono and Berg 2010). Cultural diversity is increasingly a theme of contemporary studies of immigration. Immigrants often bring with them new forms of household and family formation that challenge conventional family structure. These new forms may include different traditions regarding age and other criteria of marriage and childbearing, greater emphasis on cohabitation, various blended family systems, as well as a higher or lower propensity for divorce and other forms of marital dissolution.

For example, Shaw (2004) found Caribbean and South Asian families immigrating to Great Britain challenging that society in dramatic ways, while variations in family forms were evident within immigrant groups. Transnational Caribbean families emphasize strong extended kin and socioeconomic relations with family remaining in the Caribbean. Transnational South Asian families are characterized by larger, three-generational households, made up of sons who marry and bring their wives and subsequent children into the parental household. Even there, significant variation exists among South Asian families, as between Mirpuri Muslims (who originate in Kashmir) and Jullundri Sikhs (the majority of Indian Punjab migrants living in Great Britain). The former were still adhering to patterns of close consanguineous marriages (especially to first cousins) and expressed preference for extended three-generational households. The latter were more likely to reject arranged marriage in favor of "assisted" or self-initiated marriage partner choice and neolocal residence once the couple had married (Shaw 2004).

The challenges and cultural contradictions of immigration can affect an array of family dynamics, including intergenerational caregiving and gender relations. Immigration policies themselves have a direct impact on the ability of families to adjust and adapt to transnational life (Booth, Crouter, and Landale 1997). Transnational families who are unable to reunite may have greater difficulty synchronizing members' life courses and family timetables and managing parenting and intergenerational caregiving (Leung and Lee 2005).

Regarding gender relations, Jamaican men who immigrated to New York were likely to continue to espouse the traditional double standard, while their wives, who remained behind, rejected such a standard (Roopnarine and Shin 2003). Also, migration into a society with traditional gender relations may reintroduce or fortify the traditional gender roles among migrant women. Such appears to be the case for Mexican women migrating to Montana. Although traditional gender relations may be to their detriment, Mexican women expressed preference for the more traditional Montana as a place where they could provide greater safety and opportunity for their children (Schmalzbauer 2009).

Immigration has always been a large part of globalization. During certain periods, nations such as the United States have enacted severely restrictive immigration legislation, such as the Chinese Exclusion Act of 1882 and Immigration Acts of 1921, 1924, and 1929, which placed severe restrictions on immigration from certain European countries. Bose (2006a) writes of these policies as representing a "retreat from globalization; a national acquiescence to racism, prejudice, and intolerance; and an affront to the basic fabric of a nation built by the labor of many immigrant nationalities" (p. 569).

Some courts, media, and public opinion in France, the Netherlands, the United Kingdom, and elsewhere contest the desire of immigrants to retain aspects of their home culture. For example, a tribunal court in Leeds, England, refused to overturn a school decision in which a teaching assistant in West Yorkshire, England, was dismissed for refusal to remove her veil (Wainwright 2006). In the Netherlands, the Dutch cabinet has offered a statement that "burqas disturb public order, citizens and safety" (BBC News 2006).

Host society ambivalence to immigrants and their families is hardly new. Today immigrants may be viewed as "the other," as parasitic threats to national identity, as disproportionate consumers of public resources, and even as "taking over" the dominant society. Such hysteria is common but rarely warranted. For example, Muslims living in Europe will only increase from the current 6 percent to 8 percent in 2030 (Pew Research Center 2011a). The growth rate among Muslims worldwide is expected to level off as more Muslim women pursue education and employment and more people migrate to cities with improving standards of living.

Especially after the bombings on the World Trade Center in New York City on September 11, 2001, Arab Americans and Muslims in particular have been viewed with particular suspicion and as risks to national security. However, Muslim Americans are predominantly "middle class and mostly mainstream" and express little support for terrorism (Pew Research Center 2011b). To the contrary, from her ethnographic study of Arab American communities in Chicago, Cainkar (2011) argues that anti-Arab and anti-Muslim sentiments, politics, and government actions have left Arab Americans themselves feeling particularly vulnerable and unsafe.

Hence, attitudes on immigration vary with historical events and shape that era's policy, practice, rules, and regulations regarding newcomers. The distribution of controls and restrictions, rights and privileges shape migrant families' access to economic, educational, legal, medical, and other social resources. This ultimately shapes the ease of their transition into the receiving society and their ease in becoming productive contributors to society who can enrich the host culture.

In spite of negative public opinion, the gains for the receiving country from immigrants outweigh the losses. Immigrants from poor countries provide labor in wealthy countries with the demographic challenges discussed in this chapter. Immigrant families represent what Goldin, Cameron, and Balarajan (2011) label "exceptional people."

One area in which immigrants and their families have historically contributed to American society is in the economic sector. A new report issued by the Partnership for a New American Economy (2011)—an organization led by CEOs of corporations such as Boeing and Microsoft and mayors of cities such as New York and Los Angeles—summarizes some of the ways in which the United States has benefited from immigrants' entrepreneurialism across a wide range of industry sectors:

- More than 40 percent of the 2010 Fortune 500 companies were founded by immigrants or their children.
- The newest Fortune 500 companies are more likely (20 percent) to have an immigrant founder.
- Seven out of ten of the most valuable brands in the world (e.g., Apple, Budweiser, Colgate) belong to American companies founded by immigrants or their children.
- Fortune 500 companies founded by immigrants or their children
  o employ more than 10 million people worldwide and
  o generate revenue greater than the gross domestic product of every country in the world except the United States, China, and Japan.

The postmodern immigrant experience also increasingly involves lives lived across borders with ties to home maintained. Schiller, Basch, and Blanc-Stanton (1992a) have defined transnationalism as a particular immigrant experience, a social process through which "transmigrants develop and maintain multiple relations—familial, economic, social, organizational, religious, and political—that span borders" (p. ix). From this perspective, immigrant families retain, extend, and preserve relationships, act and decide, and experience concerns and identities, even traveling back and forth across two or more societies over extended periods of time (Schiller et al. 1992a; Silverstein and Auerbach 2005).

Contemporary migration may well be linked to capitalist economic and other systems on a global scale, but migration also is grounded in the every-day experiences of the migrants themselves. Consider, for example, that immigrants to the United States are increasingly drawn not to large cities but to small towns and even rural areas, as well as to cities in the Midwestern and Southern United States (Massey 2010).

Foner (1997) has written of the immigrant family:

> The family . . . is a place where there is a dynamic interplay between structure, culture, and agency. New immigrant family patterns are shaped by cultural meanings and social practices immigrants bring with them from their home countries, as well as social, economic, and cultural forces in the [adopted country]. . . . Immigrants live out much of their lives in the context of families. (P. 961)

The literature on immigration, particularly in the last decades of the 20th century, makes clear the critical role families play in adaptation and adjustment and in alleviating the cultural and social hardships associated with immigration (see Bodnar 1987; Foner 1997; Meissner et al. 1993). For the immigrant child, youth, or adult—including marriage migrants and adoptees—the family is *home,* potentially a place of refuge and haven, where the individual is linked to larger identities through socialization, stories, and even names. Families' adaptations and adjustments to the new society are functions of stage of the family life cycle, as well as factors such as poverty, discrimination and prejudice, physical well-being, and mental health. Even aside from the traditional emphasis on family reunification in immigration policy, families are clearly critical to understanding the processes through which individuals, communities, and societies engage immigration.

Social reformers such as Jane Addams (1910), founder of the American social welfare movement, appreciated the complementary roles of immigrant parents and their children, and the particular role of children and youth as agents in their parents' assimilation, in turn-of-the-20th-century Chicago. Rumbaut (1997) reminds us that the family also constrains the immigrant, potentially binding the individual to traditions and customs ill fitted to the new society and creating conflicts across genders and generations. The potential for these schisms in the new society to compromise family cohesion and solidarity and even to lead to family conflict and disruption has long been a source of concern. More recent research (e.g., Purkayastha 2005) has emphasized how the very process of assimilation is layered even beyond generational factors with considerations of gender, race, and ethnicity.

In two subsequent chapters, Chapters 3 and 5, I discuss the challenges transnationalism presents for parenting and global cultural systems across intergenerational relationships. A compelling body of research has documented the extent to which social–structural factors, such as residential segregation, life in ghettos, inferior education, and racial discrimination in employment, as well as serial migration and changes in lifestyle in the destination country, can corrode the ties that bind immigrant parents and their children (Waters 1994). Further, immigrant parents may find themselves working long hours in locations distant from their homes. Coupled with greater isolation from kin and community than in the home country, immigrant parents may thus find themselves less able to supervise their children in the new society. Those factors may all compromise parental authority for immigrant families (Landale 1997).

Still, in many ways, immigrants and their families endure and even triumph. In the United States, while immigrants and their second-generation family members tend to be poorer and have lower incomes, lower-status occupations, and lower levels of education than do members of the general population, immigrants and even second-generation immigrants are less likely to be divorced and children are more likely to live with both parents than are other Americans. Thus, the persistence and resilience of family ties serve as critical economic, cultural, and social capital for their immigrant families (Rumbaut 1997).

In the 21st century, transnational migration defies and spans the usual concepts of culture and society, nation and tribe, race and ethnicity in a world shaped by globalization. Thus, Schiller et al. (1992b:11) describe the identities of transnational migrants as "complex," "multiple," and "fluid," and as variable from individual to individual. In the following sections I elaborate on some of the effects of immigration on families, including gender, marriage, transnational adoption, and parent–child relationships. I address in Chapter 5 the particular implications for families of migration across national borders by those seeking employment.

Gender and Migration

Historically, men have greatly outnumbered women as migrants. Today, women constitute a growing proportion of migrants worldwide and even outnumber men as migrants from some areas, such as the Philippines and

Sri Lanka (Seager 2003). This has led some researchers (e.g., Anthias and Lazaridis 2000:1) to refer to the feminization of international migration. Still, women's role in international migration has received less attention, in spite of the fact that women are critical nodes in the creation, maintenance, and extension of social networks before, during, and after migration (Wilson 2009).

Both the existence of a large informal economy in which irregular employment is common (with the accompanying issue of undocumented workers whose legal status rests in the hands of their employers) and an increase in female employment among local women support increasing demand for women's migration into the destination country. Thus, the feminization of migration correlates with the following factors in the destination country:

- A concentration of women in the service sector, particularly as domestic maids in the homes of women employed outside of the home
- Poor welfare provisions
- Poor facilities for child care
- A demand for women as sex workers, often recruited for these dangerous and vulnerable positions through sex trafficking (see Chapter 4)

Until recently, migrant women have been almost invisible in migration studies. Anthias and Lazaridis (2000) note the extent to which the sexism explicit in migration "intersects with different forms of 'othering' and racialization" through the "crosscuttings of gender, ethnicity, and class" (p. 11). For example, those writers describe how policies originating in the European Union make little reference to migrant women, leading them to be critical of welfare systems, such as those found in Italy, that fail to provide basic support for migrant women and their families. An absence of training and infrastructures for employed migrant mothers ensures that these women will be permanently relegated to domestic work or illegal sex work or, if reunited with their husbands, to continued subordination in their own families. These gendered effects have consequences not only for the female migrant but also for the longer-term quality of life for her family.

Bologna, in the Emilia-Romagna region of Italy, seems to be an exception. In that city, migrant women from the Philippines, Somalia, Eritrea, and Ethiopia significantly outnumber migrant men, and the Bologna City Council seems to have made a concerted effort to take gender into account when providing services to migrants. The Bologna City Council aims to document the presence of migrant people bearing in mind the differences between men and women and between different nationalities. If we were to have aggregate statistics under the "blanket" of the word *extracomunitari*, without specifying anything about sex or nationality, we would not face these issues properly and in their complexity in the Bolognese area. (Bernardotti, Capecchi, and Pinto 1994:2, as quoted in Orsini-Jones and Gattullo 2000:132–3)

In fact, the very decision to migrate may be mediated by gender. Toro-Morn (1995) studied working-class and better-educated middle-class Puerto Rican women who immigrated to Chicago after their husbands. While working-class women reported migrating to care for their children, husbands, and families, middle-class women reported migrating for professional reasons. While working-class husbands supported their wives' employment as a temporary accommodation to life in the United States, traditional division of labor in the household remained unchanged. In contrast, the middle-class women in Toro-Morn's study developed strategies that gave equal standing to career goals and family. Toro-Morn's research demonstrates how migrant women experience the dual worlds of productive work in the social economy, including experiencing reproductive work in their families differently than do men, as well as how gendered migration experiences intersect with social class.

Personal and group networks also shape the content, direction, and timing of migration, provide housing and social needs, and enable the migrant to assemble a support system to assuage the privation and isolation of separation from family and home. Chell-Robinson (2000) describes a series of concentric spheres with close relatives at the center, followed by more distant relatives, friends, and others from one's home country on whom one may depend for support. In this last category, she includes migrant traffickers, religious organizations, and the national governments. The closer a relationship is to the core of the sphere, the greater the degree of obligation among the individuals involved. These relationships can assist the migrant woman in building a sense of identity in her new location. Ironically, the very existence of these spheres of obligation—for example, the requirement to send money home—can impede the migrant woman's achieving independence in the host society.

Finally, migration, even when to a country promising greater economic, political, religious, or other opportunity, carries with it significant gendered risk in terms of safety and security. While the discontent among young male immigrants in the impoverished housing projects of the Paris suburbs has received a great deal of attention in the news media, the plight of girls and women has received very little. According to Fadela Amara, founder of

Ni Putes Ni Soumises (Neither a Whore nor a Submissive), women and girls are "double victims" in France's immigrant society. First, females experience racist and sexist discrimination in employment and social opportunity. Then, some Muslim females also suffer from sexual harassment and violence, including domestic violence, rape, and gang rape, in their own families and communities (Faramarz 2005:A20).

The incidence of domestic violence among immigrant and refugee women in the United States is likely consistent with incidences of domestic violence in other populations (Alvi et al. 2002; Immigrant Law Center 2003; Minnesota Advocates for Human Rights 2004). However, refugee and immigrant women face significant obstacles in securing safety for themselves and their children and in prosecuting their abusers. I discuss domestic violence among immigrant populations in greater detail in Chapter 4.

Marriage Migrants

Sometimes lost in the discussion of immigration as movements of large groups of people across national borders for economic, political, religious, or other opportunity is the reality that some immigration occurs because individuals wish to form or build new families. Marriage and adoption across national borders are both a continuing part of global migration.

The number of marriages in which the spouses are of different nationalities is increasing dramatically, especially since the 1990s in places such as Southeast and East Asia (Yang and Lu 2010). With more than 250 marriage bureaus and catalogs operating in the United States alone, an estimated 150,000 women are advertised each year as available for marriage across national borders (Seager 2003:56). For example, in Germany in 1995, the proportion of marriages in which one partner was *Ausländerinnen oder Ausländer betreiligt* (i.e., holder of a foreign passport) was only 1 in 25. However, just 4 years later, by 1999, the proportion of such marriages in Germany had risen to 1 in 6. In the United States, a quarter of men and more than 4 out of 10 women who enter the country do so as marriage migrants (Beck-Gernsheim 2001:79).

The transnational business of agents and agencies that match men from more affluent societies to women from struggling ones is the subject of considerable, often sensational, attention in the media. Research on the husband's side of the equation (e.g., those who use international services for second marriages and families) is sparse. However, Beck-Gernsheim, Butler, and Puigvert's (2001) analysis of advertisements for marriage placed in newspapers by professional marriage agencies suggests that transnational marriages are most favored by men with serious social shortcomings and, at their worst, are arrangements characterized by gendered oppression, abuse, and violence. Thus, transnational marriages may best be described as grounded in the interactions among disparate worldwide socioeconomic dependencies, international labor migration patterns, and universal gender inequalities.

Popular views of marriage between American men and women from other countries are clouded by stereotypes (Williams 1991). Noting assumptions of "a fusion of passion and calculation, desire and deception" that accompany the terms *mail-order brides, visa wives,* and *imported husbands,* Beck and Beck-Gernsheim (2010) charge that academic and public discourse about marriage migration tends to be biased. The oppression of women and girls when they are trafficked or forced into marriage is a horrible reality. For many women, however, especially those from the poorest regions of the world and in the lowest strata of their societies, "women's 'marriage migration' may often be the most efficient and socially acceptable means available to disadvantaged women to achieve a measure of social and economic mobility" (Palriwala and Uberoi 2008:23).

Marriage for social mobility is nothing new and "is becoming increasingly linked to marriage for transnational mobility" (Beck and Beck-Gernsheim 2010:402). In this global age, finding a marriage partner has never been easier. The options include the international commercial marriage-brokering industry composed of professional and semiprofessional agents mediated through the Internet, newspaper advertisements, matchmaking tours, and even sex tourism. Families who have relatives already settled in the global North or West have another option: kinship-based networks (Beck and Beck-Gernsheim 2010).

Three factors—economic inequality, national inequality, and gender inequality—are problematic in many migrant marriages. In such marriages, the economic disparity between the husband, who is usually of higher status, and the wife is often significant. Also, women in these marriages often come from countries that are politically unstable or economically stagnant, thus complicating their unsteadiness in the world. Further, the agencies that broker such marriages seem to cater to different, more traditional gender expectations, depicting the women as "loyal, home-loving," "demure," and "all heart and soul for the man and the family." In combination, these conditions set the stage for a husband to exert power over a wife, or even violence against a wife who disappoints (Beck-Gernsheim 2001:70–1).

In Japan, the largest group of international marriages (75 percent) is between Japanese men and foreign women, usually of Philippine, Korean, Chinese, or Thai origin. Piper's (2000) study of international marriage between Japanese men and Southeast Asian women views such marriages as part of a global, gendered, political economy. She describes the marriages among participants in her study as "marriage of convenience," with the women leaving relatively low-status or low-paying positions with little opportunity for advancement for immigration and work in the Japanese entertainment industry (p. 212).

The number of foreign women entering Japan increased dramatically in the last decades of the 20th century (Herbert 1996), and the largest number of immigrants to Japan are young Filipina and Thai women (Muroi and Sasaki 1997). The women in Piper's (2000) study originally immigrated to Japan as autonomous, yet vulnerable parties, relegated to work in the flourishing sex and entertainment industries. Such systems reveal not only a need for the lowest-skilled labor in countries such as Japan but also an existing system of patriarchal gendered realities. In Southeast Asia, the "hospitality" or tourism industry provides sex tours for men traveling alone or with other men from Japan or other more-developed societies with the expressed intention of purchasing the services of prostitutes. The women employed in this industry work at low wages in hazardous circumstances that compromise their health and well-being. The shift from prostitution by indigenous Japanese women to prostitution by immigrant women from other Southeast Asian countries is a by-product of an increase in more legitimate employment opportunities for Japanese women.

While some of the women who immigrate to Japan or other affluent Southeast Asian countries are employed as domestic and child-care workers and in other low-status occupations, the burgeoning sex industry offers strong competition for women seeking better employment than they could secure in their home countries. Although the connection between gendered sex trafficking and transnational marriage has been largely ignored in migration studies, the connection has been explored by Barry (1995), Lee (1998), Truong (1990), and a few others.

The transnational sex trade also provides an opportunity for marriage migrants in some countries to meet their future husbands. Chant (1997) estimates that of foreign visitors to the Philippines in 1990, in some regions 8 out of 10 of the tourists were male, 4 out of 10 were men traveling alone, and 1 out of 3 were men traveling with male friends. Only 1 out of 8 were traveling with a spouse. In fact, the majority of the participants in one study met their future husbands at their place of work, which was a bar or a club. The same study found that the circumstances under which these husbands met their future wives contributed to the husbands' subsequent treatment of the wives as "property" and "domestic slaves." In the words of one respondent, "many men do not marry to have a wife, but . . . they 'buy' these women to be their slaves" (Piper 2000:217).

These foreign-born wives face additional discrimination, not only based on their past status in sex work but also from a stratification system in which race and social class place them even further toward the bottom in Japanese society. These women's short duration in Japan, their lack of understanding of the culture, and their isolation often lead to harsh circumstances, including living with drunkenness and violence, but with few resources to leave.

A neglected part of the research on marriage migration is immigrant men who return to their country of origin to select and marry a woman from their home country. *Viet Kieu* are Vietnamese living abroad. According to Thai (2002), Vietnamese men who have immigrated to the United States are increasingly returning to Vietnam to seek brides. Further, such marriages are often between two of the least marriageable in society: a highly educated woman and a man with a low-wage job. These marriages are often arranged, or at the very least suggested by a close friend or family member, and, in contrast to the transnational marriages described above, these individuals rarely meet on their own (e.g., at bars or clubs) but, rather, are likely to be introduced by kin.

Further research is needed regarding the stability of migrant marriages, let alone the quality of satisfaction in such marriages. Research suggests that couples such as those in Thai's (2002) study, made up of more traditional husbands and more liberated wives, are often ill prepared for disparities in their understandings of marital gender relations. Yet, at least some manage to process a complicated calculus of exchange in this regard. In the words of one *Viet Kieu* man:

> I know many men . . . who go to Vietnam to marry beautiful young women. . . . Those women . . . will leave their husbands when they get the chance. They can use their beauty to find other men. . . . The educated women, they know it's important to marry and stay married forever. . . . Educated women must protect their family's reputation in Vietnam by having a happy marriage, not have it end in divorce. (P. 251)

Thai (2002) sees such a "marriage squeeze" as directly related to global processes. High male mortality during the Vietnam War and high male emigration during the subsequent years created an acutely skewed ratio of women to men in Vietnam. Likewise, male emigration created a parallel tilted ratio of men to women in Vietnamese communities abroad. Globalization expanded the market for Vietnamese capital, goods, and labor while opening opportunities for more personal exchanges of emotions and marriage partners. But while goods and capital tend to flow in two directions, the divide between the First World economy of the West and the

Third World economy of Vietnam makes it impossible for women in Vietnam to go abroad to look for grooms but very easy for *Viet Kieu* men to go to Vietnam for brides. Just as global corporations and factories moved to Vietnam to partake of its large supply of labor, *Viet Kieu* men go there to choose among its large selection of potential brides.

Global transfers apply not only to populations but also to culture and values. Thai (2002) concludes that globalization may appear to offer Vietnamese women an avenue to escape patriarchal norms by marrying abroad; however, to the extent that highly educated women marry men with more traditional marriage values, these women may find themselves disappointed. The high value placed on marriage in Vietnamese culture—and the fact that these marriages are transnational—enables these nontraditional couples to transcend the usually strong norms regarding the marriage gradient in Vietnamese culture.

Transnational Adoption

As in the case of marriage migrants, global demographic analysis rarely takes adoption into account. However, transnational adoption offers an opportunity to reveal the intersections among not only gender, race, and ethnicity but also culture, nationality, and family, as they are woven together through immigration and identity. (For a comprehensive examination of adoption practices worldwide, including the place of adoption in family formation and kinship identity, see Riley and Van Vleet 2011.)

Today, the United States is the largest receiving country in the world for international adoptions, the largest number of children coming from China and Ethiopia. The U.S. State Department issued more than 22,000 visas for incoming to-be-adopted children during 2005 (Hamwi 2006:17). In 2004, 21,449 Americans completed international adoptions, but by 2009 that number had dropped to 12,753. The number of foreign adoptions by Americans has dropped, largely due to external factors. Other countries have increased efforts to place children in adoptive families in-country. Countries have increased their regulation and oversight of adoptions. The number of Americans seeking to adopt abroad has increased, due perhaps in part to publicity surrounding adoptions by celebrities (e.g., Angelina Jolie, Madonna). Some countries (e.g., Romania, Russia) have set moratoriums in light of scandals involving international adoptions. Others (e.g., Nepal, Sierra Leone) have ceased adoptions in the face of widespread civil unrest ("Tough Times, Longer Waits" 2010).

The U.S. State Department does not track the number of such visas for American children to be adopted in another country, but the latter number is likely less than 300 annually, primarily black and biracial children whose birth mothers seek a society in which their children will experience less racial prejudice. Beginning in 2007, however, with the United States scheduled to ratify the Hague Convention on International Adoption, the State Department will begin monitoring the outplacement of American children (Hamwi 2006:17). When ratified, the Hague Convention will prohibit ratifying countries from approving adoptions from countries that have not ratified. In that case, adoption of children from countries such as Guatemala to the United States will no longer be possible (Ode 2007).

What, then, in this increasingly globalized world makes a child *belong* to a particular society? The literature surrounding transnational adoption focuses almost exclusively on adoption by American parents of children from other countries. That research indicates that developmental, family, and other outcomes of international adoption are highly variable. For example, most children who are adopted, even after living for periods in deprived institutional settings, "catch up" developmentally, although some may lag in physical growth and attachment. While children who are internationally adopted have some elevated risks, "most respond well to the warm and welcoming environments of their adoptive parents" (Britner, Mossler, and Eigsti 2008:F9).

Dorow (2006) has attempted a critical analysis of this oft-romanticized aspect of what can surely be considered a part of global family formation. Her study focuses on one of the most common forms of international adoption today—Americans who adopt children from other countries, especially infant girls from China. The adoption of Chinese daughters is sociohistorically situated in inequalities that make possible this particular global exchange. Adoptable Chinese daughters reflect China's strong male preference and "one-child policy." Further, China represents an extension of gender and racial ideologies and hierarchies present in the United States, ideologies that discount African American children while considering Asian children as "model minorities" and girls as more easy to assimilate.

Jacobson (2008) extends the analysis of cultural effects of transnational adoption—in this case of Chinese and Russian children, again by American parents. She finds that Chinese-adoptive parents are more active and more public culture keepers (e.g., organizing language lessons and culture-specific activities for their adoptive children) than are Russian-adoptive parents. Furthermore, the former associate such culture keeping (often mandated by the Chinese adoption industry) as essential to raising a "well-rounded child." Jacobson's research also reveals the availability of networks of similar international families and the significance of those networks in socially constructing racial/ethnic (and, I suggest, national) identity.

Migration for marriage and transnational adoption constitutes a small but significant piece of the global demographic puzzle. Another piece of that puzzle, LGBTQ families, remains almost totally ignored in considerations of global demographics, including migration.

Lesbian, Gay, Bisexual, Transgender, and Questioning Families in Global Demography

Several scholars (e.g., Adam, Duyvendak, and Krouwel 1999b) have argued that the modern capitalist world system has reorganized public and private spheres of social life, diversifying family and kinship codes in unprecedented ways. The resulting changes in traditional family structures have resulted in greater personal autonomy (albeit not without significant resistance) in family formation, including more frequent cohabitation outside of marriage, young adults returning to the family of origin, and long-term committed partnerships between LGBTQ individuals.

Adam (1995:13–4) speaks of these emerging new relationships and institutions as "oases of refuge and intimacy" in a globalizing world. At least one group—gay expatriates—exemplifies how one manifestation of globalization—transnational travel—may help explain discourses of normative gender, race nation, and gay desire. Collins's (2009) research indicates that gay expatriates see their mobility as a way to escape heteronormative controls and homophobia at home.

In some contemporary societies, homophobia is one of the ugly legacies of colonialism. In 1995, after the end of apartheid in South Africa, the South West African People's Organization (SWAPO) in Namibia initiated a period in which political homophobia was used to stifle dissent, reinforcing a masculinist position and the organization's liberation heritage. This repression took the form of urging police officers to "eliminate" lesbian and gay Namibians, using allegations of homosexuality to discredit political opponents, and issuing public statements that linked homosexuality with the destruction of the newly liberated nation. SWAPO thus used "political homophobia to expel gender and sexual dissidents from official accounts of [Namibian] history" (Currier 2010:110).

Just as social movement theory largely neglected the organization of LGBTQ communities (Duyvendak 1995), the demographic literature on global changes shaping the family has given short shrift to global patterns of morbidity and mortality, family formation and fertility, and emigration and immigration among LGBTQ individuals and their families. The paucity of research and theory on demographic shifts among LGBTQ populations is, at the very least, inopportune for scholars wishing to secure a full understanding of global change. Continued exclusion of consideration of LGBTQ populations in demographic analyses seriously compromises a full understanding of family characteristics and societal transformation.

Adam et al. (1999b) posit that the reasons for the inattention to immigration dynamics in LGBTQ populations are both social and epistemological. First, the concept of being "gay" or "lesbian" is contested, not only among but also within societies. Second, same-sex association does not always involve construction of either a personal identity or an identifiable shared community. Third, a variety of social conditions continue to limit the formation of social movements around LGBTQ issues, thereby hindering the very study of those communities. In a postmodern, global world,

> national traditions shape discourses through which homosexually interested people come to understand themselves and their "rightful" place in the societies in which they live. . . . Any sense of commonality that might be evoked by the widespread adoption of such terms as "gay," "lesbian," or "bisexual" must be tempered by the diversity within and among national cultures. (Pp. 8–9)

Whether examining the more traditional features of demographics—mortality, fertility, morbidity, and migration—or the burgeoning area of LGBTQ studies worldwide, inclusive globalization studies have the potential to extend scholarship. In doing so, 21st century demography not only will be more inclusive of groups previously invisible but also will expand the power of demographic theories to explain a wider range of social phenomena while recognizing the diversity within those phenomena. In order to do so, diverse voices of immigrants and others are required to advance our understanding of demographics in a global world.

In the essay that closes this chapter, Margaret L. Kvasnicka, CSJ, describes the lives of one group of women whose voices have often been silent: immigrant and refugee women finding a home and relationships at Sarah's . . . an Oasis for Women. These women struggle to secure legal immigration status for themselves while acquiring the language, education, and employment skills necessary to support themselves and their families. Their words provide first-person testimony to both the hardships and the achievements of women and their families seeking refuge and asylum. Such narratives provide scholars and students with an authentic sense of the impact of demographic forces such as immigration on families.

Summary

Three major demographic trends dramatically affecting families across the globe are (1) mortality, (2) declining fertility, and (3) the rise in immigration. These three trends are in turn fueling a series of changes in family structure. Demography—mortality, fertility, and migration, and the processes of demographic transition—offers a first glimpse into the impact of global changes on families. Infectious and parasitic diseases remain prime causes of death and disease in less-developed parts of the world. The case of HIV/AIDS again demonstrates the gendered nature of social and family life as that disease erodes the capacity of adults to provide for their families by straining caregiving systems, forcing children to leave educational pursuits, and leaving family members vulnerable to sexual and economic exploitation.

World fertility, even in the least-developed parts of the world, shows steady decline due to myriad factors related to shifting norms and values around mortality, direct and indirect costs associated with children and childbearing, improved methods of and access to birth control, delayed marriage, and cultural diffusion regarding fertility practices. Population control today has a global dimension, both in terms of nations' satisfaction with their own fertility rates and the involvement of international organizations in shaping population policy. Like other factors related to globalization, changes in fertility patterns seem to be associated with postmodern influences on culture and society.

Obviously, migration is a key component of global demography. Historically a one-way path, migration today is more complicated than ever before, with family members emigrating and immigrating in different streams. While traditional perspectives on immigration viewed the family as a cornerstone of assimilation, more contemporary views see greater diversity in immigrant experiences. Yet, even in the best of circumstances, migration can be a significant stress for families both as a gendered process, which may include marriage migrants and transnational adoption, and a process with implications for the parent–child relationship.

Some immigrant families and their members flourish, even in the face of adversity, as demonstrated by the stories from Sarah's . . . an Oasis for Women, discussed in the essay that follows this chapter. The study of globalization and demography is limited by inattention to death, birth, and migration among certain populations, including lesbian, gay, bisexual, transgender, and questioning individuals and their families.

IMMIGRANT WOMEN, NEW NEIGHBORS, GLOBAL FAMILIES[1]

By Margaret L. Kvasnicka, CSJ

Sarah's . . . an Oasis for Women[2]

Mantras:

You come to Sarah's in order to leave.

Sarah's will always be your home.

You can do it!

You are a good woman.

May peacemaking prevail on Earth today!

One day at a time. One lesson at a time. One woman at a time.

Mission:

Sarah's provides hospitality to women in transition who are seeking housing, community, and safety.

Vision:

Sarah's fosters the self-empowerment of women in community through life skill development, advocacy, and referral services.

Values:

Respect
Opportunity and possibility
Diversity
Sharing lives and changing lives
Simplicity
Right relationships
Beauty
Responsibility and accountability
Healing and hope

---

[1]Kvasnicka adapted this essay from a longer work she authored. She retains the right to use the original work or any portion of the work.

[2]Strategic Plan, 2008–2013.

Ada and Malena[3]

The phone rang late in the evening of December 23, 2006, and a young mother's voice came through clearly. "Sister, my children are on the plane!" Ada's voice carried an excited lilt I had not heard before. "They will get to Minneapolis St. Paul International Airport at 1:30 p.m. tomorrow, Christmas Eve! I paid the extra fee to make sure they were placed in first class so they will be really safe!" And then a stream of memories poured through the phone line. "You know how hard I worked in this country and in my own country with my husband, waiting and praying for this day to come. Now it is finally here, and it is Christmas! All that paperwork and waiting, and paying fees and then there was more paperwork. It was never done. You know that I haven't seen them for more than 3 years, and now they are coming!" Ada is a refugee[4] from an African nation.

On another day I accompanied Malena, also a refugee, to the same airport to welcome her three adolescent children to the United States. "I won't be crying," she said to me. "I know that God loves me because my children are coming. My children are coming! I won't be crying today. God loves me." Assuring her I would be crying for both of us, I continued to listen to her joy. "I have worked so hard. I wandered through many countries to get here, and I have waited 10 years to see my children again." Over the years, Malena faced serious health issues, including cancer, but through the supportive network of the Sisters of St. Joseph,[5] she recovered her health each time, while managing other personal and family challenges in a new country.

Sarah's . . . an Oasis for Women: A Ministry of the Sisters of St. Joseph of Carondelet

Two women from two different nations in Africa came to the United States with refugee status. Each found home, safety, and community for a period of

---

[3]Names and nations have been changed to protect individuals where necessary.

[4]As defined by the U.S. Refugee Act of 1980 and the United Nations, a refugee is a person who leaves her country of origin because she has dire fear of persecution for her race, religion, nationality, membership in a particular social group, or political opinion (Minnesota Advocates for Human Rights 2004).

[5]The Congregation of Sisters of St. Joseph is a congregation of Catholic women founded in LePuy, France, in 1650. These communities of sisters remain dedicated to "the practice of all the spiritual and corporal works of mercy of which woman is capable and which will most benefit the dear neighbor" (Primitive Constitution). The Sisters of St. Joseph of Carondelet have U.S. provinces in Albany, Los Angeles, St. Louis, and St. Paul; vice provinces in Hawaii and Peru; and a region in Japan. They belong to the U.S. Federation of Sisters of St. Joseph.

time at Sarah's . . . an Oasis for Women, which is a ministry of the Sisters of St. Joseph of Carondelet in St. Paul, Minnesota. Each woman fled her home nation for her own safety and that of her family. Each came to the United States, eventually arriving in Minnesota, a federally designated refugee resettlement area. At Sarah's, these two women restarted their lives in a strange and new country.

In 1995 a convent of the Sisters of St. Joseph of Carondelet in St. Paul became available when the work of another ministry was completed. A year later Sarah's . . . an Oasis for Women opened its doors to women who were homeless, needing safety, and willing to share a community experience with other women. This new ministry welcomed any woman in any kind of life transition willing to live together with other women and do life planning. Over the years sisters lived with them when possible. Sarah's was named for Sarah of the Old Testament, the elderly biblical woman who faced the impossible in her life with humor, hospitality, and faith.

Homelessness among immigrant and refugee women in Minnesota remains severe, with a majority of those served today at Sarah's being women new to the United States. Over 15 years, this home has served more than 600 women from nearly 60 nations. Sarah's is one expression of the overall ministry commitment of the Sisters of St. Joseph to direct service among those most in need and to advocacy for change wherever there is systemic injustice affecting people from across the globe.

By now, Ada and Malena have probably met each other through one of Sarah's reunions, or perhaps while shopping at St. Paul Halal Grocery near University Avenue in St. Paul, or at the Midtown Global Market on Lake Street in Minneapolis. Because they both profess Orthodox Evangelical Christianity, they may have found each other at church on Wednesday, Saturday, or Sunday. With the safety and support of a home setting, they found educational, employment, health, language, legal, and social services. Each learned English in a St. Paul English Language Learner (ELL) program while at Sarah's. They found jobs and began to plan for their own living spaces. They repaid loans and sent funds to their families "back home," while acquiring the skills to live in the United States. They learned that women can live together well and can heal themselves and each other in community. The security of "home" at Sarah's empowered them to reclaim their lives and plan for their futures.

Through shared lives and household responsibilities, and through stories, laughter, and tears, lifelong relationships are established in this place many women call "their mother's home." All at Sarah's learn to treasure the power of hospitality, of meal preparation, and even cleaning—across nations, cultures, and unique family practices. The ordinariness of daily life becomes a way of creating and "homemaking." Ada has written, "I have learned so much at Sarah's that enables me to live with people of diverse backgrounds and cultures. It is at Sarah's that I discovered my love for *injera* (an African flat bread). The household jobs at Sarah's are essential for they offer responsibility as well as accountability. Sarah's is like a mother who gives responsibility to her children. We learn how to do all this work in preparation for our own homes. What a home this is!"

Beauty and Healing: Women Among Women

Located in a residential neighborhood with access to public transportation, Sarah's is carefully managed, with beauty evident everywhere on its grounds and throughout the household. The house is set back on the property, adding natural beauty to the neighborhood and providing a spacious welcome. Split-level construction disguises the size of the 30-bedroom home. The interior of the house features public spaces for community gatherings, a learning center equipped with computers with high-speed Internet, a laundry and storage space, an interfaith chapel and reflection space, parlors for visiting, and, of course, the kitchen and dining room.

Beauty and color, including art from around the world, frame every space in the house, inviting each new woman into a place of care, compassion, and peacefulness with the security and safety of home. At the entry of the house a basket of flags representing the nations of residents welcomes both visitors and newcomers. Naima from Somalia walked through the hallway at her residency interview tearfully exclaiming, "This is a peace place. This is a peace place! It is so beautiful here. How can a home be so beautiful? Is it just for me? Can this be my home?"

Beginning with their first interview, women learn that "Sarah's will always be your home." Wednesday dinners and annual reunions celebrate this mantra as past and present residents share times of homecoming and reconnection. "You come to Sarah's in order to leave" is another mantra learned along the way. Everything about the experience in this household prepares each woman for an independent, contributing lifestyle in her own neighborhood, work, school, faith, and civic communities. While at Sarah's, she has her own bedroom and phone service. She has access to all the public spaces, to food and food storage, and to the leisure spaces in the house. She has a household job that changes every few months, sharing the tasks of group living. She has the support, respect, and care of every woman and every staff member in the household.

"We are sisters to each other in this place," says Everlyne, a woman of Kenya. "Our sisterhood as women from so many nations makes this a global home. We respect each other." This home for women among women is inter-faith and intergenerational, as well as international. Solitude and community are offered to each woman.

Drawing Out the Potential Within:
Education and Learning

Every woman comes to Sarah's desperate and alone—most without English, nearly all without a penny—and determined to make a new life. Sarah's is all about responding to a woman's homelessness and desperation and support-ing her determination.

Teaching and advocating are the daily work of Sarah's staff members. Education is how the mission and vision come alive for each woman. She learns new life skills to manage a home or apartment (e.g., using a gas range, a washer and a vacuum cleaner) and to navigate technology (e.g., voice mail and the Internet), while gaining confidence with public transportation; pro-curing banking, health, and language services; and, for most, moving through high school or language school to postsecondary education. One woman who is an asylum seeker has said:

> I came from having nothing; I was hopeless and desperate. Now I am a graduate of the College of St. Catherine. I am a nurse, and I am starting a new job. All of these accomplishments go back to Sarah's and the Sisters of St. Joseph. Yes, I am still having problems with immigration in this country, but I am supported here. I know I could not have survived alone, even though I try to be strong. I don't think I could have accomplished all of this without the support of living at Sarah's.

Selam moved from Sarah's several years ago and remains deeply con-nected with this community of women as she pursues asylum[6] in the United States. While at Sarah's she learned English in a local ELL program, found full-time work, and regained her health. She completed her Bachelor of Arts degree in nursing and found full-time employment as a nurse in a skilled nursing senior facility.

> The problems we've faced sometimes make us feel like we are worthless. Sarah's women have become my family and my friends. Sometimes you don't

---

[6]Asylum refers to legal permission to live in a country, given by the country's government, to people fleeing danger or persecution in their original homeland (Minnesota Advocates for Human Rights 2004).

know all that you have inside you. There should be somebody who can look through all of that with you and tell you, "You can do it." I am not alone here with all my immigration struggles.

Following the denial of her asylum request, Selam appealed the judgment and prepared for even more grueling, lengthy, and costly legal work. Words fail to tell the whole story of the sheer grit, faith, conviction, and struggles of this young woman seeking legal status and eventual citizenship in this country. Today she continues her nursing profession in a Twin Cities medical center and recently earned a graduate degree in nursing.

Some of the immigrant and refugee women completed their high school educations while living at Sarah's. One of these women, an immigrant[7] named Keshauna, graduated with honors and became a U.S. citizen. She was so proud the day she arrived at Sarah's door with her citizenship document. "Come, be in a picture with me and my United States citizenship papers!" She now lives and works in the Twin Cities with her husband, whom she was finally able to bring to this country. They made plans for their future here knowing that their dual citizenship allows them to return to their home country and families of origin, should they choose to do so. "I am so happy for all I learned at Sarah's and in this country. I want to go on to college for more education, and I know I will," she says.

For these women, education is self-empowerment opening doors to opportunity, influence, and power in the world. Education can end poverty, ensure health care, and reunite families. It can create communities of possibility among women with diverse life experiences. Peacemaking will prevail over violence, and Earth, "our Mother's home," will survive.

Making a New Life

"Sarah's became a place to practice what I want to be and do in the rest of my life, and I found so many new friends," said Amey as she prepared to move to Illinois after a time at Sarah's. From Ethiopia, Amey came to the United States through what is known as the diversity lottery,[8] which allowed her to procure the documents needed to move here, including a Minnesota identification card, a work permit, and a Social Security card. She said she was "ready for

---

[7]An immigrant is one who comes to a country intending to settle permanently and obtain citizenship (Minnesota Advocates for Human Rights 2004).

[8]The U.S. State Department makes 50,000 to 55,000 immigrant visas available each year through this method of selection.

work." Her English language skills were limited, and with no income or even relatives or other connections in this country, she was documented but alone, desperate, and determined. Several months later, with improved language and work skills, she was reenergized. With a community of new friends and living skills, she was on her way to a new state, a new job, and further education.

Another woman, Elena, said: "Here I am, Sister. Will you teach me how to write a check so I can give something to Sarah's?" The pride and delight on Elena's face was amazing to see as she came with pen and checkbook in hand! "Finally, I can give some money to Sarah's for all Sarah's has given to me."

Any adult woman in any kind of life transition who is willing to do basic life planning soon becomes a contributing resident at Sarah's, based on her income. Through regular individual conferences with the director, goals are set, revised, and added to. These most often are reached with the assistance of the staff of area agencies. When leave-taking time arrives, a final visit with the director at Sarah's allows each woman to name and claim all her accomplishments. Often she sets additional goals, as new hopes and dreams are possible by then. Each woman is invited to continue her connections with Sarah's after she moves on to become involved in her new neighborhood, faith, and civic communities. Each woman is encouraged to make a financial contribution to Sarah's as she gets settled so that another woman might have a similar opportunity. Two women stated:

> This truly is a home, a nurturing place, and a spring of hope for women. I found a social life here, and I really learned responsibility for myself and my home. I found love here. I got my health back, and my education. Now I am going to be a social worker and work in Minnesota. I am going to become a United States citizen.

> Confidence! I found my confidence in myself. I finished high school, and now I am in college to become a nurse!

These women have recently moved from Sarah's into public housing. They will do well. They have the self-confidence that got them to this country in the first place and the new courage gained by overcoming the hurdles of being alone and new and poor. These self-empowered young women have the impetus to live their individual dreams and to make a difference in the lives of others as well.

Following Dreams

Eleanor Roosevelt once said, "The future belongs to those who believe in the beauty of their dreams" (Quotations Page 2007). A woman of Sudan, mother, grandmother, sister, aunt, poet, and businesswoman in her own nation, Maria tells parts of her story humbly and with great courage.

Maria came to the United States fleeing political oppression, war, and violence. She witnessed the murder of many family members, including her husband, and she now lives with HIV/AIDS. She, too, seeks asylum from the terror and torture she experienced and witnessed. She learns regularly of the illness and death of victimized family members and relatives, some now living with HIV/AIDS. Her daughters ask, "Can you ever return to us? Is it possible for us to come to America?" Maria's time at Sarah's allowed her to obtain good health care and support from HIV/AIDS communities while also learning English. Now living in another state, she stays connected with Sarah's and longs for higher education and employment. The long legal process as an asylum seeker limited her accomplishments when she lived at Sarah's but never her dreams or her hope. Yet, in her words, "I know that Sarah's will always be my home. It was my first home in this new country and Sarah's is my mother here." More recently, Maria was denied asylum and now has another appeal in process. She faces another legal battle with both hope and apprehension.

"I will become a doctor and return to my own people in Kenya," says Everlyne, a fourth-year nursing student at what is now St. Catherine University. Everlyne is in the United States on an international student visa,[9] which also allows her to work part-time on campus. She came to Sarah's when her living arrangements off campus became unsafe and says, "Sarah's became my lifesaving moment. Sarah's has a plan that helps me achieve my dream, and I know I can!" Her dream includes graduating to become a physician and return to her native Kenya to work, especially among children, where HIV/AIDS is epidemic and health care greatly needed. Systemic violence and oppression worldwide create gaping needs for health care, education, and courageous work, including in the African nations that are home to most of Sarah's women. Those who know Everlyne's ability, energetic spirit, and determination know that she will achieve her dream.

Sarah's is a global home that has become a place to learn the commonality and the diversity of nations, people, and cultures. The experience of Sarah's allows those who live and work there to learn firsthand of the issues and systems that need change in order to create more just societies. Part of Sarah's work is to "watch over and watch out" for women and children of the world and for potential laws that might affect their lives. The voices of Sarah's women are shared to inform those who make law surrounding critical issues involving immigration. Letters to state legislators and to Congress on potential legislation that will impact the women's lives are sent regularly. The experiences of Sarah's women are shared with policymakers

---

[9]An international student is one issued a visa to study in this country for a given period of time (Minnesota Advocates for Human Rights 2004).

through the Sisters of St. Joseph, a nongovernmental organization of the United Nations.

Sarah's has become a provider of healing and hope for women. It is indeed an oasis for women in need of another chance at life. What community of religious women dedicated to "all of which woman is capable and which will most benefit the dear neighbor" could ask for more? What more would Sarah and Hagar, symbols of three faith traditions, dream for women and the world?

Meanwhile, the blessing at each community meal at Sarah's includes another mantra, taken from the Peace Pole standing in the gardens near the front door of the house: "May peacemaking prevail on Earth today."

Margaret L. Kvasnicka, CSJ, served on the founding task force for Sarah's . . . an Oasis for Women in 1995 and was the first chair of its advisory council. She served as Sarah's director from 2002 to 2010. Kvasnicka's professional experience includes education and religious education ministry in parishes, leadership in her province of the Sisters of St. Joseph of Carondelet, and work in adult spirituality and ritual, especially with women. She is a graduate of St. Catherine University, as it is now known, and a current trustee. She holds graduate degrees from Loyola University of Chicago and the University of San Francisco.

"It is a privilege to witness the self-empowerment of women among women in community. It is awesome to imagine the power and influence of these women to create a better, more whole world in their own circles, families, and larger communities. With each of them, their nations and our world, we pray: May peacemaking prevail on Earth today."

CRITICAL THINKING QUESTIONS

1. This chapter has examined three features of population growth: death, birth, and migration. Compare and contrast the ways in which each of these features impacts families in more- and less-developed parts of the world.

2. Families can easily be seen being swept along in the general tide of demographic transition. In what ways can families be active agents in social demography? What forces inhibit families' abilities to do so?

3. The HIV/AIDS pandemic has been described as one of the most serious crises facing the world today. Why is this pandemic a critical issue for families?

4. Consider the inattention paid by researchers to LGBTQ populations and the accounts of women and their families at Sarah's . . . an Oasis for Women (described in the essay that follows this chapter). What cutting-edge demographic trends do you predict will affect quality of life for the world's families during your lifetime?

3

Families and Worldwide Culture Systems

Media, Technology, and Consumption

The concerns that many in the media, politics, the pulpit, and even my students have expressed regarding the threat of globalization to cultures around the world prompted me to write the present chapter. Does globalization inevitably mean some sort of transnational corruption of what is good in societies? Does globalization warp norms and values that are vital to the well-being of families and their members? This chapter explores how globalization exposes families to new cultural systems, for better or for worse.

The concept of global culture, even a unified global culture, is not a new one. More than a half century ago media theorist Marshall McLuhan (1964) coined the term *global village*. Smith (1990) traced the rise of such transnational cultures from the aftermath of a divided Europe following World War II through the formation of a transnational European Union with economic, political, and even cultural traits that transcend any single nation-state. He wrote rather of a "postindustrial global culture" as

> a pastiche of cultural motifs and styles, . . . operating on several levels simultaneously: as a cornucopia of standardized commodities, as a patchwork of denationalized ethnic or folk motifs, as a series of generalized "human values and interests," as a uniform "scientific" discourse of meaning, and finally as the interdependent system of communications. (P. 176)

That which is being transmitted through globalized media and consumption goes beyond marketing products and services to transmitting and socializing powerful messages about what is beautiful and desirable, what is good and valuable. Spybey (1996) argued that the resulting world culture socializes individuals into different patterns of knowledge and awareness that may displace traditional, local institutions in favor of novel, transnational ones.

The U.N. Educational, Scientific, and Cultural Organization (UNESCO) collects data on a wide variety of selected cultural goods and services, including heritage goods, books, newspapers and periodicals, other printed matter, recorded media, visual arts, and audiovisual media. UNESCO (2005) defines core cultural goods and services as follows:

> Cultural goods [are] consumer goods which convey ideas, symbols, and ways of life. They inform or entertain, contribute to build collective identity and influence cultural practices. . . . Cultural services [are] the overall set of measures and supporting facilities for cultural practices that government, private and semi-public institutions or companies make available to the community. Examples of such services include the promotion of performances and cultural events as well as cultural information and preservation (libraries, documentation centres and museums). (P. 84)

Using official customs declarations (and therefore not reflecting all foreign sales—or thefts—of cultural goods and services), UNESCO (2005) estimated the global market value of cultural and creative goods in 2005 at 1.3 trillion U.S. dollars (USD). Between 1994 and 2002 the value of cultural goods and services exchanged across national borders increased from 38 billion to 60 billion USD. The magnitude of these cultural exchanges only continues to increase, and dramatically so, with the growth and dispersion of the World Wide Web and other computer-mediated communication technologies and multinational and even transnational economic institutions. Technological advances are reducing time and space barriers between people with access, beyond even television to the Internet and cell phones.

The present chapter focuses on what Appadurai (1996) has called mediascapes (flows of images and information produced by television and film, as well as the written word) and technoscapes (flows of technology, especially cyber technology). Young men and women—those on the cusp of forming new families—and non-elites across the less-developed nations are particularly amenable to such globalizing cultural innovations (Lukose 2009).

More than a half century ago, Park (1950, 1952) delineated five processes (which he called "sociation") that may come into play when cultural groups encounter one another: contact, competition, conflict, accommodation, and assimilation. These concepts have been successfully applied to understand cultural diffusion in a variety of contexts (Karraker 2004, 2006), but the extent to which globalization has resulted in a truly global culture (and the extent to which any such culture is predominantly Western) remains somewhat contested. As discussed in the first chapter, global skeptics contend that transnational movements of populations and individuals, as well as the flow of cultural features across the global landscape, have always influenced cultural identity. Even beyond that, skeptics argue that commercial and public-service broadcasting, the press, and even the news, often have a local or national quality (MacKay 2000).

In other words, perhaps the focus should not be on globalization but on glocalization. Marling (2006) argues that local cultures—in everything from language and eating habits to education systems and land use—are remarkably resilient and even resistant to the importation and wholesale adaptation of American or any other predetermined cultural direction. For example, Venice, Italy, a city notorious for its maze of streets, represents preservation of *local* culture in land use even in the face of Western tourism. McGregor (2006) has recorded that

> tiny streets that led everywhere within an islanded neighborhood and nowhere beyond it . . . posed no problem. Obviously, Street of the Priests meant street of *our* priests, Boatyard Street referred to *our* boatyard; there is only one neighborhood warehouse, one parish church. . . . [Today,] though the street names are carefully painted on uniform white blocks at nearly every corner, Venetian postal addresses make no mention of them. (P. 319)

To the contrary, global hyperglobalists offer a powerful argument that worldwide cultural diversity is losing ground to more homogeneous Western, particularly American, culture. The international flow of cultural goods and services does appear to be dominated by a very few countries. In 2002 (the most recent year for which data are available), the largest single exporter of cultural goods was the United Kingdom at 8.5 billion USD, followed by the United States at 7.6 billion USD. Together, the United Kingdom and the United States accounted for almost 30 percent of the world's core cultural exports. Likewise, the largest single importer of cultural goods in that year was the United States at 15.3 billion USD, followed by the United Kingdom at 7.8 billion USD (UNESCO 2005). See Table 3.1 for a summary of the top five exporters and importers of core cultural goods.

Some hyperglobalists argue that globalization has led to the insinuation of Western values of individualism, materialism, and secularism into other more

Table 3.1   Top Five Exporters and Importers of Core Cultural Goods, in U.S. Dollars (USD), 2002

Top Five Exporters	USD
United Kingdom	8,548,772,100
United States	7,648,414,300
Germany	5,788,930,800
China	5,274,900,700
France	2,521,273,300
Top Five Importers	USD
United States	15,338,583,000
United Kingdom	7,871,901,800
Germany	4,162,119,700
Canada	3,829,892,500
France	3,406,846,100

SOURCE: Based on UNESCO (2005).

collectivist, less avaricious, and more spiritual cultures. They see global consumption and media as compromising unique, historic ways of life among indigenous people while increasing the gap between families who have access to Western cultural resources and those who do not. They see the erosion of barriers between cultures caused by globalization as propelling the world toward a massification of culture on a global scale (Albrow 1997). Such massification is aggravated by a tendency toward monopolistic control over consumption, media, and other cultural systems, resulting in cultural imperialism by the West. From such a perspective, the current violence directed at the West can be seen as reflecting the efforts of more tradition-bound societies to reject Western decadence while laying claim to traditional norms and values.

A more moderate position might question such a simplistic view of cultural diffusion from more- to less-developed societies. For example, one of the most powerful cultural forces at work in the world today is religious fundamentalism; however, fundamentalism is not the purview only of less-developed societies. Marty and Appleby (1991) assert that the Christian right of a more-developed society such as America and Islamic fundamentalism of the less-developed world have much in common. In *Jihad vs. McWorld*, Barber (1995:205) draws parallels between certain tenets of Islamic fundamentalism and other forms of "fundamentalist opposition to modernity," including fundamentalist Protestant movements in contemporary American society. Perhaps certain Islamic fundamentalist clerics "are not so far from . . . the Christian Right's campaign for a return to nineteenth-century family values—family values understood as direct emanations of church going, school prayer, and a Protestant Christian America" (p. 211).

Affirmation of traditionalism and opposition to structural changes faced by families around the globe are not limited to religious fundamentalists. In endorsing "the marriage covenant, whereby man and woman establish a permanent bond," Benedict XVI, head of the worldwide Catholic Church, extols not only traditional norms regarding family structure but also a conviction that such a structure "is a great good for all humanity" ("Pope Extols Virtues" 2006:A9). Certainly, contemporary families faced with demographic transitions, international violence, and transnational employment need all the help they can get, but some ask if such statements defy the rich diversity of intimate bonds that serve families confronting postmodern global realities. In the extreme, such statements may even provide support for those who seek religious endorsement for discriminatory behaviors against lesbigay, single-parent, and other families that do not conform to such a marriage covenant.

Global optimists such as Featherstone (1990) acknowledge the tendency to see American mass consumer culture as the prototype of homogenized, cultural imperialism "riding on the back of Western economic and political domination" (p. 2). However, they do not see a single, unified global culture but the "extension of global interrelatedness" that can be advanced by continual cultural interaction and exchange. They also hope that globalization may stimulate new ways to view gender, class, and other social structures, thereby challenging sexism, racism, and other systems of privilege while moving societies in more humane directions. The next chapter reveals how some global responses to international systems of oppression, including war and its collateral damage, have done just that. The final chapter (Chapter 6) describes some of the ways that international and transnational social policies can better position families around the world in the global landscape.

UNESCO has acknowledged the inequity in the export of cultural goods between the northern and southern hemispheres and the threat such inequity poses to vulnerable cultures. Mounir Bouchenaki, assistant director-general of the Culture Sector for UNESCO (2003a), opined:

> Globalization in trade has undeniable consequences for cultural diversity, pluralism, and intercultural dialogue. Cultural diversity also heightens the sense of identity as the source of creativity and living culture. Globalization can contribute powerfully to bringing people closer together. But in doing so it must not lead to world-wide cultural uniformity or the hegemony of one or a few cultures over all the others. (P. 19)

These cultural transmissions can influence age and gender roles, childhood and sexual socialization, and youth and other family cultures. For example, Japanese women who immigrate to Great Britain may relinquish values of family reciprocity in favor of individualist values. In the words of one such woman, 60 years old, living in Britain since 1958:

> When I need old-age care, I'll sell this house if financially necessary, and move to a nursing home. Although I want to leave the house to my children, they may also suggest that I sell it. My son's partner said, "Don't worry about your sons. They both have a job. Just look after yourself." Even between parents and children, we need to respect each other. Old-age care is hard work even for professional nurses, not to mention ordinary individuals. . . . Even if I have to sell this house, I would hire a professional helper. (Izuhara and Shibata 2002:164)

Contrary to traditional Japanese cultural expectations, these women do not expect their children to support them in old age. Thus, cultural changes wrought by globalization often force families to confront the reproduction of Western social institutions through patterns of values and norms across shifting global boundaries. In this chapter, I consider the implications of global culture on family life, including the significance of the media and patterns of mass consumption. I conclude with a discussion of the impact of global forces on family norms and values.

Global Media in an Era of Information Revolution

Beck-Gernsheim (2001) describes the mass media as a "driving force behind transnational life plans."

> More persons throughout the world see their lives through the prisms of the possible lives offered by the mass media in all their forms. . . . People are beginning to imagine other worlds and to compare them with their own. So life for the ordinary person is no longer determined just by the immediate situation but increasingly by the possibilities that the media (either directly or indirectly) suggest. (P. 62)

Mass media educates, entertains, and can bring geographically diverse groups together across time and space. Globalization changes the influence of media impact by increasing reach to virtually any part of the world. In the 21st century, media and especially computer-assisted networks enable viewers to move from being witnesses to virtual or even actual participants in social events. This was powerfully demonstrated in the Arab Spring, a social movement that began in December 2010 when a Tunisian fruit vendor set himself on fire to protest his treatment by police—a story subsequently shared around the world through Facebook and mainstream media (Fahim 2011; Giglio 2011). Global communications are challenging "borderline racist" images of the rest of the world, and "the West is paying attention" (Khalidi 2011).

Developments in mass media and particularly the Internet have lowered economic and other obstacles to communication and even interactions across societies. These more globalized exchanges have the potential to provide new pathways to knowledge and understanding about world events and even to foster sympathy and interaction across national and other borders. Images projected through the mass media also broaden access to experiences in which individuals cannot participate but to which they may nonetheless aspire. Potentially, this creates relative deprivation, a sense of hardship in the face of comparisons with now global others (even if the hardship is not absolute).

Allen and Massey (1995) contend that the globalization of the mass media, prompted by new communication technologies, has resulted in cultural imperialism, the standardization of culture on a worldwide scale. Worldwide, more than 40 percent of television programming hours originate in the United States (MacKay 2000:63). The increasing domination of mass media by American, European, and Western images may shift local culture as those images prompt consideration of new visions of culture and society, including social and family structure, gender and intergenerational relations.

The same factors contribute to a hegemonic view of "the other" to audiences in the West. For example, only recently have Western media begun to cover resistance in areas such as modesty in women's dress, standards of sexual propriety, and gender relations in marriage. In fact, some Muslim women (and men) have for some time criticized "unqualified, ignorant imams [who] make back-alley pronouncements on the lives of women, men, and children" (Korteweg 2008:445).

The massification of media may be a consequence of an oligopolistic worldwide media. Five firms—Bertelsmann, Disney, News Corporation, Time Warner, and Viacom—are not only the largest in the world in terms of sales but also the most fully integrated across news and entertainment production and hardware and software businesses (MacKay 2000). Australian-born Rupert Murdoch's News Corporation owns Fox News, the *New York Post, The Wall Street Journal,* and 20th Century Fox film studios. His control of news and sports, film and books; his access to political leaders (e.g., British prime ministers); and his newspapers' ability to endorse candidates who later win elections lead to concern that Murdoch's power extends from the media to politics and beyond ("Rupert Murdoch" 2011). News Corporation-owned television stations, in 2000, covered 40 percent of households in the United States (MacKay 2000).

News Corporation has long held stakes in several American, Asian, Australian, German, Indian, Japanese, Latin American, Spanish, U.K., and other global television, cable, satellite, radio, and music video networks (Herman and McChesney 1997). It remains to be seen if recent illegal hacking into celebrities', politicians', and others' phones by newspapers belonging to a British subsidiary of the conglomerate (Chu 2011) will substantially reduce News Corporation's media domination in the long run.

The rise of a sizable middle-class consumer base in less-developed countries in central Asia and even the least-developed countries in sub-Saharan Africa has generated tremendous expansion of the mass media in societies in those regions. As in more-developed regions, a globalized mass media in less-developed regions can educate and entertain and can sell consumer and cultural goods. Also in less-developed societies, globalized mass media can symbolize and promote a sense of community identity and can mobilize societal support for social movements (Ong 1999). Such appears to be the case, as seen in the influence of mass-marketed popular films distributed worldwide that shape race and sexual orientation identification beyond local communities (Gabilondo 2002)— as well as in the previously mentioned Arab Spring and the protests in Tiananmen Square in Beijing, China, in 1989, also broadcast worldwide.

Global media have the capability to construct what Morley and Robins (1995:64) call "electronic communities" beyond local, regional, and national borders. Modern global media can be said to be "constructing new geographies [while] bringing together otherwise disparate groups around the common experience of television . . . [and] bringing about a cultural mixing" (pp. 128, 132). Unfortunately, the impressive potential of global mass media to transform societies and families in less-advantaged parts of the world in terms of education and literacy, health and wellness, and other quality-of-life issues is yet to be fully realized.

Television as Global Media

Broadcast media have long played a pivotal role in connecting audiences at a mass societal level, thus "promoting national unity at a symbolic level" (Morley and Robins 1995:66). UNESCO (2003b) has recognized television as "one of the most influential forms of media in the present time," even establishing a World Television Day in 1996. Morley and Robins (1995) argue that television and the new globalized media and electronic technologies play a substantial role in the "transnationalization of culture" by "disrupting established boundaries . . . and . . . rearticulating the private and public spheres in new ways" (p. 64).

The explosive potential of global media imagery—and the potential impact on families—is evident in the widespread availability of television, with its unique characteristics of accessibility, immediacy, and privacy. Worldwide, the number of television sets per thousand individuals tripled in the last three decades of the 20th century, from 81 television receivers per 1,000 inhabitants in 1970 to 240 television receivers per 1,000 inhabitants in 1997. As with other cultural commodities, significant differences persist among continents, with Europe having the highest and Africa having the lowest number of receivers per 1,000 inhabitants (UNESCO 1999).

Responding to concerns around cultural imperialism, in some markets, some receiving societies acted to regulate the representation of television programming produced in or originating from another society. For example, in response to criticisms that children in places such as Canada know more about New York City than they do about Toronto, the Canadian Parliament adopted broadcasting legislation in 1968 and again in 1991 that had as a primary objective "the maintenance and enhancement of national identity and cultural sovereignty," with the observed effect that the amount of foreign broadcasting in Canada is higher than in the United States but lower than that in other industrialized societies (Tremblay 1992:1).

In cases of other widely distributed cultural icons, distributors have responded by recasting and re-envisioning the original television program concept. For example, by 2002 the award-winning children's educational television show *Sesame Street* was distributed in 20 markets, including China, Egypt, and Russia. In some markets, characters derived from the local society are drawn to reflect those populations and customs. For example, the South African version of *Sesame Street* features a puppet named Kami. Kami is 5 years old and HIV positive. Kami's mother died of AIDS, and she is depicted as living with a foster mother (Orecklin 2002).

Readily turned on and tuned in, television can be a critical part of family leisure activity. As such, the social functions (and dysfunctions) of television include structuring the day and punctuating family time and family activity (Morley 1986). As the presence of television extended and expanded to families worldwide, these globalized images of meal time, homework, leisure, and bedtime may have reshaped the rhythms of daily family life in peculiarly Western, capitalist ways. Established family rituals, such as attentive deference to elders as they communicate knowledge and skills or conversations around meals about the days' events, may be reorganized around normative authority reflected in televised situations or conversations regarding demand for marketed products.

Television is rapidly being replaced by cyber technology. While 98 percent of Americans own a television, less than two thirds of them consider television a necessity. Two thirds of Americans own a home computer and a cell phone and more than half consider those devices a necessity (Pew Research Center 2011c). Still, to the extent that televised images disproportionately represent Western culture, television brings a hegemonic image of values and norms into families' homes (or, in less-developed societies, community gathering places). In the words of David Walsh (2006), psychologist and founding president of the MediaWise Movement (a program of the National Institute on Media and Family), "Who tells the stories defines the culture." Families are thus faced with cultural images that may enrich but also compete with or even challenge local, traditional values and norms.

Wired and Wireless Families on a Global Scale

Go to the website for V-Day (http://www.vday.org/home) and you will be met by multilingual text and multiethnic images for this "global movement to end violence against women and girls." That organization has mobilized women across the world around missing and murdered, raped and battered women in Afghanistan, Egypt, India, Israel, Jordan, Palestine, and other countries.

According to the U.N. International Telecommunications Union (UNITU 2011), by 2011 the number of mobile phone subscribers exceeded 5.3 billion while the number of Internet users exceeded 2 billion worldwide. In light of these statistics, the previous discussion of television as a cultural icon seems rather anachronistic. Globalizing new technologies in the form of mobile phones and the Internet represent not only a new way to educate and entertain but a new, powerful form of social capital. These technologies can produce both cultural homogeneity and cultural complexity and transnational cultures (and, as in the case of the Arab Spring, even social disorder) that may transcend the interests of nation-state societies. After all, information flow can be among the most difficult aspects of a society to control. As any parent who has attempted to control his or her child's Internet use can testify, information has a way of oozing around any efforts to contain it.

Castells (2000), author of *The Rise of the Network Society*, studies the history, politics, and technology surrounding the emergence of new social structures associated with what he calls "informationalism." Led by radio and then television broadcasting, the new information technologies have resulted in a "communication explosion throughout the world" (p. 361), including microelectronics, computers and software, and telecommunications. Computer-mediated communication technologies, in particular, challenge conventional national boundaries. The Internet and the World Wide Web, especially, have the capacity to revolutionize aspects of social life, including community and family, socialization and work, self and identity.

As with other forms of technology, access to the Internet is unevenly distributed worldwide and even within societies. After observing a live-action map at Google headquarters depicting all the Internet activity across the world, Barack Obama (2006)—then the junior senator from Illinois—wrote:

> The physicist in Cambridge, the bond trader in Tokyo, the student in a remote Indian village, and the manager of a Mexico City department store were drawn into a single, constant, thrumming conversation, time and space giving way to a world spun entirely of light. Then I noticed the broad swaths of darkness as the globe spun on its axis—most of Africa, chunks of South Asia, even some portions of the United States, where the thick cords of light dissolved into a few discrete strands. (Pp. 140–1)

As described in Table 3.2, the highest concentration of key telecom indicators is found in the more-developed world. The difference between

Table 3.2   Key Telecom Indicators by Continent and Region (per 1,000 Inhabitants), 2010

Indicator	Fixed Telephone Lines	Mobile Cell Subscriptions	Internet Users
World Total	17.2	78.0	29.7
Continent			
Africa	1.5	45.2	10.8
Arab States	9.8	87.9	24.1
Asia and Pacific	13.6	69.2	22.5
CIS[1]	26.2	134.8	34.0
Europe	40.7	117.7	67.0
The Americas	29.5	94.5	50.7
Region			
Developed	41.6	114.2	68.8
Developing	11.9	70.1	21.1

NOTE: 1. The Commonwealth of Independent States (CIS) includes Armenia, Azerbaijan, Belarus, Georgia, Kazakhstan, Moldova, Russia, Tajikistan, Turkmenistan, Ukraine, and Uzbekistan.

SOURCE: Compiled from UNITU (2011). © International Telecommunication Union, 2010.

more- and less-developed regions is lowest for mobile cell subscriptions (at 114.2 and 70.1 per 1,000 inhabitants, respectively), suggesting that inhabitants of the developing world may be "skipping" fixed-location Internet technology in favor of more portable access through cell phones. Differences across continents are much less striking. Although Africa is last on all three key telecom indicators—and economies such as Brazil, China, India, and Russia account for much of the growth in cell phone subscriptions— the greatest rate of growth is found in Africa (Tryhorn 2009).

Internet costs remain highest in the least-developed parts of the world. Worldwide, the typical Internet user is urban, higher income, and male (Seager 2003:82–3). What has been termed the *digital divide* exists not only locally and globally but also along age, social class, gender, and race lines within some countries.

Desire to own a computer and employment in technology-related occupations are also important factors in access to computer technology. However, education and income are the two largest variables associated with differences in computer ownership. A study in California revealed that the technology gap for immigrant youth is significant and widening (Fairlie et al. 2006). In 2006, 70 percent of native-born individuals and 56 percent of immigrant individuals had home access to a computer. Gaps exist within immigrant groups as well, with the highest percentage of home computers found among youth in immigrant Asian households and the lowest (36 percent) found among youth in immigrant Latino households. In the United States, Latinos and blacks are more likely than are whites to access the Internet through cell phone technology—at 51 percent, 46 percent, and 33 percent, respectively. Ironically, such higher access may actually be contributing to a greater digital divide. "It's tough to fill out a job application on a cell phone, for example" (Washington 2011).

In 2011 the United Nations declared access to and freedom of expression through the Internet to be a human right (U.N. Human Rights Council 2011). In order to reduce the growing digital divide, Fairlie et al. (2006) advocate not only programs to make computer ownership more affordable and school-centered programs to make computers more home accessible but also community education programs to socialize the entire family—parents as well as children—on the value of digital technology.

The social meaning of Internet-derived communication is complex (Castells 2000). On the one hand, the Internet has the potential to draw people into online interaction around shared values and concerns, with new virtual communities eventually providing face-to-face meetings, friendly exchanges, and even aid and assistance in the form of material and other support for their members (Rheingold 1993). Today, migrant and other transnational families in which one or more members are employed, attend school, or otherwise live away from the family can use not only telephones and innovations in lower-cost long-distance calling but also the Internet to enhance communication.

The Internet tends to increase contacts among individuals who are just beyond the reach of usual, everyday contact (Hampton and Wellman 2004). However, if any member along the family chain does not have access to, cannot afford, or cannot use the technology, the potential of transnational families to network in an increasingly globally wired world is diminished. Also, in contrast to the perspective that a wired family is a closer family, some critics express concern regarding the potential of such communications to dehumanize relationships, at least in everyday life (Slouka 1995; Wolton 1998). Psychologists have found greater Internet use to be associated with decline in size of social circle and decline in communication with family members in the household, thus generating a possible increase in depression and loneliness for some family members (Kraut et al. 1998).

The United Nations has assessed the effects of information and communication technologies (see UNESCO 2005; United Nations 2005). The importance of global mass media for families lies, broadly, in (1) the ability of the media to structure time and space and (2) the role of the media in socialization. Any definitive conclusions regarding the impact of Internet would require far more controlled, systematic study on more populations than seen to date. However, Castells (2000) may be correct in concluding that Internet is best suited to developing and maintaining many weak ties (as opposed to fewer strong ties) at relatively low material cost. New communication technologies have the potential to dramatically transform time and space and, accordingly, human life and relationships by enabling families whose members are miles or even continents away to remain virtually connected.

As described above, global transformationists contend that cultural transmission is complex, nuanced, and sometimes contradictory. The example of the adaptation of the telephone, the Internet, and cell phones to social relationships represents another such case. "The telephone was adapted, not just adopted. People shape technology to fit their own needs" (Castells 2000:293). The same can now be said of computer-mediated social media.

Lack of effective communication technology has long been a barrier to economic growth and societal development. To Hamadoun Touré, secretary general of UNITU, cellular technology has the potential to act as a catalyst to help the world achieve the goals set for the new millennium, including reducing poverty (UNESCO 2008).

In India, more people have access to a cell phone than to a toilet (U.N. News Centre 2010). Cellular and mobile phone technology has had a significant and rapid impact on families. Mobile phone technology enables people to make instant money transfers, to seek health and other advice, and to secure Internet service on the spot. The United Nations has developed protocols to use mobile and other wireless technology to deliver education to girls and other underserved groups in less-developed, particularly rural, areas of the world. Doing so could revolutionize women's status and social inclusion in those countries (UNESCO 2010).

For those with access, this technology enhances the abilities of children, parents, and other family members to remain in contact, securing lower costs for families living apart and even permitting family members to locate one another. Cellular phone technology still serves as a primary means to call for help. Finally, families' access to communication and other technology is linked to other patterns of global consumption.

Global Consumption and Families

Culture, in particular mass culture, has been conceptualized as a commodity in much the same way that the products of factory labor are commodities (Adorno 1991). Lash and Lury (2006) describe a "global culture industry" in which material objects (e.g., designer labels, sportswear) vested with globally recognized brands mass-marketed through global capitalism have become powerful transnational cultural symbols. Most of the world's consumers of material goods live in the global North (Lawson 2001a). That means that individuals and families in the more-developed world are the focus of enormous, global marketing organizations. However, advertising and other marketing efforts across national borders increasingly make mass consumer systems global consumer systems (Mattelart 1994).

Such global marketing seems to rely on and generate a system of increasingly universal values in which consumers are socialized into the hegemonic consumption of products. Globalization promotes a particularly universal, insatiable consumerism because, in a world in which capitalism serves as the globally dominant economic system, consumers' desires are never satisfied. Globally derived mass consumption thereby becomes a primary part of the construction of identity and lifestyle (Miles 2000).

Several studies reveal the extent to which global patterns of consumption have in fact been glocalized, co-opted by the local culture via face-to-face relationships. For example, Billington, Hockey, and Strawbridge (1998) have examined the preference of young men in the Congo who are members of a low-status group (the *sape*) to consume global goods. These men wear clothing with ostentatious designer symbols and display in their cars global products, such as internationally marketed soft drink cans. Billington et al. argue that these young men are not merely imitating Western culture; they are using these cultural artifacts as a means of establishing a high-status identity and, thereby, enhanced social power.

Lest cultural diffusion appear to be an exclusively North-to-South phenomenon, consider that Americans may also seek to purchase the latest fashions and technology in order to appear "on the cutting edge" of cultural trends. For example, in recent years Australian wines have begun to replace French wines as among the most desirable on American and even some European tables.

While some societies and cultures may resist the forces of global capitalism and even develop functional alternatives, the pervasiveness and invasiveness of mass-marketed, iconic goods make this a Herculean undertaking. For example, Barbie, that most successfully marketed idol of hypersexualized, hyperconsuming American femininity, was banned for sale in Iran in 1996. In doing so, Iranian political authorities were indicating their perception of the power of American consumer goods to cultivate, compromise, or corrupt traditional culture in that Middle Eastern society. A "counter-Barbie" named Sara was introduced in Iran in 2002. However, even at a cheaper cost, sales of the chastely dressed Sara are poor and consumers seem still willing to pay $40 for a Barbie doll on the black market ("Dolls No More American Whore" 2002). A new doll developed by a toy company based in the United Arab Emirates was introduced in 2003. About the same size as Barbie, Fulla comes dressed in a long, black abaya (but no bikini). The storyline that accompanies the doll portrays her as a doctor and teacher who likes sports and respects her parents. The "real test [of the doll's success in the Middle East] will be . . . whether this is something that only adults will collect or whether [it's something] kids will want" (Shah 2007:E3).

Postmodernists have argued that such American means of consumption, which include not only dolls and other specific projects but also superstores, mega shopping malls, cybermalls, as well as television shopping networks and family-oriented theme parks, are imposing themselves in ways that compromise family intimacy (Baudrillard 1988). George Ritzer (2005a) sees a relentless, globally ubiquitous propulsion toward an extreme version of Weber's formal rationality in mass-consumption patterns. In a series of works including *The McDonaldization of Society,* first published in 1993, *Expressing America,* published in 1995, and *Enchantment in a Disenchanted World* (2005), Ritzer describes what he has termed "McDonaldization" in the exceedingly bureaucratized, highly efficient, predictable-if-mundane, technology-driven, and above all rational escalation of fast-food eating places (Ritzer 1996) and credit card retail purchasing (Ritzer 1995, 2005b). In this way, the massification of not only consumer goods but also consumer leisure experiences moves the family further from cherished, spontaneous, intimate connection and closer to anonymous, standardized, rationalized interface.

The global family should not be viewed as a purely private domestic institution. Rather, the family is an active player in every other public system, including religion, government, education, and most certainly economics. For example, globalization changes dietary cultures. Men living to greatly advanced ages in Crete have a lifelong pattern of nutrition following the traditional Mediterranean diet, rich in homegrown, unprocessed natural fruits, vegetables, and grains, with liberal doses of healthy fats from olive oil and fish, but sparse on foods heavy in saturated fats from meat and dairy products. In contrast, the new generation represented by teenagers in the same culture demonstrates a decided preference for an American-style diet, heavy in processed foods, sugar, and saturated fats, resulting in a diet typical of what some have called a "world-wide epidemic of heart disease" (Schmickle 2006:A7).

Like Baudrillard (1988), as well as Bauman (1992) and Featherstone (1991), Ritzer views postmodern society as a consumer society. These theorists argue that the focus of capitalist society has shifted from concern with the means of production to concern with the means of consumption. In Ritzer's (2005b) words: "Although producing more and cheaper goods remains important, attention is increasingly being devoted to getting people to consume more and a greater variety of things" (p. 282).

This shift requires an increasing emphasis on marketing and advertising, including infomercials, telemarketing, and even product placement in television shows and movies. Baudrillard (1988) even describes the new means of consumption as a new kind of labor. In Ritzer's (2005a) analysis of the McDonaldization of society, the consumer engages in labor to arrive (and wait in line) at fast-food destinations. Once there, the consumer performs tasks related to serving food that were previously performed by paid employees. All the while, the hapless consumer is increasingly besieged by objects of consumption.

As a result, an American family traveling anywhere in the world is rarely far from McDonald's golden arches. Others are not persuaded of the global extent of consumer McDonaldization, or at least the validity of that most American metaphor, McDonald's restaurants. While effective as a rhetorical device, McDonald's is not the ultimate, ubiquitous global symbol that Ritzer (1993) and others have made it out to be. In *Globaloney*, Veseth (2005) agrees that McDonald's is highly visible to Americans abroad searching for recognizable branded symbols in the global landscape— another such symbol is Coca-Cola—even if the glocalized McDonald's in India serves vegetarian cuisine ("The Case Against Globaloney" 2011).

In fact, the number of "reasonably authentic" Italian restaurants outside of Italy is more than double the number of McDonald's in all the world, the signature fast food in Great Britain is Indian curry, and McDonald's is no more and perhaps less globally ubiquitous than Chinese cuisine. Veseth (2005) argues that observers

> constantly encounter images of home as they travel the world, and they associate them with their particular visions of globalization. Their reactions to what they find are likely to differ, however, because, although they see the same world, they process the images through different cultural filters, which yield predictably different conclusions. [The observer] assumes that the fast food he finds abroad is the same as at home and takes comfort from that. But he's wrong. In fact, McDonald's menus are not all the same. . . . What made the original McDonald's distinctive was price and efficiency. (Pp. 126–7)

Veseth (2005) sees cultures today not as monolithically global but as diverse and complex. If so, then families may be faced with less pressure from global mass culture than what the McDonaldization thesis would suggest. Further, the local construction of meaning for community, household, and family life attached to such cultural icons as McDonald's should not be overlooked. Reflecting a family development theme,

> Some women in East Asia . . . seem to use McDonald's stores as a "sanctuary" from male domination. . . . McDonald's has become a gathering place where children and grandchildren are specially celebrated. . . . McDonald's is the home of "conspicuous consumption" . . . but it is also the great leveler. . . . [In Taiwan] the choice of McDonald's (versus a restaurant owned by a mainland Chinese family) makes a [political] statement about independence from mainland influence. (P. 134)

To the extent that the interaction behind the fast-food counter, credit card payment counter, or theme park concession is carefully scripted, patterns of interaction surrounding the new means of consumption can best be described as "simulated," resulting in a loss of authentic interaction (Ritzer 2005b:284).

Some of these new means of consumption have further, specific, identifiable effects on individual consumers. Parents in particular face social dilemmas: short-term advantage in responding to mass-marketing appeals or long-term costs associated with sometimes deleterious effects. As in the case of the shift from the traditional Mediterranean diet in Crete, fast-food establishments stimulate unhealthy food choices, to the detriment of physical health. Credit cards encourage people to spend beyond their means. Shopping malls stimulate people to buy things they do not need, to the detriment of fiscal well-being.

Television, cybermalls, and mass-distributed catalogs enable people to shop without space and time constraints (Ritzer 2005b). Baudrillard (1989) and Ritzer (2005a) both describe American society as emotionally hollow, where every place seems like every other—meaningless, monotonous, superficial, a reminder of Gertrude Stein's (1937/1973) pithy description of Oakland, California: "There is no there there" (p. 289).

Lipovetsky and Charles (2005) frame the problem of "hyperconsumption" as patterns of consumption that absorb and integrate ever-increasing aspects of postmodern life. Hyperconsumption encourages individuals to consume for individual gratification, hedonism, and pleasure. Such a condition creates anxiety, tension, and anguish as the individual fails to find comfort in increasingly uncertain times void of traditional systems that had previously restrained individualistic impulses.

Baudrillard (1990) and Ritzer (2005b) depict these hyperconsumptive experiences as occurring in the context of "enchantment," "magic," and "spectacle." Ritzer (2005b) writes of these new means of consumption as "fragmented" and "discontinuous." He writes, "We find ourselves adrift in an ecstatic system in which fast food restaurants . . . and their endlessly different, but surprisingly similar, products whirl about us. We are lost in a world of relentless, but meaningless, expansion" (p. 285).

What is the impact of this "enchantment" on parenting and families around the world? Is a "good parent" the one who succumbs to the seduction and provides his or her child with the fullest measure of enchantment? What is the impact of parental competition to mount the most extravagant birthday party at a themed restaurant, complete with a fantasy-character host? Is a family failing or ensuring a special form of relative deprivation if the parents do not provide the children with a Disney or other theme park holiday? How does hyperconsumerism create wider gulfs between the "haves" and the "have-nots" of families worldwide?

Some social critics argue that these new means of consumption can be injurious to family cooperation, connectedness, and intimacy, even beyond the social class implications for parents who are unable to conform to the pressures of this mass consumerism (or who financially "express," thereby overextending themselves in an effort to conform). Lemert and Elliott (2006) argue that both this mass consumer capitalism and globalization (and, I would argue, the emphasis on "enchantment") have had dramatic impacts on eroticism, sex, and intimacy. Global capital, ideas, and ideologies coupled with increasing geographic mobility form increasingly global views of sexuality through worldwide advertising, mass media, and information culture and technologies. In particular, Lemert and Elliott cite the increasing consumerist emphasis on youth, sensuality, playfulness, and physical attractiveness. They fear that some of these increasingly global exchanges may be replacing family norms and values favoring family cooperation and durability with wide-ranging views of enchanted consumer culture.

These negative effects aside, global patterns of distribution also offer the potential to provide, on a large scale, both a wide variety of goods and also information that can significantly enhance the material quality of life and well-being for families. Mass distribution of materials for health, literacy, and other areas of life may be more effectively and efficiently distributed, perhaps even with increased economies of scale, if markets are defined in global terms. The successful global marketing of products such as Coca-Cola soft drinks—but also world health efforts to eradicate scourges such as polio and small pox, as well as female genital mutilation—gives but a hint of the potential for the worldwide distribution of goods and services.

In 1998, the United Nations (1998/1999) convened the Technology and Families workshop in Dublin, Ireland, to provide an opportunity to examine the impact of technology on families. The development and diffusion of technology has "contributed immensely to the improvement of living standards of millions of people in many parts of the world," resulting in reduced poverty, improved health, greater opportunities and choices, and access to products that have enhanced the quality of life (p. 4). The report says that technology also has the potential to strengthen the family unit.

> The effect [of technology] is to alter, often dramatically, how people live, how they earn their living, what their prospects are—for better or for worse—and how they relate to each other in and through their social institutions. Technology impacts the institution of the family through various channels, among them the education system, the mass media, the world of work and social services, in particular those relating to health and social well-being. (P. 2)

The report concludes that technology, including computer and other digital technology, changes the ways families nurture and socialize children and alters the quality of relationships among spouses, parents, children, and siblings, as well as near and extended kin. In the next section, I explicate the effects of global media and consumption on family norms and values.

Cultural Globalization and Families

Every family in every society—to a greater or lesser degree—is confronted with the issues that globalization portends for culture (Nederveen Pieterse 2004). Some of these issues involve increasing uncertainty and insecurity for families. Lemert and Elliott (2006) remind us that "the changing world all about is filled with risks—risks that prevent any life, even among the well-heeled, from reclining into self-satisfaction" (p. 154). If nothing else, the increasingly frequent "bumping up against" diverse folkways and mores, languages and traditions presents families with challenges and opportunities on an escalating scale. Moreno (2002) argues:

The changing demographic characteristics of our society as well as the increasingly global nature of all enterprises are rapidly propelling us into ever more frequent close encounters of the cultural kind with persons quite dissimilar from ourselves. We are largely unprepared to adequately cope with this quiet but significant revolution taking place in our society and our world. (P. 1)

Families are the primary agents through which their members can acquire the skills to contend with globalization, what Bourdieu (1998) calls cultural capital. Cultural capital is articulated through the family in the form of socialization of values and norms, habits and customs, which in turn enhance or inhibit the accumulation of educational, economic, and other forms of capital. Families that can provide access to diverse cultures enable their members to accumulate symbolic capital in the form of language, education, and other traits that increase cultural adaptability.

In Wallerstein's (1990) world-system analysis, culture is an "ideological battleground" but one in which might arise "a new rendezvous of world civilizations" (p. 54). The globalization of culture compromises local cultural integrity and challenges traditional family patterns in favor of global cultural homogeneity—or even just pervasive change along nontraditional lines—in families. Globalization can challenge family autonomy and authority in many areas but perhaps in no area more than gender.

Globalization and Gender

The patterns of family life associated with globalization, including demographic transitions, international violence, transnational employment, and especially global cultural exposure, challenge traditional gender roles and the socialization that produces them. Abdi (2007, 2012) uses a feminist perspective and a multimethod approach including interviews, participant observation, focus groups, and literary analysis to reveal how the Somali civil war in the late 1980s and the subsequent migration, resettlement, and transnational experiences of Somali men and women underscore changing gender dynamics on ideological, economic, and social levels.

The absence of formal institutions in the aftermath of the conflict rendered women's economic pursuits in the informal sector salient for family survival. In the American setting, refugee women's access to public assistance, and/or jobs in the lowest tier of the economy, where most refugee men are also clustered, has led to a male perception of women's "empowerment" in America. . . . New discourses supported and driven by mostly male community leaders demonize women's "transgressions" of cultural and religious boundaries, which are seen as "emasculating" Somali men. (Abdi 2012)

Abdi's findings on the shifts and conflicts surrounding gender norms and values, as experienced by Somalis living in the United States, are presented in an original essay, "Contested Norms and Values in Transnational Families," at the end of this chapter. Abdi posits that boys and young men are more likely than girls and young women to have the opportunity to adopt the cultural practices of inner-city youth, therefore bringing young males into more direct confrontation with the older generation.

Likewise, Timera (2002) found that Sahelian[1] girls living in France are required to remain in the parental home until marriage and to perform well in school to prepare to be good wives and mothers. On the other hand, Sahelian boys leave school and enter the labor force at an early age and are unlikely to be sanctioned by their communities for marriage to a "white French" girl. Boys, who seem to be in harmony with their parents and local communities, are more likely to come into conflict with French public law.

Traditional and double standards regarding gender roles can be remarkably resilient, even in the face of globalization, perhaps because sexism is so globally pervasive. However, some girls come to conflict with family and community, as seen by the cases brought by some of these girls against their communities and their parents over issues of female circumcision or forced, arranged marriage to a member of the local immigrant community. Thus, apparently, identity formation among immigrant youth differs between girls and boys and reflects different negotiations between immigrant parents and their daughters and sons. In the next section, I address some of the challenges—and promises—of cultural globalization for parent/child relationships in the family.

Globalization and Parenting

Contention between cultures is also evident in the case of parents attempting to navigate between two (or more) cultures in rearing their children. While some parents manage to ensure the retention of the home culture, others struggle mightily with the attractions and distractions of the new culture for the younger generation.

Al-Ali's (2002) research on Bosnian refugees relocating to the United Kingdom and the Netherlands after the wars in the former Yugoslavia in the 1990s reveals the lengths to which families will go to maintain native culture even in the face of displacement and resettlement in a safer and perhaps

---

[1]The Sahel is the geographic region between the Sahara Desert in the north and the Sudan savannahs in the south, stretching across North Africa from the Atlantic Ocean and the Red Sea.

more attractive (at least to the younger generation) Western culture. While taking pride in their children's developing skills in English language, the parents in Al-Ali's study expressed concern about their children's losing touch with Bosnian culture and language. One woman, Amra, regarding her daughter Selma's enculturation, reported:

> Selma speaks perfect English. She sometimes corrects me. Her teachers all say that she is doing really well. But her Bosnian was getting worse with time. So now I am spending a few hours almost every day reading Bosnian stories to her, practicing writing and talking. (P. 91)

Some of the parents in Al-Ali's (2002) study were even taking advantage of an official curriculum on Bosnian language, history, geography, music, and art provided by the Bosnian consulate in London. Perhaps not surprisingly, some of the parents in Al-Ali's study reported significant resistance from their children, who refused to attend the Bosnian educational programs on weekends. Bowing to the pressure, some of the parents relented, no longer requiring their children to participate in the Bosnian programs.

Timera (2002) also writes of the dilemma of second-generation Sahelian youth, children of African parents born and raised in France. She describes poignantly the situation of the relatively recently migrated parents, who remain deeply committed to their home villages in Senegal, Mali, Mauritania, and other regions through associational, religious, and national identities. While a significant part of the reality for parents is their ghettoization as an ethnic and religious community of migrants, Timera's research reveals that the assimilation and integration of this group is contested on intergenerational and gender stages. Parents who have a well-constructed identity socialized in their native country often face daunting identity tasks around adaptation and acculturation upon reaching France. Meanwhile, the children of migrants face a contradictory socialization process, beginning in the family with values and norms (e.g., names and prayers, language and body language, dietary habits and table manners, religious practices and celebrations, dressing customs and hygiene standards) that form the social structure of the parents' community.

At school, children of migrant parents may be treated disrespectfully. Sahelian youth certainly experience being foreign and "the other" in the dominant French society. Their French schools promote French values and norms, pointedly marking the difference between the parental culture and the culture of the next generation. The primary objective of French schools—to foster assimilation into the majority culture of French society— may be neither apparent nor acceptable to immigrant parents, but as these immigrant children traverse French and Sahelian societies, they face crises of their identities between home and school (Timera 2002).

Of course, assimilation is not the inevitable outcome of immigration. Some children and their families actively resist efforts of the dominant culture to obliterate the migrant culture. Yet the processes through which cultural integrity is maintained are complicated. For example, one study has examined the challenges Korean American adolescents living in the Midwestern United States face around enculturation, specifically fluency in their Korean language. Apparently, ethnic identity (i.e., "I am Korean") shapes the effects of family relations (i.e., family cohesion), which in turn shapes Korean language fluency (Park 2007). In the next section, I ask how globalization shapes cultural negotiations between parents and children and in the broader family system.

Globalization and Family Values

Conversations with parents around the world suggest that American goods, from blue jeans to Coca-Cola to rap music, are an essential part of those parents' negotiations with their children. American women traveling abroad are often surprised at the extent to which men in other countries assume all American women are sexually adventurous. After all, those same men see this titillating image thus represented on reruns of television shows such as *Baywatch* (a television show that, in reruns, remains wildly popular in Germany, along with its star, David Hasselhoff) and a constantly shifting parade of scantily clad music celebrities. Western, and more particularly American, culture seems omnipresent in global society.

As discussed earlier in this chapter, new communication technologies have expanded the potential for families to extend their worlds in terms of not only education, entertainment, and information but also communication and even interaction. A father can track his son's travels through Greece via his online credit card charges. In case of an emergency, a daughter can reach her mother across the globe using a cellular phone. Worldwide spheres of consumption play increasingly powerful roles in the formation of identity and lifestyle, including family values and norms, as illustrated by Ritzer's (2004b) concept of McDonaldization.

In a book titled *How "American" Is Globalization?* Marling (2006) responds "less than you think" but "more than you know." Marling deconstructs the assumption of cultural Americanization in the global context. He finds that the diffusion of technology (e.g., ATMs, franchising, and innovations such as bar codes and computers) not only changes the means of production and consumption but also expresses American norms in areas such as work and leisure, convenience and credit, family and community. However, the uncertain success of such quintessential American icons as Euro-Disney suggests that some culture traits do not translate well, even to other Western cultures. Further, while Americans often assume that culture traits diffuse more rapidly from the United States to other countries, one trip outside the United States challenges that assumption. For example, as ubiquitous as cell phone technology appears in the United States, that technology has been adapted faster and more extensively in Europe and other locations, initially at least because landline phone costs were so much higher in Europe.

Miller (1997) argues that, through "indigenization," local cultures are continuously changing—digesting, incorporating, and assimilating—as they encounter cultural elements from other societies. For example, in an engrossing ethnography of the construction and deconstruction of white masculine identities among youth in North East England, Nayak (2003) recounts the ability of young men and women to "splice" Englishness with whiteness and various ethnicities ranging from Anglo-Irish and Scotch-Irish to Anglo-Italian and various distinctions of color. Significant to these identities are global systems of music, fashion, and sport. However, for these youth, contact with the global is complicated and often played out in local spaces, including music clubs, playgrounds, and basketball courts. Nayak concludes:

> Whilst youth cultures draw inspiration from the global marketplace when it comes to dress, music, hairstyles and fashion, these values are invariably approached at the prosaic level of the "local," where the inflections of race, class, gender, and so forth, remain evident. . . . There remains compelling evidence that youth cultures continue to be complex, place-related phenomena. (P. 176)

In sum, Nayak finds compelling evidence that youth cultures are simultaneously local place related and complex, porous, open-ended "meeting places." In these cases, family culture clashes may be seen as a product of intergenerational conflict exacerbated by the exposure of youth to a dizzying array of global images.

Such may have been the case for the parents of the alleged bombers in London in July 2005. According to news accounts, the parents were shocked at their sons' possible involvement in a global terrorist movement. The family of one of the alleged bombers said they were "devastated" by the attacks and baffled by their 18-year-old son's involvement in terrorist activities (Frankel and Whitlock 2005).

Generalizations about differences in receptivity to cultural adaptation across generations are risky. Even though the desire to fit into the new culture in a host society may be strong among both old and young, children almost always find adaptation to a new culture easier than do older generations—whether Sahelians in France, Bosnians in the United Kingdom, or Hmong in Minnesota. The young also may actively attempt to distance themselves from being different, as well as from their parents' strong ties to the native society and repeated desires to return.

"Hmong Families, Frogtown"

Photograph by W. Y. Huie. Reprinted by permission of the photographer.

Acculturation appears to increase the risks involved in parenting across two cultures (Martinez 2006). Some research suggests, albeit inconclusively, that acculturation is linked to psychological problems, including depressive symptoms (e.g., Katragadda and Tidwell 1998) and suicidal thoughts (e.g., Hovey and King 1996). More powerful research offers more compelling evidence that acculturation as indicated by English-language adaptation and participation in other aspects of the dominant culture places first- and second-generation Mexican-origin youth at increased risk for alcohol and substance use, conduct problems, early sexual activity, juvenile arrests, and other problem behaviors (Gonzales et al. 2002).

Some groups will go to extraordinary lengths to manage and retain their native values. For example, in research on British Asians in the Swaminarayan movement,[2] Barot (2002) found transnational families whose adherence to shared beliefs about religion, business, and welfare (including values and norms emphasizing contributing to the common good of movement members and endogamous marriage) has resulted in effective business networks and a high level of family welfare that has extended over a century and across four continents.

The explanations for negative associations with acculturation include decreased family cohesion and parental authority and increased conflict between youth and their parents (Gonzales et al. 2006), as well as greater exposure to negative stereotypes and discrimination and increased susceptibility to deviant peer role models (Gil, Vega, and Dimas 1994; Rotheram-Borus 1989).

According to Baca (2006),

> the most recent waves of immigration have brought new Americans into a culture that is more complex, more technology- and bureaucracy-driven than it ever has been. When immigrants' command of English is lacking, sometimes they turn to the closest available interpreters, their children. (P. 1E)

Bicultural families, especially in cases where the children are becoming acculturated at a much faster rate than the parents, may find themselves in situations in which the roles of parents and children are reversed or compromised. For example, in Minneapolis, Minnesota, students speak almost 100 different languages. Given the diversity in languages spoken in family homes, some immigrant children are placed in the position of serving as interpreters for their parents in the marketplace but also in the child's own teacher conferences and personal counseling sessions and even in the doctor's office for parents seeking medical care.

---

[2]The Swaminarayan movement takes its name from Sahajanand Swami, a Brahmin from Uttar Pradesh, India. The movement originated in the 19th century as India was transitioning from Mogul to British colonial rule and developed in response to perceived moral decline. Followers from a range of castes aspired to salvation through adherence to the teachings of the charismatic Swami and supported social changes that would result in improvements in the ritual and social status of lower- and middle-rank caste members (Barot 2002).

While children can derive a sense of responsibility and maturity from these roles, they also may become overburdened and parental authority may be compromised (Baca 2006). Youth also may share their parents' regret at absence from the home country. Anisa, a 15-year-old living in the Netherlands grieves over the culture she left behind in Bosnia.

> Bosnia is so different from the Netherlands. I am looking forward to the summer when we will go back to Sarajevo. It is so much more fun there. I go out with my friends and cousin all the time. People are so much nicer and warmer there. Most of my best friends here are from former Yugoslavia, not just Bosnians. We try to have fun here as well. But here everything is so expensive and my parents won't let me stay out as late as in Sarajevo. And the food . . . I hate Dutch food! Have you tried our pies? (Al-Ali 2002:92–3)

This contrast in rates and levels of adaptation can result in parental disappointment and even intergenerational conflict, as demonstrated in Al-Ali's research. Such differential rates of adaptation to the new society—and estrangement from the native culture—may even set the stage for alienation between children and their parents, as the latter adapt more readily and more comfortably to the values and norms of the adopted society.

Far beyond the usual meaning of assimilation, some families and their members engage in what Bryceson and Vuorela (2002) call reverse cultural alienation—that is, "the tendency to alienate oneself from one's original cultural background as opposed to the more common form of cultural alienation in which newcomers feel estranged and out of harmony with their new adopted surroundings" (pp. 21–2). Bryceson and Vuorela posit that this reverse cultural alienation may be most common among elites who more closely identify with elites in the host society and who may feel comfortable speaking other languages. They welcome living in the host country and may avoid others from the native country out of concern for becoming "ghettoized expatriates." Izuhara and Shibata (2002) have observed this phenomenon among Japanese migrant women living in the United Kingdom with their English husbands.

Globalization shapes "the fluidity of intra- and inter-family relations in the face of far more fixed cultural norms" (Bryceson and Vuorela 2002:24). Therefore, appreciating the effects of globalization on real families requires understanding how families live out cultural values and norms in everyday life. Globalization tends to take a "top-down" approach (Flusty 2004). Emphasizing the sublimation of the local, regional, or national to transnational economic or political processes reveals the global context of immigration, colonization, and other social processes. However, such a hyperglobalist or world systems approach overstates the significance of economic and political systems and understates the importance of cultural systems in everyday/everynight life. In other words, the smaller-scale contexts and practical consequences of global forces on families are overlooked. The permutations of globalization on real families require examination of everyday practices and members with multiple identities in diverse localities. Theoretical and methodological creativity, including more research of an ethnographic or other observational nature, are needed to reveal what Flusty calls the "inside-out" or "from-below" implications of globalization on families.

Bauman (1992, 2001, 2004, 2007) and Lemert and Elliott (2006) are among the social scientists who have tried to unravel the impact of globalization and postmodernity on individuals, their identities, and their relationships. Those authors charge that globalization does have dire consequences in terms of emotional costs and culture. They see a world increasingly characterized by individualism, which is a "current preoccupation with the self in terms of narcissism, emotionalism, the manipulation of individual needs or desires, and a quest for self-realization and self-fulfillment . . . with traumatic consequences for people's emotional lives and relationships" (Pp. 10–1).

Lemert and Elliott (2006) also see heightened individualism in the shift from custom and tradition to what they call the "internal world of the individual" and the production of competing polarities of freedom and alienation. For Lemert and Elliott, the consequences of globalization can be seen not only in accelerating patterns of international contact and worldwide social problems and in rapidly expanding communication technologies and more rational consumption patterns but also in more diverse cultural cosmopolitan life worlds and relationships that are more experimental, open, and privatized than in the past.

The "new individualism" (Lemert and Elliott 2006:18) has personal and cultural implications, more felt in the more-developed world but with an increasingly universal reach due to globalization and revolutions in communication technologies. This new cultural identity is highly "privatized," meaning that the individual is required to be independent and autonomous.

Bauman (2003) terms these "liquid" relationships—associations that are temporary and frail and destined to produce a sense of anxious impermanence in the actors as they seek secure bonds they are unable to establish and maintain in an uncertain world. In *Wasted Lives,* Bauman (2004) describes as an inevitable consequence of globalization a greater emphasis on rapid response to changing cultural, economic, political, and other forces. Ultimately, such rationally grounded relationships, organizations, and networks trend toward expendability.

Perhaps with an overly romantic view of family and intimacy, Lemert and Elliott (2006) lament the loss of secure, reliable intimacy and bemoan the arrival of fleeting, casual, impersonal, clandestine sexual encounters as a symptom of narcissism and psychic withdrawal, all enabled by the new technology that allows men to establish sexual contacts and engage in experimental encounters in a whole new way. Is this not just new technology laid over old patterns? How different is this, really, from anonymous sexual encounters experienced by men as they traveled away from wives and families and landed in different ports, countries, and communities as part of their mobile work lives? One major difference is the extent to which these options are increasingly available to women as well as men. As seen in the dramatic increases in American women's participation in the labor force during World War II, nothing shifts gender roles as quickly and as radically as an urgent macrosocial situation. However, while globalization has clearly generated significant shifts in gender roles, greater egalitarianism is a long-term trend in gender roles across societies.

Any discussion of the impact of globalization on family culture should be framed around the reality that geographical place has never been perfectly correlated with community and identity.

> Communities can exist without being in the same place—from networks of friends with like interests, to major religious, ethnic or political communities. . . . The instances of places housing single "communities" in the sense of coherent social groups are probably—and . . . have for long been— quite rare. Moreover, even where they do exist this in no way implies a single sense of place. (Massey 1994:153)

Globalization challenges scholars and citizens to re-envision space and place, community and identity, which does not necessarily deny the uniqueness of local space but sees culture and space as

- dynamic, rather than static, processes;
- associated with boundaries, as well as linkages to the outside; and
- characterized by internal conflicts.

Postmodern families are increasingly on the frontier of a globalized world, at an "interface between two (or more) contrasting ways of life" (Bryceson and Vuorela 2002:12). These transnational families are "frontiering" in the sense that they are breaking new cultural ground. Families must be able to hold values and priorities, norms and strategies in ways that take into account changing demographics, employment, and other realities in a global world. Thus, global families are challenged to use creative approaches to structuring family life, including gendered ways of organizing care work and responding to violence and other threats. In doing so, families face new stressors and possible conflicts in the face of oft-reduced intimate connections in which associations and identities are more open to negotiation in postmodern, globalized cultures.

Summary

Globalization impinges on the reproduction of social institutions, values, and norms and the conduct of everyday life among families whether or not they are experiencing transnational population shifts. Families increasingly experience flows of cultural goods and services across national borders, with a clear tendency for Western (particularly English-speaking) nations to dominate as both cultural exporters and importers.

The mass media not only inform, entertain, and educate; they also virtually extend reference points beyond that which the individual and family actually experience. In doing so, mass media (television and, increasingly, the Internet and cell phones) can create "electronic communities"—essentially transnational mass culture, considering the oligopoly of mass media production. Transmitting cultural messages to families beyond the local, regional, and national through international levels thus situates families in global context.

The globalization of culture also involves ever-broadening and deepening patterns of mass consumption, which impact family values and norms. Therefore, globalization affects families in terms of the goods and services available for consumption, the information disseminated concerning economics and politics, but also the environment, health, medical, and other critical issues of family life. Globalized culture is a powerful force in shaping attitudes and behaviors; systems of stereotyping, prejudice, and discrimination; likes and dislikes; values and norms. Globalized culture offers an enormous— some say homogenized—range of entertainment and information options but also influences our deepest belief systems in terms of gender and age roles, parenting and other family relationships, and youth and other civil rights and social movements.

CONTESTED NORMS AND VALUES IN
TRANSNATIONAL FAMILIES

By Cawo M. Abdi, PhD

Following a civil war brewing since the late 1980s and reaching its climax in 1990, Somali women, men, and children fled from their war-torn country to seek asylum in countries in the Horn of Africa. Some eventually found their way to other places, including the Americas, Europe, and Australia. Dispersal of families became the norm rather than the exception. Somali refugees went not necessarily where they wanted to go (e.g., Canada) but, rather, where they could go (e.g., Scandinavia). To escape the war and precarious life in remote refugee camps in Kenya, Ethiopia, or Djibouti, Somali people used legal routes, such as family reunification and government settlement programs, as well as illegal routes, such as paying traffickers, traveling with false documents, and/or taking dangerous boats to cross the Mediterranean. This dispersal has resulted in family networks that often span more than two countries and has also led to myriad challenges for the Somali family.

Drawing from research in Canada, the United States, and Kenyan refugee camps, this essay examines some of the challenges Somali families face. I collected original data in Dadaab camps, Toronto, Minnesota, and three provinces in South Africa from 2001 to 2011. This data comprises in-depth interviews, participant observation, and focus groups with hundreds of Somalis of both sexes and different ages. My research illustrates how the dispersal of Somalis around the globe, in regions where the language, religion, and ethnicity of the majority differs from that of this group, is affecting their identity by challenging some of their norms and values. Refugees' accommodation and resistance to these new practices result in a complex web of gender and generational power contestations and discourses within the community.

From the onset of displacement, refugees face problems requiring rapid and innovative adjustments to new realities. To provide an example, the role of men as providers is greatly undermined in the context of civil war, when these men are either absent partaking in the war or are the first to leave the country. The latter is due to the nature of civil war, when men are the first killed.[1] Thus, migration challenges gender norms dictating the roles of men

---

[1] Women also are killed in war. In addition, as discussed in the following chapter, they are subjected to gender violence, including rape and torture.

and women in the household, which, in turn, inform the gender power relations within the household and society.

My research revealed that these new challenges, though real, did not really shift Somali gender power relations. In the period of transition, when refugees were still settled in temporary areas within and immediately outside of Somalia, the wider context of refugee life did not change. That is to say, refugees were still within or very near the country of origin, where strong cultural and religious edicts dictated the subordinate position of women. While the Somali civil war undermined the gender order, the war did not translate to overt gender power contestation between the sexes, at least in the early stages of the conflict.

Conditions undermining gender power relations become more drastic when the settlement area is not only distant from the country of origin but also when the gender practices prevailing in the place of settlement greatly differ from the practices in the country of origin. My interviewees report that the main factors destabilizing traditional Somali gender order are the institutions catering to newcomers and the socioeconomic opportunities and challenges refugees experience in their new places of residence. For instance, similar to the previously mentioned challenge to the male "breadwinner role" in transit settlements, the new context in developed countries, such as the United States, offers new opportunities in the form of public assistance for refugee women and their children. Most of these women arrive with low human capital, in terms of education and other transferable skills, making initial integration into the American workforce difficult. I found that these new sources of income for women with children become arenas of dispute and conflict within families, with claims that women's access to these opportunities is destabilizing the Somali family and that these opportunities are leading to conflict and higher divorce rates within the community.

Interestingly, rhetoric on the disruption of Somali traditional gender practices brought about by settlement in a Western country is not limited to those dependent on social assistance for their livelihoods but, rather, is a widespread belief among Somalis, including women. When the economic opportunities refugee women access in the Diaspora, in the forms of welfare and/or employment, are not deemed the culprit in gender disruption, Somali men fear the institutions and values of the mainstream community may be triggering a revolt amongst women in contesting Somali gender relations. Some men argue that, in addition to economic opportunities, the legal system in place in the West encourages women to "break up" their families whenever they feel they are being denied anything. These claims border on paranoia, with some refugees going as far as asserting that the

Western system seeks the breakdown of the Muslim family. While it is more the men who resent and dwell on the dangers confronting the Somali family in the West, many women also support these claims. Most of these men and women place the responsibility of the danger the Somali family faces in the Diaspora on women's shoulders, saying women are abandoning their cultural and religious practices under the influence of Western values made by and for a different type of society.

A contradiction between what was regarded as sacred in the Somali context—that is, women's culturally and "religiously" sanctioned subordination to men—and the new institutions and gendered practices in the countries of settlement (especially in the West) has led to a vigorous debate about the future of the Somali family in the Diaspora. A proverb often cited by my interviewees states, *"naagi waa saar, saarna kaligii geed kama boxo* (women are vine, and vine does not grown on its own),"[2] and is currently challenged by Somali women's prominence in the economic and emotional sustenance of their families since the collapse of the Somali state. From my research, I conclude that the Somali civil war exposed the contradictions between gender rhetoric and practice and the prominent roles women played and still play in society—roles unacknowledged and, thus, invisible in a patriarchal society.

In addition to gender, a topic considered most pertinent for the Somalis in the Diaspora is related to the wedge emerging between young people and their parents. Many parents expressed the danger of losing their children to the mainstream culture, perceived as greatly different from that of Somali culture. Intergenerational conflict is nothing new in society, including in migrant and refugee communities; however, this conflict is exacerbated by the myriad other settlement issues refugee communities confront in their new homes. For example, consistent with their low socioeconomic status as recent refugees with low human capital, the residential areas available to most Somalis in the West are in urban inner-city areas. Concentration in these areas means that young Somalis, especially boys and young men, adopt some of the cultural practices of inner-city youth in terms of dress and behavior. As these poorer areas are subject to more police scrutiny and as affordable or available extracurricular activities in such neighborhoods are limited, refugee/immigrant youth perceive their new country as excluding them. They often identify with those most marginalized in these societies. For example, in the American

---

[2]This proverb is often stated to support a woman's dependence on her father, husband, or brother during the life course, thus justifying the necessity for women to remain dependent on and, therefore, subordinate to men at all times.

context, many Somali youth identify with African American youth, who, like them, are often concentrated in poorer neighborhoods and feel excluded from the "American dream."[3]

Unlike the youth, Somali parents, who were brought up in a completely different society, panic at their children's future prospects in their country of settlement. Most parents I interviewed asserted that they escaped their war-torn country to provide better opportunities for their children. They detailed the sacrifices they made to come to the West in the hope that their children's futures would be brighter than their own. Again, parents fear the new institutions in the West are disrupting cultural childrearing practices. The parents fear power reversal between parents and children. Illustrating this dilemma for parents, a male community worker in his late 30s stated:

> Here the child is raised by the state....The state is the authority. In Somalia, it was different. When you are a child, the highest authority is your parents. Other higher authorities were the teachers, the Koranic one, and the school one. You could not smoke cigarettes in front of them; you could not misbehave in front of your teacher, just like your parents. Here the teacher is nothing. He is just a service provider; he is selling something to you. The parents are just here to provide you services, food, shelter; and, if you don't like them, you can even complain to the school, or you can call 911. What exacerbates this is the existence of cultural barriers, language barriers with the parents. Here the kid has become the authority; so when there is a meeting with the teacher, or they go to the hospital, or to a governmental agency, or to an office, it is the child who is interpreting. The parent does not know anything.

This excerpt highlights refugees' interpretation of the intergenerational conflict existing between parents and children. The speaker was, in fact, an educated man, and most parents expressed this conflict in more daunting language, with some expressing regrets of bringing their children to this new land and others detailing plans to return with their children before they lose them to the "system."[4]

---

[3]It is also true that male Somali youth in many urban areas (Toronto, London, and Minneapolis–St. Paul) are in conflict with other black youth. Many incidents of violence and confrontations in and out of schools have been reported.

[4]Intergenerational conflict is gendered, with most problems identified with boys. Girls often experience intense scrutiny compared with boys. Girls are thus closer to their families and remain more connected to Somali tradition, even if the tradition is adapted to the new country. Boys, on the other hand, enjoy great freedom, coming and going as they see fit—something that was okay in Somalia but is now said to be leading to the deviant behavior of some youth.

The gender and generational conflicts within the Somali family as a result of forced displacement and settlement in the West are currently salient in the debates on the family, as highlighted in Chapter 5. This debate is occurring in a transnational context, with emerging developments often circulating between Somalia and the countries of settlement in the West. The debate is even held on Somali websites. There, diverse viewpoints are presented, though opinions often dramatize changes deemed inherently to undermine Islam and Somali cultural practices. Inevitably, these conflicts will continue as the second generation of Somalis in the West comes of age in the next decade.

Cawo M. Abdi, PhD, is an assistant professor of sociology at the University of Minnesota and research fellow at the University of Pretoria in South Africa. Her areas of expertise are gender, family, Islamic societies, transnationalism, and development. She is currently finishing a book comparing Somali migration to the United States, South Africa, and the United Arab Emirates.

CRITICAL THINKING QUESTIONS

1. What are the potential benefits of globalized media and consumption to families of the global North? To families of the global South?

2. Outline the research design for a study that would deepen our understanding of the impact of global mass media, including the Internet and cell phones, on socialization in the family.

3. Are you a skeptic, a hyperglobalist, or a transformationalist regarding the impact of cultural globalization and families? Do you agree or disagree with the contention that "McDonaldization" increasingly threatens families' ability to forge an authentic culture for their members? As some cases offered in this chapter suggest, societies are remarkably able to construct local meaning from even the most American of cultural icons. How might a globally presented aspect of Western culture (e.g., McDonald's restaurants) be adapted by families to improve the quality of family life?

4. Frontiering refers to "interfacing between two (or more) contrasting ways of life." To what extent do the gender roles described in Abdi's (2007, 2012) research demonstrate that globalization fosters frontiering in family values and norms around gender roles?

4

International Violence

Family Legacies of Oppression and War

Whether it is actual warfare, civil strife, the spread of AIDS, the sale of children into the sex trade, grinding poverty, or sewage flowing in front of the doorway of a shanty, violence is present whenever those with the means use their means to protect their privileges against those who want a share of them. And, to come to the unique feature of globalization, when money and time move as rapidly as they do today on the wings of a digital bird, everyone knows that he or she is at some risk—even those most securely ensconced in their gated villas. (Lemert and Elliott 2006:155)

The Sisters of the Good Shepherd (*Buon Pastore*) provide safe houses, counsel, and pastoral care to prostitutes in Rome (and other locations across Europe) who wish to leave the life. Sister Helen Ann Sand (personal communication, January 5, 2004) has described the processes through which these women (some of whom are mere girls, my own teenage daughter's age) enter Italy illegally. They often land by boat along Italy's relatively uncontrolled coastline, arriving from Africa, Asia, the Middle East, and Eastern Europe—with Albania, Romania, China, Iraq, and a growing list of African countries leading the list. Often trafficked by men who promise they will secure a position for these women caring for children or performing domestic work in affluent Italian households, the women hope to be able to send desperately needed euros home to their families and, eventually, achieve citizenship and reunification with their families in a less violent, more civil society than that from whence they came.

For anyone who enters Italy illegally—and especially for someone who is not only undocumented but cannot verify gainful, legal employment since arriving—attaining Italian citizenship (or citizenship in any member of the European Union) is virtually impossible. Cut off from educational, employment, health, and other social services, the outlook for these women is grim indeed. Although the European Union requires member nations such as Italy to control their borders effectively, an investigation into trafficking throughout Italy resulted in the arrest of 2,000 people, most of them foreigners, and uncovered "hundreds" of trafficking rings (Sanminiatelli 2007). Efforts to stem the flow of trafficking for sex have been largely ineffective and seem futile in light of the scale of the problem, especially with the growth of information technology to assist traffickers and consumers in securing women and children (Hughes 2001a, 2001b). As Anderson and O'Connell Davidson (2002) argue, the trade in human beings for sexual purposes appears to be a "demand led" problem.

The heartbreaking effects of international violence on families make this a most difficult chapter. Certainly, covering a range of issues related to international violence inflicted against families and their members is a daunting task. A particularly painful undertaking was reading personal narratives concerning how colonization and sex trafficking, rape, sexual slavery, and other violence disrupt and disturb families in the most profound and tragic ways. However, perhaps nothing shapes the quality of life, well-being, and even the survival of global families more than international violence.

I begin this chapter with a discussion of international systems of oppression, including the legacies of colonialism for families and the impact of sex trafficking. I then address the effects of war: sexual domination and exploitation, including rape in war, military sexual slavery, and other collateral violence against women and girls. I consider the marital consequences of war as well, including the marriage squeeze, heterogamous marriages, and marital instability. I also offer a discussion of military and refugee families, as well as consideration of the extent to which the greatest man-made horrors inflicted on human kind also reveal the deep promise of family resiliency. I hope this chapter captures a measure of both parts of this story.

International Systems of Oppression

Many Euro-Americans are accustomed to conceiving of colonization from the perspective of the early history of the United States. From that point of view, colonization refers to the establishment of imperial colonies peopled by settlers from the dominant society—English from England to Australia, Dutch from the Netherlands to South Africa, French from France to Vietnam. An almost romantic social legacy exists around people who may share nationality or ethnicity with the colonial power. Sometimes early colonists were part of the aristocracy or at least sponsored bourgeoisie. More likely, many early colonists were social cast-offs and misfits—criminals, debtors, heretics, or other social nonconformists—from the dominant society. (See Grochowski's essay on Australia's global families at the end of Chapter 1.)

An alternative, oppositionist perspective of colonialism began to emerge toward the end of World War II (Said 1978). Colonial administrations lasted well into the last half of the 20th century, and only within the past three decades has critical theory toward decolonization become mainstream (Miyoshi 1993). The concept of global diaspora is being extended beyond reference to catastrophic dispersal of a people across wide geographic areas to include imperial, labor and trade, as well as cultural dispersion through societal domination (Cohen 1997). Sociology, psychology, history, economics, and other disciplines continue to expand the analysis of colonialism, slavery, and other oppressive legacies to include these resistance paradigms. The best of those paradigms include the principle that violence against women is part of the social construction of sexuality (Itzin 1992).

A review of the hardships, turmoil, and often violence faced by inhabitants of former colonies makes clear that decolonization did not automatically result in economic, political, and social liberation for the formerly colonized. Former colonial societies often confronted long-standing systems of inequality across race and gender but also religions, tribes, ethnicities, and other characteristics. Further, former colonies were often left with abbreviated time frames in which to resolve the problems of fractured and inefficient economic, political, and social systems. Miyoshi (1993:731) notes that "peaceful progress [including to nation-statehood on the global stage] has been structurally denied" to Third World states. Former colonies, now Third World societies, simply cannot compete on a playing field dominated by the General Agreement on Tariffs and Trade, the International Monetary Fund, and the World Bank.

Perhaps war is an inevitable legacy of the clash of civilizations (Huntington 1996) and especially empire building (Hardt and Negri 2000, 2004). The legacies of colonialism die slowly, as demonstrated in the Democratic Republic of the Congo. The early 20th century sociologist Robert Park began his career as a journalist and activist in the Congo Reform movement, seeking to address an unfolding social tragedy as that former Belgian colony sought to establish itself as a free, democratic republic (Karraker 2004, 2006). Still today, the Democratic Republic of the Congo stands as an archetype of a society where military authorities directed an excessive level of violence against civilians. The country's natural resources continue to be plundered, while perpetrators of the genocide in Rwanda operate openly from within the Democratic Republic of the Congo's borders.

Families in the region have been particularly affected by the history of war in that nation, a history that grew out of colonialism and now stretches into a third century. The International Criminal Court (The Hague) pressed charges against a Congolese warlord for impressing children into service as soldiers in that country's rebel conflict (children who are part of the estimated 300,000 child soldiers participating in armed conflicts worldwide; "War Crimes Court" 2007). The war that began in 1998 involved Angolan, Namibian, and Zimbabwean armed militias operating within and outside of the Democratic Republic of the Congo, at a cost of almost 4 million lives (U.S. Holocaust Memorial Museum 2006g).

Colonialism and Families

The societal legacies of colonialism, bound as they are with violence and power, are reflected in the social reproduction of family patterns. Colonial authorities often seek to dominate the indigenous society with critical institutions, including reinforcing family structures that will be consistent with colonial economic, political, and cultural systems. For example, in the case of Nyasaland, Africa, British colonial agents operating in the small, land-locked colonial state in the early-to-middle 20th century enacted practices that effectively replaced family farming with low-wage labor and the extended, matrilineal family with the nuclear, neolocal, highly mobile family (Brantley 2003). In another case, the British successfully reshaped the family structure of Egyptian *effendiyya* (the political ruling class) to emphasize monogamy and the nuclear family, more conducive to de facto economic and political colonial rule (Pollard 2003).

Families, but also gender relations within families, have often been transformed by colonialism. Colonial agents viewed gender relations through a Western, patriarchal lens. For example, by defining the African men as farmers in a culture in which women historically had far-reaching authority over feeding their families—including cultivating, harvesting, storing, and preparing all food—British authorities undermined the existing status quo. Men were privileged and women were denigrated by disrupting family structure and spheres of authority. Colonial agents thus ensured that men were available to perform wage labor (and to pay taxes), with the family changed to a monogamous, nuclear family consistent with British ideals of family as a husband–father with economic control over his wife and their children (Brantley 2003). These kinds of changes have disrupted and damaged women's roles and status across African families and society.

A flourishing sex trade often has been integral to regulating the dominant colonial population in absentia from the imperial society. Briggs (2003) takes the argument even further, proposing that ideologies of family, sexuality, and reproduction direct imperialist and racial agendas. Briggs outlines how the United States operating in Puerto Rico between 1849 and 1916 engaged in colonial discourse that was both biomedical and familial, resulting in the requirement that prostitutes be registered, that they submit to medical examinations, and that they be treated if found to be infected. The historical precedence for such a model can be found in Western programs to address matters of sexual access in military and port towns. As such, these colonial policies protected "various forms of sanctified domesticity" (i.e., white, nuclear families of the colonists), as well as armies and labor forces, while serving to "organize disorderly women, often limiting their mobility in segregated districts, enrolling them as imperial citizens through the . . . bureaucratic process of registration, sometimes restricting their clients by race" (pp. 41–2).

Not all prostitutes in colonial towns were women of the indigenous population. At the turn of the 20th century, European prostitutes in colonial Bombay, India, occupied an intermediary status in a racially stratified sexual order. British colonial authorities managed, monitored, and segregated European prostitutes to a much greater extent than indigenous women involved in sex work. Such a system enabled the colonial state more effectively to control the racial and sexual order through coerced medical regulation and licensing by the police and brothel mistresses. From a transnational feminist perspective, European prostitutes were an "evil" necessary to maintain access to safe sexual recreation, but within acceptable racial parameters (Tambe 2005).

Apparently, "the British saw prostitution wherever they looked" (Levine 2004:159). On the one hand, prostitution was a "problem, but it was also both a necessity and a convenient canvas on which to illuminate the greater evils or dangers of uncivilized peoples" (p. 159). Colonial commercial interests depended on missionary Christian interests to "civilize" the colonized population, thus enabling the conforming colonized population to be subdued by Christianity and exploited for capitalist interests. Colonial authorities used prostitution, in all its varieties, as a means to reproduce colonial economic, family, inequality, and other social systems necessary for a successful colonial enterprise (White 2004). Prostitution disturbed the moral social order, but prostitution also helped demarcate and institutionalize social hierarchies of race, social class, and gender. Thus, social control agenda provided opportunities to channel sexuality into commercially productive boundaries while reinforcing the dominant and subordinate statuses of the colonial and the indigenous people, as well as the relative statuses of men and women.

On another level, some scholars place prostitution in the context of rationally chosen sex work that a woman sometimes deems necessary to support herself and her family. In such cases, prostitution may be viewed as consistent with cultural values that permit unmarried women to control their own bodies. From this perspective, prostitution is a means to achieve or retain relative economic and social independence. Bliss (2004) arrived at such conclusions regarding the regulation of prostitution in Mexico City during French occupation in the 1860s, through the subsequent dictatorship, revolution, civil war, and reconstruction, culminating in the political and social reforms of the 1940s. Bliss found substantial contradiction between official public pronouncements of prostitutes as deviant, morally depraved women who were a threat to family and society and prostitutes' perceptions of themselves as acting out of economic responsibility, supporting a network of children and others through their earnings.

Undeniably, prostitution exposes women to a host of short- and long-term hazards, including violence, disease, and death, as well as economic, legal, and other vulnerabilities. In a study of the estimated 1,000-strong sex workforce of young Nigerian women engaging in prostitution in Italy, Achebe (2004) documented that sex workers remain in subordinate, dependent, dangerous relationships relative to the sex traffickers, pimps, and madams who control prostitution.

Sex Trafficking

Prostitution in colonial societies calls to mind the age-old problem of human trafficking and the growing problem of sex trafficking in women and children. The U.N. Office on Drugs and Crime (UNODC 2011) defines human trafficking as a crime against humanity and notes that "every country in the world is affected by trafficking, whether as a country of origin, transit or destination for victims."

Trafficking for sex or labor involves the often violent transportation of men, women, or children for exploitative, illicit purposes, including slave work or undocumented work ("Trafficking in Persons Report 2006" 2006). The Palermo Protocol from the U.N. Children's Fund (UNICEF 2000) specifically defines trafficking as

> the recruitment, transportation, transfer, harbouring or receipt of persons, by means of threat or use of force or other forms of coercion, of abduction, of fraud, of deception, of the abuse of power or of a position of vulnerability or of the giving or receiving of payments or benefits to achieve the consent of a

person having control over another person, for the purpose of exploitation. Exploitation shall include, at a minimum, the exploitation of the prostitution of others or other forms of sexual exploitation, forced labor or services, slavery or practices similar to slavery, servitude or the removal of organs. (P. 2)

Although the underground, criminal, international nature of trafficking makes accurate estimates difficult, the United Nations offers a conservative estimate of 2.5 million victims trafficked at any one time, with tens of billions of dollars in profits every year (UNODC 2011). In response to the Protocol to Prevent, Suppress, and Punish Trafficking in Persons enacted by the United Nations in 2003, by 2008, 80 percent of 155 countries surveyed by the United Nations had passed specific legislation on trafficking in persons, and the number of convictions is growing. However, African nations in particular have been slow to adopt legislation, and convictions still occur in only a few countries (UNODC 2009).

The United Nations estimates that 66 percent of trafficked persons are women, 13 percent are girls, and 9 percent are boys. Sexual exploitation is involved in 79 percent of human trafficking. While forced labor is the most frequent type of human trafficking, the sexual exploitation of women is often the most visible. The typical human trafficker is a man, but women have a more visible role in human slavery today than in other forms of crime. For example, in Latvia, an estimated 53 percent of those who traffic in persons are women (UNODC 2009).

Again, estimations are difficult, but a half million women and children are believed to be trafficked into Western Europe from poorer countries, and women are trafficked out of Southeast Asia at the rate of a quarter million per year (Seager 2003:56).

Every year, as many as 1.2 million children are trafficked around the world. They are taken from their homes in West and Central Africa for domestic, farm, industrial, and sexual slavery. A third of all sex workers in the Mekong region of Southeast Asia are 12 to 17 years old. Thirteen-year-olds from Asia and Eastern Europe are trafficked as "mail-order brides." More than 16,000 children are engaged in prostitution in Mexico, especially in tourist destinations. In Lithuania, children 10 to 12 years old living in orphanages or other shelters have been used to make pornographic movies (UNICEF 2010).

Trafficked women and children are isolated, powerless, and at great risk of violence and death. The multibillion-dollar global sex trade is built on social–structural inequalities of economics, gender, and ethnicity. Such inequalities oppress women and children into global prostitution and fuel the market for sexual consumption among men. Sex trafficking also draws on the economic and political disparities between regions of the globe.

Global poverty can be said to provide incentive for societies to enter the global sex trade circuit, which is sustained by coercion, torture, rape, and other forms of violence and intimidation (Davidson 2006; UNICEF 2004).

In some countries, families sell their daughters as part of systems in which the trafficking in human beings, especially women and children, is normalized as socially acceptable. Such appears to be the case among the men involved in sex trafficking as a "family business." As Blank (2003) described in her thesis, as well as in the essay that follows this chapter, she found many of the men to have generally indifferent, dismissive, or even hostile views of their female cargo. As verified in the UNICEF (2004) report, patriarchal views of females as inferior, along with myths that HIV/AIDS can be cured by having sex with a virgin, contribute to the ease with which women and girls are commercially exploited. The report continues:

> The links between poverty, violence, and trafficking have been compounded by the effects of HIV/AIDS. Women and girls trafficked for prostitution are among the most vulnerable groups exposed to HIV infection. Insufficiently informed, seduced or forced to have unprotected sex, once infected with HIV/AIDS they are left without care or support. Furthermore, children orphaned by AIDS can be more vulnerable to trafficking due to the increasing poverty of their households and communities, and as a result of the stigmatisation, rejection, or marginalization to which they are exposed in their communities. (P. 6)

UNICEF (2004) has endorsed a human rights approach to combat trafficking of women and children. The UNICEF proposal requires nations to enact major legislation to address five areas of concern: immigration; child labor and employment; child welfare and protection; protection from abduction, torture, slavery, and unlawful detention; and prostitution and related sexual activities, including pornography, statutory sexual contact, and other sexual offenses. Clearly, effective response to the problem of trafficking will require concerted global effort on many fronts.

War and Social Disorder

Between December 1937 and March 1938, in what has come to be called the Rape of Nanking (or Nanjing), Japanese soldiers killed an estimated 300,000 Chinese people (many of them women and children), raped 20,000 women, and proceeded to torture, bury alive, freeze to death, decapitate, mutilate, and cause dogs to tear apart uncounted others. The number dead exceeded those killed by bombs dropped on Hiroshima and Nagasaki (Chang 1997; "Scarred by History" 2005).

Globalization does not cause war or collateral horrors such as rape. However, as Barkawi (2006) argues, "war itself is a form of interconnection" (p. 92). War is not only an example of globalization; war is one of the principal mechanisms of globalization. War shapes cultural frameworks, influencing how people view the world, their place and the place of their nation in the world, and the experience of other places in the world. Put another way, war draws individuals from the local to an awareness of their connection to other places, including national–international identities.

War destroys communities, forces migration, and creates refugees. War obliterates agriculture and other forms of subsistence while eroding education, government, religion, and every other core institution on which social equilibrium rests. War uproots families from familiar environments and forces them to live in new situations with strangers, where existing government or international assistance programs are often sorely taxed to provide for the newcomers. War costs families kinship networks and social and economic exchanges with extended kin. War deaths create impediments for those who wish to marry and those who depend on children for support in their old age. By engendering social disorganization and status inconsistency, war is an enormous stressor for families (Aghajanian 2008).

In the following section, I address issues that result from the broad category of war-related crises: international warfare but also "ethnic cleansing" and inter-tribal disputes, internal insurgencies, and other armed conflicts. These conflicts impact families directly through the maiming and murder of their members, family absence during periods of service, family dislocation, and the collateral effects of economic disintegration, political upheaval, poverty, famine, and other shortages that accompany such large-scale violent crises.

Many readers of *Global Families* remember where they were on the autumn morning of September 11, 2001. Some readers will remember frantic calls to loved ones, both those close by and those in more distant locations. Perhaps some

Cartoon editorial by David Horsey titled "A Nation at War," dated July 12, 2006, which originally appeared in the *Seattle Post-Intelligencer*. *d/b/a* Seattlepi.com, an operating unit of Hearst Seattle Media, LLC.

readers experienced the loss of a brother or sister, a father or mother, a husband, wife, other life partner, kin, or friend in the events in New York, Pennsylvania, and Washington, DC.

For the first time in many Americans' lives, the events of 9/11 brought home the fear of war and the deadly effects on family and personal life. The continental United States has not been a battlefield location since the end of the Civil War, almost a century and a half ago. Still, as this book goes to press, 4,408 American military personnel lost their lives in Operation Iraqi Freedom between March 19, 2003, and May 31, 2011 (U.S. Department of Defense 2011). The death toll for Iraqi civilians during the same period has been highly contested, with estimates now far exceeding the 35,000 dead estimated in 2007 (MacAskill 2007).

These direct and indirect results of the most recent wars in the Middle East leave reverberations of grief in every family touched by those deaths. Even families that have been spared loss of life in that conflict live with everyday uncertainty regarding the safety and well-being of their loved ones. Further, veterans now count for one out of every five suicides in the United States (Hotakainen 2011). Pauline Boss (2006), Professor Emerita of Family Social Science at the University of Minnesota, describes the particular stresses faced by families who lost a loved one through a veteran suicide, the attacks on the United States on September 11, 2001, or other terrorist attacks as "ambiguous loss."

I am moved to ask: Do not all societies and families want to shield their most tender members from not only the lived experience of war but also the vicarious horrors war inflicts on others? In the following section, I address that question, focusing on sexual domination and exploitation, including rape in war, military sexual slavery, and other collateral damage particularly affecting women and girls.

Sexual Domination and Exploitation

Rape is one of the most effective weapons of social control. In countries as varied as Switzerland and the United Kingdom, India and Zimbabwe, between one out of eight and one out of four women or more report being the victims of sexual assault or attempted sexual assault by an intimate partner (Seager 2003:58–9). Rape is a threat to women and girls and a traditional male privilege everywhere in the world. As a tool of patriarchy, rape serves as a violent mechanism used to assert male dominance. Even among spouses and intimate partners, the rape of women and girls is far from uncommon.

Rape in War

Across the globe, rape has been used as widespread and systematic action by soldiers, paramilitary troops, or others involved in warfare. During the second Sino-Japanese war in 1937, an estimated 20,000 women were raped, with some 200,000 then kept as sex slaves for the Japanese army during World War II. The Soviet army raped an estimated 100,000 to 2 million German women during World War II. The Indian Army raped an estimated 200,000 women during the Bangladesh war of secession in 1971. More than 50,000 women were raped between 1991 and 1992 during the Sierra Leone civil war. In Bosnia-Herzegovina (the former Yugoslavia), 20,000 Muslim women were raped in 1992. A half million women were raped during the Rwandan genocide in 1994. In Indonesia, ethnic Chinese women were targeted for rape in 1998. In the Sudan in recent years, 50,000 girls have been captured, raped, and kept as sex slaves by government forces in the northern territories (Seager 2003:99; "War's Overlooked Victims" 2011:63).

Reliable estimates of the number of women raped are difficult to come by. Many victims are murdered by their attackers, others die of their injuries, and many others do not report the rape because of the stigma. Rapes are more likely to be reported where victims have access to health services, but access to not only health but also legal and other services are among the most compromised during war ("War's Overlooked Victims" 2011).

> The anarchy and impunity of war goes some way to explaining the violence. The conditions of war are often conducive to rape. Young, ill-trained men, fighting far from home, are freed from social and religious constraints. The costs of rape are lower, the potential rewards higher. And for ill-fed, underpaid combatants, rape can be a kind of payment. (P. 64)

The genocide in Darfur reminds us that the very preparation for war, and especially mass killings, requires dehumanization and creating a sense of "the other" (Hagan and Rymond-Richmond 2009). Nationality but also race, ethnicity, religion, and gender intersect, providing a necessary condition for the slaughter and rape of innocents.

Rape is both a tactical weapon of and a strategic approach to war across all nationalities (Brownmiller 1975; Farwell 2004). Rape can serve as an "international metaphor for [national] humiliation" and national subjugation. Rape has been used to terrorize and humiliate, for military retaliation or reprisal, or as an element in psychological warfare. Viewed as one of the "spoils of war," rape underscores the intersections among gender and patriarchy, as well as ethnic, racial, religious, and regional political identities, and militarism. Globalization and feminism enable us to see the long-lasting effects of rape and sexual slavery in wartime on family formation and quality of life. As systematic, ritual pollution—such as during a pogrom of ethnic cleansing—rape can render substantial portions of the female population unmarriageable or can so severely depreciate women's honor and status that an entire generation is impaired in its ability to form families, solidify kin networks, and ensure the care of children in conjugal pairs, even beyond the physical and psychological injury to the victim. Rape can compromise long-term, even lifelong circumstances for the woman or girl who survives rape, including her sense of safety and security in intimate relationships.

Brownmiller (1975:34) argues that rape provides ordinary men with a legitimate outlet for exercising misogyny in a group dynamic of conformity. Throughout history women (and children) have been viewed as regrettable but incidental and unavoidable casualties of war and conquest. Virtually no attention has been given to the rape of boys and men, although their rape serves many of the same functions in war. Regardless of the gender or age of the victims, capture and subsequent rape and enslavement are a collateral acquisition in war, much like the acquisition of territory and property.

War, along with genocide and other crimes against humanity, creates an atmosphere in which protective institutions fail, leaving civilians—but especially women, the young, and the old—most vulnerable. The sexual violence that occurs at these times is even more brutal, intense, and pervasive than during more stable times. Sexualized violence during war generates terror not only for the immediate victims but also for their communities.

This "brutalization of the body" in war is not inevitable (Cockburn 2004). Rape was rare during El Salvador's civil war. When rape did occur in that conflict, the assailants were most often state forces. Rape was absent during the Tamil Tigers' displacement of Muslims from the Jaffna Peninsula in 1990. Tamil mores prohibit sex across caste lines and between people who are not married ("War's Overlooked Victims" 2011).

Rape is a criminal act under international rules of war, punishable by imprisonment or death under Article 120 of the American Uniform Code of Military Justice. Rape is prohibited under the Geneva Conventions, but the U.N. Security Council did not formally recognize rape as a tool of war until 2008. However, sexual violence has been less rigorously prosecuted than other war crimes. The Balkan War was a turning point, when rape (along with torture and sexual enslavement) during war was treated for the first time as a crime against humanity. In places such as the Congo, however, where the legal system remains in great disarray, trials and convictions have been rare, leading some to call for greater international involvement and to criticize the United Nations for not doing more to protect civilians ("War's Overlooked Victims" 2011).

Military Sexual Slavery

Another gendered aspect of global warfare that has long-lasting effects on families is military sexual slavery. Between 1930 and 1945, especially during World War II, between 100,000 and 200,000 Asian women were forced into sexual slavery by the Japanese armed forces. *Ianfu* or "comfort workers" was the name given to the women who sexually serviced Japanese military men during World War II (Nozaki 2001). Hicks (1995) described the "comfort station" in Shanghai, first of a series of officially sanctioned brothels. His research reveals the extent to which women, many in their early teen years, were coaxed or deceived but often coerced to service the sexual desires of the Japanese armed forces. Many of these women were transported from rural villages to military bases. In the desire of nations to move forward with postwar reconstruction, these women were all but forgotten. Even if they returned to their communities and families, these women were never repatriated in the full meaning of the word. Many carried with them extensive trauma that affected their social–psychological and family adjustment throughout the rest of their lives.

Howard (1995) compiled in a translated volume powerful testimonies collected by the Korean Council for Women Drafted for Military Sexual Slavery by Japan. An article by Chung (1995) in the same volume summarizes some of the characteristics of the women thus enslaved, including the effects on their subsequent family lives. Eighty to ninety percent of the women were Korean. The other 10 to 20 percent of women enslaved by the Japanese were Taiwanese, Indonesian, Filipina, and Dutch. Ruff-O'Herne (2008) offers an autobiographical account of her passage from being the daughter of a wealthy Dutch colonial family to serving as a comfort woman for Japanese officers. Although, at the time of the war, the legal age for licensed prostitutes was 18 in Japan and 17 in Korea, no age restriction applied to comfort women, and girls as young as 11 were forced into sexual slavery. Most of the women had little education and came from poor farming families. Very few were married.

Not surprisingly, comfort women recall fearing for their lives (T'aesŏn 1995; Yongnyŏ 1995). The women who survived sexual slavery under the Japanese during World War II report feelings of lost youth and opportunity (Okpun 1995; P'ilgi 1995; Yongsu 1995), embitterment (Haksun 1995), and struggling against resentment (Yŏngsuk 1995), as well as continuing to be treated with contempt after the war ended (Kŭmju 1995). Some grieve over continued rejection by their families of origin after the war (Sangok 1995) and their inability to bear children (Sunok 1995). The repercussions of military sexual slavery on family life were still being felt almost a half century later.

The "comfort station" system was part of a larger effort on the part of the Japanese government and armed forces to enforce a wartime policy exploiting Japan's long-standing colonial control over Korea (Chung 1997; Min 2003).

Initially, these brothels were organized and regulated by military authorities, but by the 1940s civilian authorities had been placed in control (Chung 1997). However, as discussed in Chapter 1, a structural oppression theory, which examines the intersections among multiple systems of oppression, often offers a richer explanation of global contact. While the case of Korean comfort women (*jūgun ianfu*) reflected Japanese military and imperial policies, some authors argue that such an interpretation neglects the political and social discourse of the time. Not only military subjugation and colonization but also reinforcement of social class and gender hierarchies were at work (Min 2003). Nozaki (2001) and Yang (1997) argue that the case of Korean comfort women should be viewed in light of the role of Japanese masculinity, racism, and imperialism. Japan's comfort system was viewed by the Japanese Imperial Army as a method of enhancing the masculine efficiency of its fighting force (Hicks 1995; Mendoza 2003).

The situation of comfort women should also be viewed in the larger context of traditional patriarchal mistreatment of daughters (Soh 2004). Daughters fled or were driven from their homes into public domain, where they may have a chance to flee the domestic oppression of their father's households but were made more vulnerable to victimization in the Japanese military brothel system. Thus, Howard (1995) emphasizes the devaluation of daughters, the prevalence of domestic violence against women and children, and the pervasive poverty in Korea at the time of World War II to explain why families sold their daughters into sexual servitude.

Some nations, such as the Netherlands, brought criminal charges against Japan immediately after World War II. However, Asian nations took much longer to take action on this issue. Eventually the Japanese established the Asian Woman's Fund to compensate victims. While the government of the Philippines accepted Japan's offer of redress, Indonesia, Korea, and Taiwan did not (Soh 2000b). Still, the case of sexual enslavement of women by the Japanese during World War II has received little attention in Japanese textbooks and other official war records. Until recently, testimony from the aggrieved women had been missing. Beyond that, the Japanese response has not included authentic remorse accompanied by "apology, compensation, and historical reflection" (Field 1997:38). Perhaps this policy is consistent with Japan's postwar ideology portraying itself as a war victim (Chung 1997), but ignoring and trivializing this case has strong sexist and patriarchal overtones (Chung 1997; Nozaki 2001). Again, such reactions marginalize, and even make invisible, the lower status of women and daughters and the impact this practice had on thousands of Korean, Taiwanese, Filipina, Indonesian, Dutch, and other families.

Not until the early 1990s was debate fully engendered at the level of the United Nations to consider sexual enslavement by the Japanese as a war crime. In doing so, the debate shifted from considering these women not as prostitutes but as sexual slaves. The debate surrounding the enslavement of *ianfu* serves to symbolically represent the view of women's rights as human rights in the arena of global politics (Soh 2000a).

More than 50 years after the end of the War in the Pacific, in December 2000, the Women's International War Crimes Tribunal for the Trial of Japanese Military Sexual Slavery met in Tokyo. Seventy-five women from Korean, India, Japan, the Netherlands, and the Philippines testified to the long-term consequences of their experiences (Askin 2001). At least some of the initiative and effectiveness of the efforts to gain recognition and redress for these women came about through transnational feminist women's activism, with women in Korea and Japan using transnational legal means to both popularize and politicize the issue at both regional and global levels (Piper 2001).

Other Collateral Violence Against Women and Girls

The poverty and lawlessness that accompanies life in a combat zone does not portend well for anyone's quality of life, even beyond rape in war and military sexual slavery. A long-standing history of embattlement seems to ensure that the safety and security of girls and women will receive little or no attention. A society that teeters precipitously on the brink of collapse of its civic, economic, educational, and other social systems may have difficulty devoting economic and political resources, to say nothing of emotional resources, to concern over the well-being of a part of the population that may well be viewed as invisible and of depreciated status.

A report based on research conducted in the West Bank and Gaza confirms that violence in besieged territories has dramatic impacts on the lives of girls and women. In a report titled "A Question of Security: Violence Against Palestinian Women and Girls," the Human Rights Watch (2006) charged that, due to the current political and economic crisis, the Palestinian authority has failed to address violence and abuse of women and girls as a priority security issue. The report documents violence ranging from wife and child abuse to rape (including that within marriage) and incest. The report cites honor killings (in which men kill female family members suspected of adultery or even of having been sexually violated) and cases of rape victims being required to marry their assailants. In such cases, patriarchy, which indulges domestic and broader-scale violence against women and girls, can remain uncontested as the society struggles against external enemies.

While the Human Rights Watch (2006) study was welcomed by some Palestinian officials, perhaps a signal that some in the society are ready for a change, violence against women and girls tends to go unreported in Palestine and, when reported, unpunished or only mildly punished in a society in which a quarter of women said they had experienced domestic violence and even more (two thirds) reported experiencing psychological abuse in their homes.

Of course, Palestine is not alone. Data collected by the World Health Organization confirms that sexual abuse continues to be a "stubborn scourge" in not only sub-Saharan Africa but in Brazil, Japan, and Peru (LaFranier 2006). Poverty makes securing children's safety especially difficult. Legacies of violence, oppression, and cultural mores that indulge child sexual abuse create a climate of relative tolerance toward a crime with heart-wrenching consequences in a world inhabited by the HIV/AIDS pandemic and poor health and medical care.

Almost one third of American women report being physically or sexually abused by a husband or boyfriend. In Europe, domestic violence is the leading cause of death and disability for women aged 16 to 44 years old. The World Health Organization estimates that worldwide, 10 to 70 percent of women are physically abused by their male partners. Immigrant and refugee women are at particular risk for domestic abuse. The immigrant experience may transpose the pattern of male economic and social dominance over wives in the host society. Further, language barriers, including inadequate interpretation services; fear of removal and legal obstacles; cultural barriers and community pressures; and reduced funding in social service areas create significant, unique risks for immigrant and refugee women (Minnesota Advocates for Human Rights 2004).

War then disproportionately affects women and the care systems they provide through families. "War and terror have the effect—sometimes deliberately achieved, sometimes incidental—of rending the fine fabric of everyday life, its interlaced economies, its material systems of care and support, its social networks, the roofs that shelter it" (Cockburn 2004:35).

In the next section, I examine the effects of war and military service on marriage.

War and Marriage

Another effect of any armed conflict is the impact on family formation patterns. Family effects are shaped by such factors as conflict duration; mortality or injury; military and civilian population characteristics; occupation and collaboration; economic, spatial, and other hardships; and family and societal resources for recovery. Researchers have documented several impacts of armed global conflict on patterns of marriage, including opportunity to marry, the likelihood of heterogamous unions, and the likelihood of marital stability.

The Marriage Squeeze

The opportunity to form a marriage is first and foremost shaped by the availability of eligible partners. Wars disproportionately remove from the marriage pool the most suitable male partners. Men who volunteer, are drafted, or are otherwise mustered into military service during wartime tend to be among the youngest and fittest (even if sometimes the most socially disadvantaged). These are desirable characteristics not only for soldiering but also for marrying, establishing a household, fathering children, and supporting a family.

This demographic situation has been referred to as the marriage squeeze. Studies conducted on different war experiences illustrate the impact of war on marriage rates. Goodkind (1997) has studied the deficit of male partners in Vietnam during the 1970s and 1980s, the years immediately following the withdrawal of the United States from and the ending of the war in Vietnam. In addition to loss of male population due to war, Vietnamese men emigrated at higher rates than did women. The consequence of such a marriage squeeze was, not surprisingly, delayed and forgone marriage (Goodkind 1997; Thai 2002).

Researchers also have observed a severe marriage squeeze in contemporary Lebanon, another country beset by decades-long armed conflict. Using the Population and Housing Survey—a representative sampling of 64,472 households in Lebanon—Saxena, Kulczycki, and Jurdi (2004) found that the proportion of single women of childbearing age doubled in proportion to men during a 25-year period ending in 1996. The mate availability ratios (calculated as the number of single adult males available for single adult females in adult age groups) declined to 75 by age 25 and to 50 by age 30.

Heterogamous Marriages

Another testimony to the impact of global forces on marriages and families can be seen in the number of marriages between women and men from different sides of an armed conflict. Racist ideology is sometimes relaxed when the dominant regime finds itself in need of workers or future population growth. Outlawing marriage and sexual relations between a group and the oppressor never completely restricts intimate relations, as in the case of Jews and people designated Aryan in Nazi Germany (Kallis 2005). While the picture of these marriages is often encumbered by stereotypes (Williams 1991), research reveals interesting facts about the nature of marriage formation and consequent impacts on marital quality, gender roles, and other couple dynamics.

The research in this area is almost exclusively on women who marry men from the dominant—often winning—side of an armed conflict and adopt the country of their husbands. These "war brides" may well be enhancing their socioeconomic opportunity in contrast to remaining in a society that has been ravaged by war and, as discussed above, in which war has created a significant marriage squeeze resulting in a dearth of eligible men. However, research indicates that they may still face economic hardship. Further, many women struggle and grieve over the separation from their home culture and society (Footrakoon 2000).

War brides constitute a significant part of the cultural memory of some societies. Esser (2003) describes the representation of marriages between Germans and Americans in German newspapers and magazines published in the American and British zones between the end of World War II (1945) and 1949. These marriages were used to demonstrate and enhance positive relations between former combatants. Portrayals of these marriages in a flattering light contributed to popularization and dissemination of the "American dream." Part of this portrayal included the representation of the modern German woman as stylish and devoted to her husband. These same portrayals usually ignored marital instability, violence, or other problems in these marriages.

Some research suggests that the intersection of marriage and national conflict has the potential to affect previous levels of tolerance among ethnically diverse groups. Kandido-Jaksic (1999) studied attitudes toward ethnically mixed marriages and mixed-ethnicity offspring among people of former Yugoslavia. The war in the Balkans and the subsequent separation of that region into more nationalistically segregated countries may have resulted in a decrease in social tolerance toward different ethnic groups and nationalities. However, using Bogardus's Social Distance Scale, Kandido-Jaksic found that the offspring of ethnically mixed marriages appear to be uniquely unwilling to adopt negative attitudes toward other ethnic groups.

Other research from Croatia's Center for the Investigation of Transition and Civil Society suggests that ethnic conflict promotes both in-group polarization (attachment to Croatian nationalism) and out-group polarization (distrust of "others"). Kunovich and Deitelbaum (2004) suggest that out-group polarization, in particular, is associated with a return to conservative values, including attitudes toward gender roles and family policy on issues such as abortion and divorce. These findings suggest that heterogamy may, through the next generation produced by such unions, decrease the level of prejudice and increase the level of tolerance for diversity in a society.

Marital Instability

Careful research does not always confirm stereotypes of military life's negative effects on families. In particular, research is contradictory regarding the effect of military service in general and the lived experience of war in particular on opportunity to marry and probability of subsequent divorce. American marriages formed during World War II and especially those formed during the Korean War appear to have had higher rates of divorce than did American marriages formed during peacetime (Ruger, Wilson, and Waddoups 2002). The effects of time of marriage (before, during, or after the war) and even the gender of the military spouse are more variable for subsequent cohorts.

Pavalko and Elder's (1990) classic research on the effects of military service during World War II drew on longitudinal studies for men representing 624 marriages, concentrating on men who grew up in California. Pavalko and Elder found higher divorce rates among men who served in the military during World War II and those who experienced combat than among men who did not serve or experience combat. Pavalko and Elder also found that prewar marriages were more likely to dissolve than were those formed during the war. Finally, they found that men who entered the service later had higher rates of divorce.

Pavalko and Elder (1990) explain the greater risk of divorce among servicemen in terms of psychological factors such as posttraumatic stress syndrome, social psychological factors such as combat bonding, life-course factors such as age-differentiated marital obligations, the presence or absence of children, and societal factors such as home-front mobilization. Some research on more recent military cohorts confirms a negative association between service and marital stability, especially during wartime. Using data on 3,800 men from the National Survey of Families and Households for 1987 to 1994, Ruger et al. (2002) found that participation in combat increased the risk of marital dissolution for American men serving in the military by more than 60 percent. However, for that cohort, the time of marriage (before, during, or after the war) did not affect dissolution.

A study using the 1992 Survey of Officers and Enlisted Personnel during the period of the Gulf War (Angrist and Johnson 2000) and another study of personnel serving later in the Middle East commissioned by the Rand Corporation's National Defense Research Institute (Karney and Crown 2006) found no effect on divorce rates from deployment of American male soldiers. However, research has found that American female soldiers serving in the current wars in the Middle East have divorce rates three times those of their male comrades (Mulhall 2009). These findings suggest that women's deployment and subsequent family absence places a greater strain on marriage than does husbands' deployment and absence. Given the greater responsibility women have for the expressive aspects of marriage and family life, the greater negative impact of their absence is not surprising.

Empirical research on the effects of war in other countries is scant. However, an analysis of the effects of war in Iran found higher rates of family dissolution among Iranians. For refugees of the Iran war, the divorce rate was 40 percent higher than the national rate (Aghajanian 2008). Another analysis of the effects of the 11-year conflict in Sierra Leone indicates that maternal mortality rose to the highest level in the world (Spencer-Walters 2008).

Although the research is limited, challenges to marital stability also have been observed among other populations who were either internally displaced or sought refuge in exile during civil and regional wars. Drawing on a 1987 survey of 254 divorced and 799 currently married women, Aghajanian and Moghadas (1998) attribute at least part of the increase in divorce rates in Iran since the 1960s to 8 years of war, as well as to social and legal changes in that country. Another study analyzing data collected in N'Djamena, Chad, from 1993 to 1994 also found a higher risk of divorce (and even transition from monogamy to bigamy) among internally displaced individuals compared with refugees (Laliberte, Laplante, and Piche 2003).

Perhaps, in comparison to refugees, those who remain behind have fewer resources available for survival strategies, while those who seek to leave must, in the most extreme cases, either marshal a more creative range of options, including family solidarity, or die. However, Granot (1995) did not find higher rates of divorce among couples living in the zones in Israel (e.g., Tel Aviv) that experienced the greatest war-related anxiety surrounding Scud missile attacks, when compared with couples living in areas less affected by the attacks. Further research is needed to examine the effects of war on marriage, including the place of unique national histories and cultures and contemporary factors such as pervasive media coverage.

The impact of war on marital stability may not transmit to any great extent across generations. One study using multivariate event–history techniques found only slightly higher risks of divorce among Germans who grew up in a family dissolved by war when compared with individuals who grew up in two-parent families (Diekmann and Engelhardt 1999). The same study did find significantly higher rates of divorce among individuals who had grown up in families dissolved by divorce. Perhaps it is not the absence of a parent per se that contributes to the higher rate of divorce but, rather, that differences in personal investments in marriage for those who lost a spouse to death, versus those who lost a spouse through divorce, contribute to the intergenerational transmission of divorce. War would seem to exacerbate these stressors.

In conclusion, the lived experience of war and the potential ensuing confusion and breakdown in social institutions has great potential to compromise marital and family stability. Even in a society with strong economic, legal, political, and religious institutional support for marriage and family, as was the United States in the 19th century, the "beginnings" and "endings" of marriages were sometimes fluid and occasionally contested. For example, Schwartzberg (2004) analyzed the records of widows who filed for the same soldier's Civil War pension. Schwartzberg found that separations (both short- and long-term), as well as abandonment and desertion, among working-class couples sometimes served as "informal divorces," setting the stage for subsequent bigamous marriages (and, hence, contested pensions). Clearly, more research is needed to support military families "shadowed by war" (Huebner et al. 2009).

Family Resiliency in the Face of International Violence

The book that can fully capture the devastating effects of war on families will probably never be written. The memory of the horrors of World War II is still alive for some readers of *Global Families*. Nazi Germany and its collaborators murdered about 6 million of the 9 million Jews living in Europe. In addition, Nazi policies systematically killed Poles, Russians, and Slavic peoples; Roma ("gypsies"); people with mental and physical disabilities; homosexuals; and political, religious, intellectual, and other groups, including Communists and Socialists, Soviet prisoners of war, Jehovah's Witnesses, and dissident Christians (U.S. Holocaust Memorial Museum 2006h).

The U.S. Holocaust Memorial Museum (2006f) estimates that more than a million Jewish children were murdered by Nazis and their collaborators. Babies and children were particularly vulnerable to morbidity and mortality due to malnutrition and starvation, insufficient clothing and shelter, and exposure to crowded, unsanitary living conditions that provided opportunities for the spread of infectious diseases. Also, as the youngest members of society were the least usable commodities for forced labor, babies and children were quickly separated from more productive members of society and murdered.

The term *genocide*, created in 1944, refers to "massive crimes committed against groups" that through "a coordinated plan of different actions [aim] at the destruction of essential foundations of the life of national groups, with the aim of annihilating the groups themselves" (U.S. Holocaust Memorial Museum 2006k). Today, the U.S. Holocaust Memorial Museum continues to track contemporary genocides throughout the world, including the following:

- Burundi, where a civil war in 1993 resulted in the deaths of 200,000 and the displacement of more than 500,000 (U.S. Holocaust Memorial Museum 2006d).
- Chechnya, where massive military action from Russia has devastated the country through indiscriminate bombing of populated areas and massacres of civilians (U.S. Holocaust Memorial Museum 2006e).
- Darfur, where tens of thousands of civilians have been murdered, thousands of women have been raped, and 2 million people have been driven from their homes. In addition, thousands die each month from living outside the areas of

conflict in harsh desert environments with inadequate food, water, shelter, and health care (U.S. Holocaust Memorial Museum 2006j).

• Rwanda, where extremist members of the Hutu majority have managed a campaign to exterminate the Tutsi majority, resulting in the murder of 800,000 people in 100 days and the rape of thousands of women (U.S. Holocaust Memorial Museum 2006i).

Families Surviving War

War and genocide displace individuals and fracture families in the most horrible ways. After all, what better way to destroy a people and a society than to separate individuals from families and loved ones or to rape, torture, or murder parents and children, siblings and elders? Such extreme violence denies families safety and security, nurturance and socialization, as well as intimate care and continuity. Stories of family resilience in the face of diaspora conditions are often lost or hard to retrieve, and accounts of slave and former slave families are particularly difficult to find (in part due to the prohibitions against slave literacy). Some accounts of the survival of such families remain (e.g., Genovese 1974; Stevenson 1991; West 2004), but just as the toll on family life was high in such families, the loss of family stories is likewise high.

However, we have enough accounts to demonstrate that, even under brutal circumstances, some families exhibit remarkable levels of resiliency. For example, during the Holocaust, ghettos were often the final location where a reasonable semblance of the traditional family structure was maintained by European Jews. Ghetto families' ability to maintain emotional bonds and construct new family structures was not only key to survival under the most austere circumstances but also served to challenge Nazi policies intended to degrade and dehumanize Jews (Cohen 2006).

While literature often describes the inadequacies of Holocaust survivors as parents (especially around issues of attachment and detachment), the research is contradictory at best. The best research in this field compares survivor and nonsurvivor families (see Krell, Suedfeld, and Soriano 2004) and employs a life-history approach (see Stanger 2005). Much of this research draws on family narratives (see Rosenthal 2000, 2002a, 2002b). Using self-reports, Kellermann (2001) found few differences between the quality of parenting by Holocaust survivors and that of a control group. Large-scale studies of survivors of wars and of their children have repeatedly found both the survivors and their children within the normal range of family relationships.

Modern technology, including the Internet and other computer-assisted technologies, may provide a means for processing and disseminating such accounts. The U.S. Holocaust Memorial Museum has established a web project that records Holocaust survivors' experiences. Among the stories included in the "Behind Every Name a Story" project is the account of Miriam (Rot) Eshel. Miriam was born in 1930, the second child and oldest daughter of a Jewish family living in Irshava in the Carpathian Mountains, in what was then Czechoslovakia. In 1944, Miriam's family was forced to move to the Jewish ghetto in Munkacs, 30 kilometers away, before being deported to Auschwitz, where Miriam was separated from the rest of her family. Miriam was later transported to a labor camp near Stuffhof and from there forced with 1,000 other women on a death march, which only 100 survived, to be liberated by the Russian army. Of 11 family members, only Miriam and a younger brother survived (U.S. Holocaust Memorial Museum 2006a). After the Holocaust, Miriam made her way to Israel (then Palestine), where in 1953 she married Jacob, another Holocaust survivor (U.S. Holocaust Memorial Museum 2006b). Jacob wrote a moving poem in honor of Miriam's strength (U.S. Holocaust Memorial Museum 2006c).

Without a doubt, ghettos, resettlement camps, forced labor, and extermination camps can fracture families. However, powerful stories have emerged that provide testimony to the resiliency of families and their ability to retain intimate bonds against all odds. Krohn (1998) recounted such a story of her father's family, which had not been together since the 1930s. Sixty-three members of this extended family, including all 10 first cousins, gathered for a reunion in Chicago, Illinois, arriving from across the United States, England, and South America. The story that emerged was one of family continuity, as, over the years and three continents, members of the family remained connected through regular correspondence and occasional, "too short and always very emotional" (p. 2) meetings. Krohn recorded impressions of that reunion:

> When we finally met . . . we noted similar family features. . . . We observed the expressions of awakening on the faces of the younger generation as they listed to elders speak about their wartime experiences. . . .
>
> After the reunion . . . family members returned to their respective homes [and] resumed their daily lives with greater awareness of how one cruel dictator had affected the lives of so many. They also returned home with a stronger, more caring sense of family. (Pp. 2–3)

Such accounts speak to the resiliency of extended family bonds across borders. In 1981, the annual International Conference on Children of Holocaust Survivors began meeting. The first large-scale gathering of children whose parents had survived the Holocaust offers the second generation the opportunity to engage in intergenerational exchange as well as contact with researchers and mental health practitioners working in the field of survivorship

(Peskin 1981). By the last decades of the 20th century, psychologists, social workers, and other professionals affiliated with organizations such as the Institute on Working With Holocaust Survivors and the Second Generation had begun to examine the impact of the Holocaust not only on first-generation survivors, including their needs as they age, but also on the Holocaust's impact on the next generation. Bergmann and Jucovy's (1982/1990) work and Lemberger's (1995) volume *A Global Perspective on Working With Holocaust Survivors and the Second Generation* brought together research and resources for a population that spans the globe and every continent.

A substantial body of research on the impact of war tends to focus on psychological impacts on and resiliency of individuals. For example, Brajsa-Zganec (2005) has investigated the prevalence of depressive symptoms among children displaced by the war in the Republic of Croatia. She found that the effects of long-term exposure to the war were lessened by social support (instrumental support, support to self-esteem, and belonging and acceptance) and tended to be greater for boys than for girls.

Another study, using in-depth interviews with a snowball sample of 55 volunteers from the 1934-to-1939 German birth cohort, found considerable variety of experiences and responses to growing up in Germany during World War II. "Engulfed in war, the individuals within those societies had to adjust to the events they experienced. They had to adopt coping strategies that allowed them to psychologically as well as behaviorally manage the events of war" (Larney 1994:206).

The participants in Larney's (1994) study had direct, personal experiences with bombings; death of parents and other loved ones; and loss of homes, possessions, and safety associated with the destruction of and changes in family and other social institutions. The participants in Larney's study also reported that their roles as children changed, as they were required to adopt productive roles in the family. That, in turn, affected their education and ambitions, as well as family life itself. As a result of growing up during World War II, the men and women in Larney's study exhibited lifelong frugality, attitudinal conservatism and traditionalism, and risk-avoidant frames of reference.

While Elder's (1974) research suggested that hardship of an economic nature leads to an increased focus on family, Larney's research indicates that individuals who experience the most severe effects of war may shift from values emphasizing family and altruism toward values emphasizing purely personal self-interest. Larney suggests that the family focus Elder observed among individuals during wartime may be temporary. Such a conclusion would be consistent with other research on the importance of the family during hard times such as the Great Depression in the United States (Elder 1974; Farber 1971), the psychological effects of war (Quester 1990), the effects of war on life course (Mayer 1988), and the place of strategies for coping with war (Elder and Clipp 1988), including situations in which a family member is a prisoner of war or missing in action (McCubbin et al. 1974).

Military Families

In addition to families experiencing war and others intimately familiar with genocide, military families represent global families in a very clear sense. Since World War II, the concept of American foreign service has expanded to include increasing numbers of families with members involved in military service, the diplomatic corps, international and multinational business enterprises, and a wide range of governmental, nongovernmental, and not-for-profit organizations. Likewise, the information, socialization, and advice offered to those families have shifted to reflect the changing demographic composition of these types of transnational employment.

Constructions of femininity and masculinity have been contested by the inclusion of women in military positions. Women are trained and serve in combat positions throughout the world—including in Argentina, Austria, Brazil, Israel, Italy, Taiwan, the United Kingdom, and the United States—ranging from flying combat missions to, in Norway, serving as submarine commander. The highest proportions of women in the active armed forces are found in Australia, New Zealand, South Africa, and the United States, where at least one out of every seven of those serving are women. Gender typing persists, however, in U.N. peacekeeping operations, where women constitute more than half the general service staff but only a quarter of local and professional staff and less than 5 percent of civilian police and military personnel (Seager 2003).

Sixty years ago, the wives of men serving in the U.S. Army could read in *The Army Wife* (a book dedicated "To Army Brides of Today and Tomorrow"; Shea 1954:iv): "Never in the history of the United States Army have American troops been allocated on such a global basis" (p. 268). Yet the chapter dealing with assignment of the family beyond the continental United States dealt with topics such as "How to Keep Cool Despite the Thermometer" when living in "the tropics"; "Clothing for the Arctic" when living in Alaska, Newfoundland, Labrador, and Greenland; "Servants in Japan" when living in that country; and shopping in postwar Europe, as well as "Schools, Medical and Recreational Facilities" in (then French) Morocco, Turkey, and Saudi Arabia. American military families facing the death of a service member were counseled to avoid outward display of mourning except in the observance of the military customs of the Service. There are no drawn shades, crepe-hung doors, muffled bells, or hushed voices, despite the deep sorry of the family of the deceased. . . . Death is accepted as an inevitable happening, and while everything possible is done to show consideration to the bereaved family, post life goes on in an uninterrupted manner except during the actual funeral services. (P. 319)

In contrast to admonitions catering to traditional conjugal couples, today's military families are more likely to be headed by single parents or women and to receive advice that better reflects the complexity of their lives. The advice offered in current guides, such as the pink-camouflage-covered *Married to the Military* (Hosek 2002) and *Help! I'm a Military Spouse—I Want a Life Too!: How to Craft a Life for You as You Move With the Military* (Hightower and Scherer 2007), offer advice on such contemporary matters as marriage enrichment seminars and pursuing a career (even starting a business). Spouses are directed to such websites as CinCHouse. com (which stands for "Commander in Chief of the House"), and spouses—husbands as well as wives—are encouraged to "find a niche" involving "purposeful activities outside the home" (R. Sick, personal communication, January 16 and 17, 2007).

In cases in which both parents are serving in the military, parents are required to maintain a Family Care Plan specifying custody and financial arrangements in the event both parents are deployed ("How to Survive Double Deployment" 2003). Those deployments can be announced suddenly and, as recent events attest, can be extended for unpredictable lengths of time over multiple periods.

A small but growing body of literature examines the adjustments of "military brats and other global nomads" (Ender 2002). Morten Ender (2000, 2006, 2009; Ender et al. 2007), professor of sociology at the U.S. Military Academy (West Point) and self-titled "military brat," has amassed a body of original qualitative and quantitative research on military families, including research about growing up as a dependent child in a military family. Ender's (2002) chapter titled "Voices From the Backseat" is a reference to the nomadic life experienced by American army families as they move from base to base every 3 years.

Such a global, nomadic life affects families in a number of ways. In the summer of 2004, the Military Family Research Institute and the U.S. Department of Defense Quality of Life Office commissioned a study on the adaptation of adolescents when a family member is deployed into combat. This qualitative study yielded findings consistent with other studies demonstrating the potential for resilience among families and members under stress. Particularly with support from the parent at home, the adolescents in this study adapted to the absence of the deployed parent with maturity and by assuming additional family responsibilities. At the same time, the adolescents in this study were well aware of the dangers associated with combat. Some adolescents experienced disruption in their lives due to interruptions in financial, transportation, or other everyday circumstances. Others exhibited certain behavioral changes, including changes in school performance and traits associated with depression (Huebner and Mancini 2005).

Military service and related effects on families have changed dramatically, especially since the events of 9/11. Deployment, separation, and reunion, often in repeated succession, stress the family unit. Some scholars emphasize the need for systems to support military families, with an emphasis on "capacity building." In this approach, formal and informal support networks come together to generate social capital in the form of resources, good will, and reciprocal relationships. Communities share responsibility for support networks and partnerships among military organizations such as the Army Child and Youth Services and the Family Readiness Center and civilian organizations such as 4-H and Cooperative Extension Services.

Refugee Families

While families in the U.S. military face such hardships as frequent moves from place to place, separations that sometimes last for years, and the uncertainty of when (or if) the service-member spouse or parent will return home from a combat assignment, military families often have in place a certain set of institutionalized supports. Refugees and their families generally have few such supports, although, today, the support for refugees (e.g., in places such as Minnesota) are certainly greater and more systematically delivered than such services in previous eras.

The U.N. High Commission on Refugees (UNHCR) estimates that by the end of 2010, 43.7 million men, women, and children had been forcibly displaced—the highest number in 15 years. Of those, 15.4 million were refugees (10.55 million under the United Nation's mandate, with another 4.82 million Palestinian refugees). Another 837,500 were asylum seekers. Finally, another 27.5 million were internally displaced persons (UNHCR 2011). Afghan and Iraqi refugees account for almost half of all refugees under the care of UNHCR.

While men (and often boys) disproportionately bear the costs of direct engagement in armed conflict, the burden of providing for families during war or other times of severely diminished resources disproportionately falls to wives (and widows) and mothers. Women constitute almost half the world's refugees (UNHCR 2011), but men have greater opportunities for

"Street Family, Potosi, Bolivia," by David L. Parker

Photograph by D. L. Parker. Reprinted with permission of the photographer and the Minneapolis Institute of Arts.

seeking asylum (presumably because women have more limited involvement in direct action; Seager 2003).

The lives faced by the children of refugee families are particularly troubled. For example, as a result of the Vietnam War, more than 2 million people fled Indochina after 1975. While at least 10 percent died in the process, more than 1.6 million refugees survived to seek asylum in the surrounding countries. Nearly 60,000 of these were unaccompanied minors (Freeman and Hũ 2003:3). Children seeking refuge may do so in the company of a parent, older sibling, or other adult but may also be alone. Freeman, an anthropologist, and Hũ , a U.S.-educated social worker with a specialization in child welfare and protection and himself a refugee from Vietnam, have chronicled in their own words the life experiences of children living in refugee camps. Their research focused on unaccompanied minors who had either been orphaned by the death of one or both parents or become separated from their parents. Some of these children fled on their own, while others had been sent on these "high-risk escapes" by parents.

Between 1987 and 1995 Freeman and Hũ (2003) visited 18 camps that housed Vietnamese people. There they found extreme neglect and abuse, with adult detainees and camp guards alike abusing the children physically and sexually. Camp officials would remove children from their families and place them in foster care and would move certain family members to other camps or across camp areas, thus further disrupting children's daily routines. In these circumstances, Freeman and Hū found children who were "traumatized, frightened, and depressed . . . who did not know what was going to happen to them next" (p. xiii). The children's narratives reflected "both uncertainty and the disarray in their lives." At the very least, these children reported missing their parents and wishing to return home. Some came away from the experience with deep psychological damage typical of children who have endured prolonged exposure to traumatic events, exhibiting feelings of numbness, sadness, fear, and rage.

The quality of adjustment to even the most devastating of refugee experiences seems, like other family stressors, to be mediated by the quality and experience of previous family relationships, as well as external role models and threats. An original study of the "dreams, drawings, and behavior" of Palestinian children living in refugee camps in the West Bank revealed that children were expressing less fear, confusion, depression, victimization, and alienation while developing more internalized locus of control in the years since the Intifada. Further, they were articulating values of bravery and solidarity in the face of hatred and revolt against the authority represented by Israeli soldiers (Nashef 1992). Thus, the refugee experience, along with lives lived under other international violence, shapes families across generations in quite direct ways.

Summary

This chapter has examined a range of issues related to international violence and families, including family legacies of oppression and war. Colonial authorities often seek to dominate the indigenous society with institutions, including monogamous, nuclear family structures and gender relations, that will be consistent with colonial systems and are to the advantage of the colonial system. Some writers argue that a flourishing sex trade likewise serves broader social agenda and regulates ideologies of family, sexuality, and reproduction, as well as imperialism and racism. The multibillion-dollar global sex trade is built on gender, national, and other inequalities that drive women and children into prostitution and fuel a world market for sexual consumption.

While globalization does not cause war, war represents a particular manifestation of global political, economic, cultural, and other forces. Rape in war demonstrates the convergence of patriarchy with militarism and yields the potential for the rape of women and children to be used as a strategy of terror and subordination during periods of armed conflict. Likewise, military sexual slavery, as exemplified by the "comfort women" enslaved by the Japanese during World War II, reveals the interconnections between gender and militarism, with tragic consequences for the women involved. Perhaps not surprisingly, in societies that have a long history of living with international violence, the physical and sexual well-being of women and children has low priority.

War changes the marriage experience, first by "squeezing" the ratio of men and women available for marriage and second by increasing a society's probability of heterogamous mate selection. Many of the latter marriages face hardships emanating from status differences between husbands and wives. Although the literature is both scant and sometimes contradictory, American military service in general and the lived experience of war not only affects opportunity to marry but also the probability of subsequent divorce.

War also displaces individuals and fractures families. Under such circumstances, however, some families exhibit resiliency, as illustrated by documents from Holocaust survivors and their families. Military families and their adjustment are a special case of work–family linkages in a highly mobile world. Including those internally displaced, about 43.7 million people throughout the world are living as refugees. These families, especially the children, face unusually severe social–psychological hardships.

SEX TRAFFICKING

A "Family Business"

By Jennifer Blank, MA

Trafficking in persons has distorted women and children as commodities in the global market to be bought, sold, and consumed by tourists, the military, organized crime, law enforcement agencies, traffickers, recruiters, and pimps (Hughes 2001b). Between 700,000 and 4 million women and children are trafficked internationally each year, at an annual shadow profit of $7 billion specifically from sex trafficking (Hughes 2001a). Such a lucrative business has attracted the attention of many governmental and nongovernmental agencies, but sex trafficking continues to grow and flourish.

Globalization, poverty, and violence against women are just a few of the macrosocietal issues associated with human trafficking. This essay briefly addresses why trafficking is such a growing, profitable business and why people, particularly men, become involved in what is often a "family business."

Globalization Fosters Sex Trafficking

The majority of women and girls trafficked into the sex industry are minority women from Third World countries. Many of these women and girls suffer from the feminization of poverty, gendered violence, and oppression of migrant populations in the host countries. Global corporations provide the lowest common denominator of wages and social services in order to best compete in the global economy (Mies 1994). Such a "race to the bottom" allows the service sector, particularly the sex tourist industry, to prosper and enables trafficking and prostitution to grow in Southeast Asian countries, Central and Eastern Europe, the independent states of the former Soviet Union, and Africa. In addition, as populations are relocated because of war, political repression, and economic displacement, women fall victim to trafficking in concert with poverty and lack of access to education and training, political power, and legal and other protection (McMahon and Stanger 2002).

The propensity to commodify sexual/erotic relations with women and children has intensified in Third World countries. Itzin (1992) believes that this industry "especially exploits black and Third World women and children, trading on race discrimination and perpetuating racist as well as sexist stereotypes" (p. 65). For the same reasons, Southeast Asia, Latin America, and Africa have become favored destinations for sex tourists. Foreign prostituted women are subject to much more harassment and abuse than are local prostituted women because of their vulnerability from being socialized into an ethos of female self-servitude and self-sacrifice. In addition, women who are trafficked are often located in environments in which people of their racial or ethnic background are considered inferior and are thus subjected to additional discrimination and abuse.

Abusive, violent treatment in the sex trade is overlooked because trafficked women are seen as merchandise; they can be used repeatedly as a source of ongoing profit for years while also being expendable. Once they fall ill, are too old, or contract HIV, trafficking women can be disposed of and replaced at low cost for high profit (Bales 1999; McMahon and Stanger 2002). However, people in the business will invest significant effort to retrieve their women who run away, thus conserving their capital investment. Furthermore, if women are able to escape and return to their home countries, which is almost impossible, they risk being shunned by their families. Found by traffickers, the women are thrown back into the prostitution/sex-trafficking ring, or they are murdered.

Dehumanization and Commodification in a "Family Business"

Women become involved in the business because they follow recruiters/traffickers who promise lucrative jobs in factories, as employees in restaurants (often fronts for prostitution), or as "entertainers" in the sex and tourist industries (McMahon and Stanger 2002). Women may be coerced, deceived, or kidnapped and sold into the sex industry, but young women also are openly recruited for work in prostitution (Anderson and O'Connell Davidson 2002; Global Alliance Against Traffic in Women 2001; McMahon and Stanger 2002). A small minority of young girls also are sold into the sex industry by their parents or other relatives and recruiters in order to pay off family debts (McMahon and Stanger 2002).

The demand for young women for commercialized sex work is very high. Some customers, especially Chinese and Sino-Thais, are willing to pay large amounts of money to have sex with virgins (Bales 1999). These men prefer to have sex with virgins first, because a girl's virginity is thought to be a strong source of *yang* (coolness), which quenches and slows the *yin* (heat) of the aging process. Second, virgins are assumed to be free of HIV (Bales 1999). Of course, the number of times "virgins" are repeatedly sold makes the latter problematic. My research, summarized in this essay, indicates that commodification and dehumanization of women and girls are inextricably linked in what has often become a lucrative "family business" (Blank 2003).

In 2003, I conducted research in London, England, and specifically focused on traffickers involved in the sex industry. This research involved open-ended interviews in a qualitative study that focused on men who traffic in persons. I addressed general questions on prostitution, attitudes about women who were trafficked for sex, and the men's experiences in the business. This essay focuses on Ahmet, a trafficker with a high level of involvement in the business (and considerable candor during the interviews), but also draws on the experiences of Demitri, a pimp, and Cyril, a bouncer in a club frequented by operators in the sex-trafficking trade in London.[1]

My research revealed that the reality, opinions, and justifications of men involved in sex trafficking are created and maintained by personal experiences of the business within their world. Before they became involved in the business, these men saw themselves as an "excluded" population. They believe they were never given legitimate opportunities to obtain material success. These men viewed greed, money, and power as motivations for maintaining a financially and personally successful life.

---

[1]The names of the men have been changed to protect their identities.

Trafficking is a low-risk, high-profit, sometimes "family business." Ahmet said he first became involved when he was 13 years old. He apprenticed under his father, first by trafficking drugs, guns, and refugees from Albania. When I asked him why he became involved in the first place, he said, "My dad owns the boats. He wanted [us; Ahmet and his brother] to [become involved]." Ahmet did not become involved in trafficking women until his family was not earning enough money to pay off the debt from their boats. He told me:

It was my idea. My mates told me about it, and it was just a way to make extra money. So I rented a boat from my dad and did it myself. I was about 14 and making 250,000 [American] dollars a month. When my dad saw me making the money he wanted to do it, too.

His family's involvement in trafficking women was motivated by money and power. He told me, "I had to do it. I had to help out my dad for a better life for myself." He also claimed:

If I had the opportunities and all the doors open, I would have done that, but we didn't have it and we aren't accepted in this society. I'm just a dirty Albanian who rapes and kills, and we have to fight back to make a decent living. I would have no other choice. I'm not gonna scrape toilets for 5 pounds [British sterling] an hour.

Ahmet wanted a better life. The same was true for Demitri and Cyril. When asked why they got involved in the business, Demitri said, "For me, it has always been about the money—do you know what I mean? It's about making money." Cyril's reasons were very similar. He got involved because of "the excitement, the money, [and] the fun. It was the money." He was 15 when he entered the business, because he was "seeing an older woman and she asked [him] to look over her and the money came in and it was easy." Each man, regardless of his current position in the business, joined for the money and the power he gained from trafficked women. The women were mere commodities, the means to an end of financial prosperity.

Of course, the tragedy of trafficking humans intersects not only with gender and economics but also with race and ethnicity. The intersecting systems of domination and oppression do not have equal effects on women in Third World contexts. Mohanty, Russo, and Torres (1991) argue for the need to recognize and explore Third World women's experiences, including their place in colonial, imperialist, and minority capital systems. Additional research and legislation must address the broader scope of the trafficking business beyond prostitution, including forced labor, debt bondage, domestic servitude, forced marriage, and child labor.

Effective social action to combat trafficking requires international cooperation on a global scale, as well as understanding the economic incentives and value systems of sex traffickers engaged in this "family business." For example, the United States has implemented a strategy to combat trafficking through the "Three Ps": *prevention* of trafficking, *protection* and assistance for victims, and *prosecution* and enforcement against traffickers (Hughes 2001a). First, trafficking must be prevented through culturally sensitive and nationally targeted educational campaigns to promote awareness. Trafficked persons must be guaranteed protection from their traffickers and provided legal, social, educational, and other assistance from government and social service agencies, while being assured that prosecution of the traffickers can be accomplished without placing the women at risk for deportation or other public sanction.

Jennifer Blank earned the Master of Arts degree in criminology at Middlesex University in London. This essay is based on original research conducted in London clubs with men involved in the sex-trafficking business. Since returning to the United States, Blank has presented her work on human trafficking and slavery at meetings of the American Society of Criminology and to educational groups. Blank is the coauthor of "Sex Trafficking: An Exploratory Study Interviewing Traffickers" (Troshynski and Blank 2008).

CRITICAL THINKING QUESTIONS

1. Referencing Blank's essay on sex trafficking as a "family business," what are the macrosocial contexts of sex trafficking? Speculate on the impact of being trafficked to a woman's broader life chances, including opportunity for family life.

2. Some scholars (e.g., Lorentzen and Turpin 1998) have written of war as a gendered experience. How does the gendered nature of war impact family life?

3. Account for the differences and similarities in marital quality for those who experience military service during wartime and those who do not.

4. Identify three variables that could account for family resilience in the face of international violence. You may reference a summary of the literature on family resilience (e.g., Chapter 3 in Karraker and Grochowski 2012) for a brief discussion of the term.

5

Transnational Employment

Work–Family Linkages Across Borders

T hroughout history, men and women have migrated, with and without other family members, in order to leave behind economic hardship and uncertainty or to pursue economic opportunity and promise for themselves and their families. The flow of human beings and their labor, including the migration of domestic, child-care, and other workers, is today a global process.

Now, more than at any other time in human history, globalization involves hypermobility (Sassen 2002). Many of the most mobile populations are seeking employment across national borders, with significant consequences for their families and societies. Thus, global hypermobility is creating an unprecedented number of transnational families: "families that live some or most of the time separated from each other, yet hold together and create something that can be seen as a feeling of collective welfare and unity, namely 'familyhood,' even across national borders" (Bryceson and Vuorela 2002:3).

Not all transnational individuals or families are disadvantaged, exploited, oppressed, undocumented, or even (by what is becoming a somewhat pejorative term) migrant. Increasingly, well-educated, unattached workers can market their skills and position themselves anywhere in the world that has demand for their skills in engineering, medicine, technology, and other fields. These individuals and their cohort, geographically separated from their families, are sometimes called "solos" or "generation S" (Edgar 2004).

Families whose members relocate or move about because of their role in multinational corporations or supranational political organizations may be transferring high levels of privilege, along with their greater educational, language, and other social capital, from one society to or across other spatial locations. Such transnational elites and their families can be viewed as mobile cosmopolitans, often welcomed and even cultivated by the host nation (Bryceson and Vuorela 2002).

A small body of research focuses on children in these privileged families. For example, Ender's (2002) edited volume on *Military Brats and Other Nomads* (cited in Chapter 4) includes a study of career orientation among internationally mobile adolescents (Gerner and Perry 2002), a postmodern analysis of the adolescent experience among expatriates (Hylmö 2002), and research on development among children experiencing international relocation (Pearce 2002). The American Foreign Service establishment is evidently aware of the complications of transnational relocation on children and family, as witnessed by such guides as McCluskey's (1994) *Notes From a Traveling Childhood,* published by the Foreign Service Youth Foundation. Beyond the study of children and adolescents, however, the lives of more privileged transnational families have received scant attention in the literature.

In contrast, less privileged migrants and members of their families are more likely to be viewed through a xenophobic lens by the adopted societies. They may be greeted with suspicion and portrayed as a potential burden, risk, or even danger in the country to which they have relocated. In this chapter I focus not on the more privileged families but on the less privileged for which globalization facilitates the transfer of certain economic and family roles, usually from less-developed societies to more-developed societies, in the interest of economic improvement.

In Chapter 5, I describe the dynamic association between economic patterns and household labor, as men and increasingly women from less-developed countries take employment in more-developed countries in a search for higher income for themselves and their families. I present the implications of transnational employment for both gender roles and family dynamics, including the impact of transnational labor on one type of care work—global care chains. Finally, while some transnational workers are single or childless, I offer a particular examination of the impact of migratory employment on transnational parenting. In doing so, I address the question, How does the relocation and potential fragmentation involved in transnational employment challenge conceptions of family across time and space?

Transnational Employment

Any discussion of transnational employment involving large transfers of labor must acknowledge the global basis of economic production today. Rosen's (2002) critical analysis of the globalization of the apparel industry in the United States is one such example. By analyzing U.S. trade policy following World War II, Rosen demonstrated the role of protectionism and policies aimed at containing communism-altered textile and apparel manufacturing and commerce, both domestically in the United States and abroad. Rosen reveals how trade liberalization, including new trade agreements, tariff reductions, and unlimited import quotas, as well as the rise of transnational retail distributors (e.g., Wal-Mart), has created favorable conditions for American apparel producers to relocate to Mexico and Central America.

Rosen (2002) and many others argue that such a neoliberal approach to transnational economics has not been to the benefit of workers. To the contrary, the new global economic order has resulted in job displacement and wage loss on the domestic front and the expansion of low-wage retail jobs both domestically and abroad. In effect, as I discussed in the first chapter, globalization has exacerbated the distances among the core, semiperiphery, and periphery nations in the world system. According to a report by an economist from the Center for Economic and Policy Research in Washington, D.C., and an economist from the Center for Economic Performance at the London School of Economics (Schmitt and Wadsworth 2006), the earnings gap between immigrant and native-born workers increased between 1980 and 2000 in both Great Britain and the United States. For example, in the United States in 2000, male immigrants earned 18.4 percent less per hour than did U.S.-born men—almost double the wage gap in 1980. The gap in earnings between immigrant and native-born women increased even more during the same period, from 3.4 percent to 10.7 percent. Further, the magnitude of these gaps persists, even when controlling for age and education (Schmitt and Wadsworth 2006).

While labor migration is certainly not limited to women, the globalization of transnational labor is increasingly a complex, often contradictory, and highly gendered phenomenon. As described in a report by the U.N. Economic and Social Commission for Asia and the Pacific (UNESCAP 2011), on the one hand, globalization has enhanced employment opportunities for women in many places where opportunities had not existed. Globalization also has helped create and strengthen women's associations and networks, increasing mechanisms for mutual support and resources. Women's migration for employment has helped reduce poverty and meet labor needs in a number of countries. In several countries, new information and communications technologies have improved women's access not only to employment opportunities but also to information on health, microcredit, and other issues (UNESCAP 2011).

Globalization has also reinforced existing gender inequities. In too many locations, traditional sexual divisions of labor have only been reinforced in new locations and forms of work. Work performed primarily by women continues to have low economic value relative to work performed by men, along with conditions of exploitation, poor job security, and violations of human rights. As discussed in Chapter 4, one persistent negative impact of globalization is the worsening situation of violence against women, including the trafficking of women and girls (UNESCAP 2011).

Adding to the complexity of gender and transnational employment, Oishi (2005) found that more men emigrate from low-income countries (e.g., Bangladesh, India, Pakistan), while more women emigrate from high-income countries (e.g., Indonesia, the Philippines, Sri Lanka). Three factors interact to determine women's migration in less-developed countries, at least in Asia: (1) emigration policies; (2) women's social autonomy, especially as related to women's education policy and nontraditional values about women's roles in the family and society; and (3) social legitimacy of emigration. In the less-developed countries she studied, the more women who emigrate, the greater the social acceptability of women's emigration.

Further, more women migrate today without their young children than would have been possible in the past (Apple 1987; Tilly and Scott 1990). Even this is related to globalization. The worldwide marketing of artificial infant formula enables women from less-developed countries to leave even their youngest children, an option much less possible when breast feeding (or wet nursing) was the only option for infant survival.

Ward (1990) has detailed the linkages between formal and informal work, as well as the part played by national and other governmental bodies, and the complex intersections among social class, race, and sex on the "global assembly line." Ward employs a world system analysis (as described in Chapter 1) in which management and profit are centered in core, more-developed nations while the actual labor is performed in semiperiphery or periphery, less-developed nations. The incentive behind this unequal economic system is diffusion of economic and political costs, access to markets, and diversity of product. Wealthier nations reap the profits and their consumers reap the lower costs, while less-privileged nations see growth in service-sector economies and increased specialization in export industries.

For example, through revolutions in transportation and technology, globalization is restructuring the tourism industry. Women working in the global tourist industry may be a nationally and ethnically more diverse workforce compared with other global industry sectors. Yet, the case of those workers has received short shrift by scholars analyzing women's employment. Such inattention is unfortunate, as the tourist industry illustrates how indigenous women may be called on in their jobs to serve as producers and translators of cultural experience for global travelers, thus profoundly affecting everyday life and interaction and perceptions of community and self, including family and family relations (Vandegrift 2008).

Ward (1990) does not see these workers as entirely passive victims of patriarchal control. She cites examples of women engaging in employment counter to dominant cultural norms, manipulating racist and sexist managers into extending special privileges, participating in informal activities, and unionizing. Ward demonstrates that men, families, and the transnational corporations themselves exert powerful control over women workers' lives, as women's wage labor often occurs in home-based or other informal sector work. Women's work is often unregulated in terms of hours, conditions, and compensation, and women's employment in these global industries falls below the low standard, even for men's wages in their home countries. Finally, the unionization that might increase women's wages and work conditions faces an uphill battle in these countries, often suppressed by military and security forces.

Women workers are exploitable and expendable, easily terminated during economic downturns. Further, Salzinger (2003:2) contends that capitalistic enterprises do not "find" workers but rather "make" workers. "Transnational capital's dream of productive femininity" involves the manipulation of gender to construct different versions (sometimes assertive, at other times embattled, at still other times docile) of the ideal female assembly worker. Salzinger's contention is that this constructed ideal worker may be variable but is always compliant, trainable, and acquiescent.

The "nannies, maids, and sex workers" of Ehrenreich and Hochschild's (2002) title represent such a case. These workers are disproportionately and increasingly women migrating from the Third World to the First World. This transnational labor movement

> enables and even promotes the migration and trafficking of women as a strategy for survival. The same infrastructure designed to facilitate cross-border flows of capital, information, and trade also makes possible a range of unintended cross-border flows, as growing numbers of traffickers, smugglers, and even governments now make money off the backs of women. . . . Women infuse cash into the economies of deeply indebted countries and into the pockets of "entrepreneurs" who have seen other opportunities vanish. (Sassen 2002:273)

Sassen (2002) refers to these complex interdependent networks of workers and traders as survival circuits. These new labor dynamics have originated in the northern hemisphere but call ever-greater numbers of migrants, especially women, from the southern hemisphere. These women either willingly enter or are forced into labor in the factories, offices, or homes of the most affluent businesses or families, for the lowest compensation and under the least secure circumstances. Even in the case of crafts advertised as "handmade," the goods are most often made by women's and children's hands.

Yet some women manage to thrive in rapidly changing global political economies. As structural adjustment policies (e.g., currency devaluations) reduced the size of and pay in the public sector that many highly educated women in Africa had sought to enter, some of those same women moved into the informal economy. There they can often make substantial incomes as traders in global consumer goods such as clothing and decorative household items. For example, Darkwah (2009) offers the example of Afrariwaa, a 31-year-old woman with a university degree who has elected to establish herself in a small business

> because trading provides her with both flexibility and more money than she would receive in the formal sector. She sets her own hours, she does not have to answer to anybody if she feels too tired or sick to show up at work at the appointed time and, besides, trading at the market pays much more than she ever made working it the formal sector. As she put it, "What more could one ask for?" (P. 44)

Domestic Employment in Global Context

As argued throughout this book, globalization is about more than the flow of economic, political, and other capital across national borders. Globalization is about the fields, factories, homes, and other locations in which employment takes place, as well as the quality of work processes and surrounding family and other social relationships.

The legacies of slavery, with the violent emigration and subsequent forced employment in masters' households, should make even a national analysis of contemporary domestic work resonate with globalists. Beyond slavery, research has examined paid domestic work by indigenous female workers in the United States, with particular attention to the intersections of race and social class, family and work. (See Dill's, 1994, research on African American women's employment and Glenn's, 1986, analysis of the lives of Japanese American women across three generations of domestic employment.)

The 1970s and 1980s saw a surge in interest by historians, sociologists, and other social scientists in the scholarly examination of housework. Lopata (1971), Oakley (1974), Strasser (1982), and others made visible and problematized work performed in the home, largely by women, as domestic labor. Later, in *The Second Shift* and *The Time Bind*, Hochschild (1989, 1997) and others took our understanding of housework beyond energy expended to accomplish tasks in the home to encompass the emotional labor that consumes so much domestic energy.

By the 1990s, Romero (1992) and others were systematically examining the lives of maids and other domestic employees. In *Maid in the U.S.A.*, Romero argued that domestic work has not been defined as employment primarily because such labor takes place in a private home, a place associated with labor expended out of love for someone else's family members. In *Doméstica: Immigrant Women Cleaning and Caring in the Shadows of Affluence,* Hondagneu-Sotelo (2001) argued that "paid domestic work is distinctive not in being the worst job of all, but in being regarded as something other than employment" (p. 9).

Other researchers have studied the lives of domestic workers in other Western countries (see, for example, Bakan and Stasiulis's 1997 compendium on studies of foreign domestic workers in Canada). Most recently, and with increasing frequency, scholars have been investigating the social, political, and economic context of transnational, migrant domestic workers. For example, Gamburd (2000) has studied migrant Sri Lankan domestic workers, Constable (2002) has studied Filipina domestic workers in Hong Kong, and Parreñas (2001) has studied Filipina domestic workers around the world.

Women involved in transnational domestic employment become relatively invisible in the global economy as they leave their own families and households in less-developed countries to travel to more-developed countries to work in the households of other, more affluent women. However, these women have a critical place in the expansion of global capitalism (Chang 2000). Dramatic improvements in the material quality of life in places such as Southern Europe (Greece, Italy, and Spain) have made it possible for families in those countries to hire live-in or hourly workers to execute their cooking, cleaning, child care, and other domestic tasks. The same accelerating national quality of life makes First World countries attractive destinations for women seeking to earn higher wages than they could earn at home, even if it means leaving behind their own children, kin, and family responsibilities (Anderson 2000).

The status of migrant domestic workers—wherever they might live—depends not only on their day-to-day relations with their employers but also on their interface with the policies of the country in which they reside. The security of a migrant worker's status in her adopted country is dependent on her maintaining employment in collaboration with immigration, employment, citizenship, and other policies administered by national governments, but is mediated through her employer. Thus, the migrant domestic worker can find herself in a condition that enforces dependence on her employer and can "institutionalize master/mistress–servant relations" (Anderson 2000:196).

National governments vary in how involved they become in recruiting and regulating domestic workers. For example, the United States has a market-driven, laissez-faire approach to the recruitment and regulation of immigrant domestic workers. On the other hand, some governments (e.g., Canada, Hong Kong) formally participate in establishing government-regulated, contract labor programs that define the recruitment and working circumstances of migrant workers. These different strategies can determine, for example, the legal parameters of hours, wages, benefits, and other conditions of employment, as well as the consequences (including deportation) if the worker ceases to be employed, whether by decision of her employer or because the worker decides to leave an abusive or unjust work environment (Hondagneu-Sotelo 2001).

In an intriguing analysis of migrant domestic workforce issues in Italy in the last decades of the 20th century, Andall (2004) found that the dominant ideology shaping domestic/employer relations in that country up through the early 1970s envisioned the domestic worker not as an employee but as an integral part of the family contributing to family well-being. That point of view may have been romantically one-sided, expressing a rationalization for the vested interest of the status quo. By the 1970s, domestic workers were becoming less willing to reside in their employers' homes, increasingly preferring to work hourly and live away from their employers' households.

According to Andall (2004), virtually all (90 percent) African and Asian migrant women in Italy in the early 1980s were employed in private-household domestic service. However, by the mid-1980s the Italian government no longer issued permits for persons wishing to enter Italy for domestic work. At the same time, the Italian government extended amnesty to certain undocumented immigrants. In 1990, another amnesty attempted to regularize large numbers of Filipino and North African immigrants, most of whom, among females, were domestic workers. As a consequence, by early 1993, the majority of non-European Union female workers granted employment permits in Italy were domestic workers.

Such policy shifts in affluent societies—especially societies like that in Italy, with increasing labor force participation of indigenous women— seriously challenge demand for and supply of potential live-in and even hourly domestic workers. For example, in 1996, the Italian government formalized policies through which illegal immigrants could be deported unless their employers testified that the workers had been in their hire for 4 months and agreed to pay social insurance contributions for the workers in advance. This policy resulted in documentation of and issuance of work permits to some of the estimated 25 percent of Italy's undocumented foreign population that was working illegally at the time (Andall 2004).

Subsequent government policies in Italy and elsewhere have ensured that migrant women workers remain relegated to and dependent on national domestic labor market policies. But supranational organizations also shape domestic employment and care work—particularly in the lives of women—in dramatic ways. Organizations such as the European Union, the International Monetary Fund, and the World Bank hold authority that transcends that of any single national government. As such, these organizations have the potential to alter dramatically the progression of opportunities, especially for women and their families. For example, Zimmerman, Litt, and Bose (2006b) discuss the role of structural adjustment policies established by the International Monetary Fund with the intent of ensuring that Third World nations reduce their foreign debt balance. Such policies often require the debtor nation to reduce national deficits by curtailing public spending on such services as education and health. Curtailments in social welfare spending shift the onus for social welfare back to the family and into the laps of women. Under these kinds of structural adjustments, girls and women can be forced out of education and driven from the labor force to assume education, health, and other caregiving functions for their families.

A global political economy makes the most vulnerable workers hostage to their employers through complicit state policies. The benefits to more affluent society are enormous. Women are more able to accept substantial, meaningful employment outside the home. While someone else negotiates traditional female tasks of family life, couples need not struggle over domestic gender roles. Women may be less mindful of the tensions between public and private spheres.

Immigrant women have streamed into the United States and other more-developed countries at times when the demand for their services has exploded. However, capitalism often carries forward both racist and patriarchal imperialist traditions. Immigrants are periodically met by waves of "racialized xenophobia" (Hondagneu-Sotelo 2001:18), which has resulted in various attempts to disenfranchise immigrants and their children through denial of education, health, and other basic social benefits and insistence on "English-only" initiatives in civic institutions. Yet they bear these costs because of the promise of very real financial gain.

Thus, the two largest employment fields for immigrant women from the Third World newly arrived to a First World society are domestic labor in private households and prostitution (Anderson 2000). Globally, the demand for cheap immigrant labor continues to grow. Worldwide, women are employed in some of the worst jobs available in terms of compensation and conditions, safety and security. The expected demand for cheap labor by women in countries such as Canada, the United States, Northern and Western Europe, industrialized Asia, and the oil-rich Middle East will far exceed the expected supply coming from such predictable Third World regions as the Caribbean, Mexico, Central and South America, Indonesia, the Philippines, Sri Lanka, and Eastern Europe (Hondagneu-Sotelo 2001). Richmond (1994) has called the international division of reproductive labor a gendered version of global apartheid. Not only the poorest women but also middle-class, highly educated women may choose transnational domestic employment at higher wage rates abroad. Gross inequalities among national economies create a type of "talent drain" in counties that can ill afford to lose their best-educated women (Parreñas 2000).

These changes in the process of social reproduction constitute nothing short of a "new world domestic order" (Hondagneu-Sotelo 2001). Earlier scholars (e.g., Chaplin 1978; Coser 1973) had inaccurately predicted that the commodification and fragmentation of household tasks and the introduction of new household technologies accompanying societal modernization and industrialization would lead to a general decline in domestic service. However, the earlier scholars (Hondagneu-Sotelo, 2001, notes that they are men) failed to predict the extent to which household tasks and the time spent on them could increase (e.g., see Vanek 1974) and standards accelerate (e.g., see Cowan 1983), thereby ensuring that housework tasks are never completed to satisfaction. Similarly, the commercialization of child care in First World countries has exacerbated the stigma attached to having children cared for out of home while ensuring that the labor force that fills that commercial need remains among the poorest compensated (Clarke-Stewart 1993; Wrigley 1995).

Implications of Transnational Employment for Family Dynamics

Thus, transnational employment has potent consequences in the lives of the women and men who pursue work across national borders, as well as for the economies their labor helps support. Labor migration quite often reduces the risk of poverty for immigrant families, especially for immigrants who can move beyond gateway cities, those border locations where other immigrants are concentrated, and into the broader society. For example, research by Crowley, Lichter, and Qian (2006) found much lower rates of poverty among Mexican immigrant families who lived outside the southwestern United States.

However, migration challenges families regarding finances, physical and mental health, language and culture, and legal and documentation issues (Dalla and Christensen 2005; Dalla et al. 2004; Vélez-Ibáñez 2004). Immigrant families that live an itinerant existence, such as Latino farmworkers in the United States who move to follow agricultural seasons, are particularly vulnerable. Problems associated with transitory residence include securing reliable, quality educational experiences for the children in the family (Roeder and Millard 2000; Rothenberg 1998), as well as health and other services, to say nothing of social associations enhanced by living in a fixed location over time. Yet, a small body of research suggests that even the most disadvantaged migrant families exhibit a level of resiliency, as indicated by their overall life satisfaction, commitment to an ethic of hard work, sense of optimism regarding their opportunity for social mobility (however gradual), and an abiding sense of the centrality of family in their lives (Parra-Cardona et al. 2006).

This kind of transnational employment also shapes family formation and family structure. Split household migration has been examined for Chinese (Glenn 1986), Italian (Foner 2000), Polish (Thomas and Znaniecki 1927), and other families migrating to the United States in the early part of the 20th century, and more recently for families immigrating from Mexico (Hondagneu-Sotelo 2001). An interesting body of research explores the impact of wives' migration from Taiwan to the United States while their husbands remain in Taiwan and send remittances to support their wives and children in the United States (Chee 2005). The research confirms that, at the most basic level, the quality of transnational family life is affected by practical considerations such as having sufficient financial resources to afford the costs associated with maintaining contact, including transportation costs such as airfare and communication technologies such as long-distance telephone calls.

Members of transnational families not only have multiple places of residence but also have more complex issues of identity and loyalty than do families whose members reside in one national space and interact in closer time frames. Transnational families may experience prejudice and discrimination on the part of the host society. They may be ghettoized, assigned to live and work in the least desirable areas. All the while, they may be pressured to hide or deny their religion, language, and other cultural heritage in order to assimilate.

Globalization complicates the transfer of wages from labor (and other factors of production, including capital) and multiplies the locations of consumption spending by households. Wages earned by a family member in one location must be transmitted across time and space—often with considerable additional time and expense—to other family members in another location. For the transnational family, consumption spending occurs in at least two locations. Not only the family remaining behind but also the family member having relocated for transnational employment must engage in consumption spending in order to survive.

Further, this globalized pattern of exchanging wages for consumption spending places both the sender and the receiver in conditions of increased uncertainty and risk. Postal or other systems of remittance can be variable, unpredictable, and unregulated. If a mother working in Europe sends school clothes to her children living in Africa, how confident can she be that these remittances will reach them undamaged in a timely manner, or at all? If her remittances or gifts do not reach her family, she has little or no recourse.

In addition to negotiating the procedures for establishing patterns of remittances involving transfers of monetary units as well as goods purchased in the adopted country and sent to family members in the home country, transnational families must also discuss expectations of rights and responsibilities of sender and receiver. Extensive kin obligations and lack of direct experience with wage and other financial norms, higher costs of living, and other economic realities in the adopted country create the potential for feelings of misunderstanding, mistrust, and even exploitation in families with even the best intentions.

Transnational Employment and Gender Roles

Women's greater participation in the transnational labor force cannot help but change family dynamics, particularly in the area of gender roles. At least in Western industrial societies, women's increased participation in the labor force has been linked to new life patterns, including some shifts in the division of labor between men and women in the home. Parenthood has been a major force in gender differences in time allocation regarding housework, a pattern especially marked in Australia and the United States in comparison with Denmark, France, and Italy (Craig and Mullan 2010). However, this may be changing. A study comparing the division of labor by gender in Swedish households found that in 1990 parenthood reinforced traditional roles. By 2000, parenthood affected women and men in more similar ways (Dribe and Stanfors 2009). Women's participation in the labor force—whether domestic or transnational—yields less traditional gender roles in the family while providing increased economic and often social, political, and cultural capital for women.

Giele and Holst (2004) have described a series of evolutionary social changes—adaptive upgrading, technological innovation, and new patterns of use of time, space, information, material, and human resources—associated with women's increased labor force participation. As goal differentiation expands in the form of wider role options for men and women, they exercise more individualized self-determination, rather than lockstep conformity to traditional age, sex, and other social ascriptors. Meanwhile, in efforts to attend to macrosocial issues of inclusion and integration, societies must coordinate new rules and policies regarding gender equity around work and family. Finally, as society becomes more complex and specialized, social values are reconceptualized to facilitate better integration of economic productivity and caregiving functions.

Giele and Holst's (2004) theory resonates with structural functional theory, including Parsons' (1966) and Johnson's (1989) paradigms linking adaptive upgrading of resources and facilities, goal differentiation of roles within groups, integration and inclusion at the institutional level, and value generalization at the cultural level. This theory predicts that, as men's and women's gender patterns converge (with more women not only in the labor force but also in positions traditionally held by men), employment structures and national policies will evolve toward greater flexibility in order to facilitate women's employment. While women may experience overload as they try to manage their work–family roles, men's and women's breadwinning roles will become increasingly interdependent. Couples and corporations will create new strategies to facilitate evolving dual work and family roles (Giele and Holst 2004).

In such a social system, the new frontier for women—employment—will be accompanied by a new frontier for men—caregiving. Giele's (2004) research indicates that women and men already on these new frontiers differ from their more traditional peers on identity, goals and ambitions, social networks, and strategies for blending education, work, and family life. In particular, these modern work-oriented women and the new care-oriented men are more likely to seek to blend work and care roles. Giele's interviews with married dual-career mothers and homemakers confirm existing research on men who are full-time breadwinners and those who reject stereotypical male roles in Western Europe and the United States. The individuals who were the most innovative in restructuring gender roles had distinctive personal identities, received approval from family and peers, were women with career ambitions and men with intimacy ambitions, and were resourceful and inventive in developing practical means to accomplishing their desired life patterns.

Policies that support such changes in the traditional gender contract include permitting work to occur in more time- and space-flexible environments. Specific practices may include the inclusion of part-time and flex-time work schedules, telecommuting, family leave and other provisions for time away from work, and early retirement, career shifts, reentry, and other shifts in employment patterns. Giele and Holst (2004) acknowledge that these national differences do not just reflect national or regional variations in societal values but also are the result of market forces, societal differences in work–family culture, and differences in social welfare establishments as institutionalized in policies surrounding family income support, child care, and gender.

Women's participation in the labor force does not inevitably result in egalitarian work and family policies at the national level. Some social democratic countries, such as Denmark, Finland, Norway, and Sweden, all with high female labor force participation, have institutionalized national policies that facilitate the blending of parental time with children and a gender-egalitarian division of labor. These policies address family leave, working-time regulations, early childhood education, and family care for both female and male workers. However, even today, most First World countries, including not only conservative countries of continental Europe such as Belgium, France, Germany, and the Netherlands but also, most notably, liberal countries with high female labor force participation, including the United Kingdom and the United States, have not implemented national policies that support egalitarian gender roles (Gornick and Meyers 2004).

Further, the trickle-down from women's employment to their greater status and power in the family and in the broader society can be slow. Cross-nationally, gender remains the strongest predictor of time spent in household labor (Kroska 2004), as well as the type of household tasks performed (Gupta 1999). Using data from the International Social Survey Program, Greenstein (2006) has documented that national context serves as a comparative reference in married women's determinations of fairness in the division of household labor. Women in nations with the highest levels of gender equity experience the greatest perception of unfairness when household labor is unequally distributed.

Even with the increasing participation of women in the transnational labor force, women continue to represent the majority (70 percent) of the world's poor. Furthermore, the percentage of women in rural areas around the world who are poor is increasing. Lower educational attainment contributes significantly to the persistent poverty among females worldwide. Almost two thirds of the illiterate of the world are women. Almost two thirds of girl children have no access to primary education. Because fully one third of families around the world are headed by women, it comes as no surprise that women and their dependents make up such a significant portion of the global poor (Butron 2001).

While women constitute one third of the world's paid labor force, they work two thirds of the hours for less than 10 percent of the wages (Butron 2001). Sørenson (2004) has calculated an economic dependence score using the difference between the husband's and the wife's earnings divided by the couples' earnings together. Even though dependency variations across and even within more-developed societies are conspicuous,[1] the most equitable economic relations between spouses continue to exist in the most developed societies.

Much like the American women described in Hochschild's (1989) *Second Shift,* women from Third World societies often bear the burden of a "stalled revolution" in which gender ideology in the family has not kept pace with the realities of women's employment. These women increasingly work outside the home, yet their husbands and other family members, and society in general, retain the expectation that these women will continue to fulfill the traditional responsibilities for hearth and home. National leaders may even issue public statements opposing migrant women's employment abroad. The mass media may provide sensationalized accounts of the horrible consequences of absent mothers who have "abandoned" their children. Thus, women who take contract work to secure higher wages and to assist in providing a better quality of life for their children are often blamed and stigmatized as selfish, neglectful mothers who have deserted their children and families. Such stigma occurs in spite of the fact that societies such as the Philippines are increasingly dependent on the wages sent home by migrant workers. In 1997, migrant workers, the majority of them women, contributed nearly $7 billion

---

[1]Ranging from −1 to 1, a score of −1 indicates the woman has no earnings and is completely earning dependent on the man. A score of 1 indicates the man has no earnings and is completely earning dependent on the woman. A score of 0 indicates perfect earnings equality between the man and the woman. The mean dependence score in Nordic countries is considerably lower than in other European countries and the United States. For example, the mean dependency measures in Finland and the Netherlands were 0.15 in 1995 and 0.063 in 1991, respectively. The mean dependency score in the Netherlands in 1991 was the same as the mean score in the United States in 1970. Further, the scores of African American women are considerably lower than those of other American women, reflecting the historical need for African American women's employment alongside the lower wages of African American men (Sørenson 2004).

to the Philippine economy, thus constituting that country's largest source of foreign currency (Parreñas 2002:41).

In conclusion, the contemporary situation of migrant workers and the implications for family continuity differ from those of previous migrant streams. Whereas in the past migrants were unlikely to return to their home countries (with women perhaps less likely than men to return), migrant workers today are often impeded from establishing a permanent residence in their adopted countries by rigid immigration policies there (Ehrenreich and Hochschild 2002). Migrant workers today are not only less likely to establish reunited homes for their families in their adopted countries, but they may be more likely to embark on a life of repeat passages between their adopted countries and households and those of their home societies and families. Such workers are transient, modern-day indentured servants who can be repatriated at economic will of the adopted country, thus remaining outsiders to the civic, economic, social, and other rights and responsibilities of their adopted countries (Huang and Yeoh 1996). These burdens are borne by individual migrants, legal as well as illegal, and their families.

Care Work

One of the most pressing consequences of transnational employment is the extent to which care work comes to be bound into global capitalist systems that impact not only First and Third World economies but also First and Third World families. Care workers are usually women who migrate to more affluent societies. These women leave behind their own families, not only to work in domestic employment but also to extend their services to emotional, expressive care work in the households of families in other societies. In this section I explore those patterns of care work and the resultant global care chains that can so dramatically impact the migrant women and their families.

In a report titled *Globalization With a Human Face*, the United Nations (1999b) identified four sources of caring labor: women's unpaid labor, men's unpaid labor, private market labor, and public services. Providing care may be guided by economic compensation but also by bonds of affection, a sense of altruism, or norms of obligation. Even when provided by non-kin who are compensated financially for their efforts, care work often involves love and emotional reciprocity. As an example of the complexities of such a relationship, see Tung's (2000) work on Filipina women as live-in home health care workers. Zimmerman et al. (2006a) have articulated these intricacies of the value of care work for individuals and societies.

All of us depend on the care work of others. The social value given to care work . . . has to do with societal arrangements such as how time for care work is allocated, whether care work is compensated, how care work fits with paid employment, and how care work is divided by gender. Social policy regimes govern these matters. Thus, we can say that care work is socially constructed in relation to communities, nations, and (increasingly) supranational organizations. (P. 300)

This care work is highly gendered. Research indicates that men's participation in housework and child care is related to national, social contexts. The level of women's employment (as indicated by employment hours) and social policies, including parental leave (and men's eligibility for parental leave), influences men's adherence to gender ideologies and norms, the "terms of bargaining" men and women employ to arrive at gender specializations in the family, and men's actual participation in housework and child care (Hook 2006). Chart (2000) reflects that these realignments in gender roles may even be creating a "crisis of masculinity," at least for some men. Based on interviews with 80 low-income men in a northwestern province of Costa Rica, Chart found that changes in labor markets, legislation, and social policy were undermining the traditional bases of family power and identity for men.

Furthermore, women and those for whom they care experience ambivalence regarding care work. Care work can exemplify conflicts between norms and cultural beliefs around not only gender ideology but also filial obligation and the parent–child bond. For example, a study of care work performed by Japanese women for their aging parents and in-laws found that norms about care work in that society create conflicting demands. Japanese women are torn among caring for parents, caring for in-laws, and changing expectations for women (Lee 2010). Traditional family culture in Asian societies (e.g., China, Taiwan) continues to require that a couple live with the husband's parents (patrilineal coresidence) and care for them as they age. Furthermore, even economic development does not appear to result in less-traditional family culture, although couples with greater personal economic resources may be able to deviate from that tradition (Chu, Xie, and Yu 2011).

Ehrenreich and Hochschild's (2002) edited volume details the extent to which women's nondomestic labor is intimately bound with their domestic lives. Girls and women play dominant and critical roles in providing care for families and in communities worldwide. The most-developed societies attract a bountiful supply of women who will work at low wages to perform care work not only for children but also for elders and other dependents requiring care in the home. As in the case of domestic labor, care work is not only gendered but manifests the complex and too often oppressive relationships among labor and the welfare state.

According to *Globalization With a Human Face* (United Nations 1999b), in a chapter aptly titled "The Invisible Heart," "globalization is putting a squeeze on care and caring labor" by changing patterns of time usage, challenging public spending on care, and encouraging a tendency for care labor to be low-wage labor (p. 77). Globalization impacts care and, consequently, human development in at least three ways. First, globalization encourages a shift in women's roles from domestic caregiving to labor force participation while at the same time leading to the feminization of labor in home work, telework, and part-time work in particular. Second, the increased scope, speed, and size of markets associated with globalization tend to disconnect markets from local communities, resulting in greater reliance on families at the time families are undergoing dramatic demographic and economic changes and instabilities. Third, the same expansion of markets devalues self-sacrifice in caring for others.

By recognizing that economic and social development involves more than considerations of income, education, health, and empowerment and that development also involves social reproduction (i.e., care), the United Nations explicitly acknowledges the value of experiences that contribute to bonding among individuals in families. The solution to the growing dilemma of care and care labor, the United Nations posits, lies in redistributing the costs and responsibilities of care across families, nations, and the private sector.

Many contemporary societies are facing a care work crisis (Meyer 2000). Hancock (2002) has described the "care crunch" facing one First World society, Australia, today. In Australia, economic globalization has resulted not only in profound shifts in labor markets but also in deep individual uncertainty about employment and financial security. At the same time, an aging population and increasing divorce rates signal major demographic shifts. These forces, when coupled with adherence to traditional assumptions about the gendered nature of family roles, are compromising Australian families' ability to care for their members.

Some organizations, such as the International Labour Organization, have concluded that the way to provide for sufficient care labor in a society is to ensure that work is adequately compensated, that the work occurs within the context of regulatory guidelines to ensure competence and skill of the workforce, and that regulatory standards are enforced (Standing 2001). However, such an agenda presents a serious challenge, given contemporary capitalist agenda with regard to minimizing wages, repelling unionization, and curtailing benefits across and within categories of workers. Feminist economists, such as Barker and Feiner (2004), advocate social policies that will ensure that both familial and societal care needs are met. Ironically, doing so may well be at the expense of conventional goals of full employment, for full employment means that no one is available for unpaid care labor.

Global Care Chains

Globalization has resulted in the commoditization of care, as care work has been rationalized and bureaucratized so as to package it better for sale in capitalist economic systems. Increasingly, affluent, First World consumers can purchase for low wages the specified services that heretofore would have been provided in private venues bound by kin obligation, if not affection. Such regulated care is characterized by fragmentation and impersonality and a system of regulation that portends to oppress the worker deeply (Zimmerman et al. 2006b).

Global care chains are personal networks based on paid or unpaid caregiving work between people across national borders. These chains usually begin in a poor country (or in the rural area within a poor country) and terminate in a rich country (or in the urban area within a poor country). As such, care chains vary in their origination and destination (e.g., from poor country to wealthy country, from poor country to slightly less poor country). They also vary in the number and strength of links in the chain. One example is the eldest daughter in a family in the Second or Third World looking after her younger brothers and sisters. Meanwhile, her mother, a migrant worker, works as a nanny looking after another woman's children (Beck-Gernsheim, Butler, and Puigvert 2001:68). Figure 5.1 provides another, graphic, illustration of a global care chain.

Figure 5.1   Illustration of a Global Care Chain

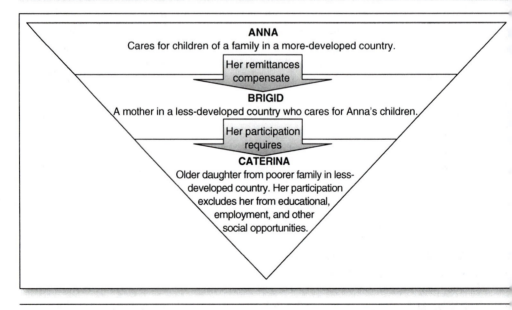

SOURCE: Based on concepts from A. R. Hochschild (2000). "Global Care Chains and Emotional Surplus Value." Pp. 130–147 in *On the Edge: Living with Global Capitalism*, edited by W. Hutton and A. Giddens. London, UK: Jonathan Cape. Original figure designed by Martin C. Doyle.

In the essay that follows this chapter, Dreby recounts the life of Paula Rodriguez, a mother of two children who manages successive migrations between Mexico and New Jersey. Part of Paula's story includes elements of such a global care chain, as Paula sends remittances to her brother and his wife, who must hire someone to care for Paula's children left behind.

Hochschild (2001) has written that care work has become a service to be bought and sold and that women are willing to migrate and leave behind their own families in order to pursue this form of employment These women do so in order to ensure higher wages than they might earn at home, with, perhaps, greater security if they can leap over currency devaluations, business failures, and other uncertainties of their home countries. At the same time, however, they may be replacing anxieties surrounding economic well-being with insecurities regarding time and space away from kith and kin.

However, the exodus of women leaves the less-developed world with a global care deficit, a shortage of women to perform the very same functions for their own families in their own countries (Zimmerman et al. 2006b). These deficits also can arise from new care needs that grow out of childbirth, illness, or disability, or out of epidemics, natural disasters, or war. Such deficits also can develop when care labor shortages develop as a result of caregiver disability, illness, or other conditions, or from societal-level shifts involving female employment outside the home or caregiver emigration.

In Chapter 2, I described the growing care crisis associated with the HIV/AIDS pandemic in certain African countries. Upton (2003) found such a case in Botswana. With one of the highest rates of HIV infection in the world, deaths among working-age adults have orphaned large numbers of children, creating a serious shortage in healthy adults who can provide for their children. The morbidity and mortality wrought by HIV/AIDS also have seriously compromised the traditional fostering system in which women could rely on extended kin for support in caring for their children.

Regardless of the cause, global shifts in care work inevitably place females as caregivers in their own countries in shorter supply. However, deficits involving the movement of females from the domestic sphere are sometimes at the explicit initiative of First World and supranational interests. Zimmerman et al. (2006b) cite the case of the recruitment of African nurses to the United Kingdom from certain African countries, leaving those African countries—some of which are battling the HIV/AIDS pandemic—with a critical shortage of trained health care workers. In a type of medical "brain drain," 43 percent of Liberian doctors now work in North America ("The Future of Mobility" 2011).

These global care chains may present dilemmas for middle-class parents, as well as for the women who care for their children (Wrigley 1995). The relationships between care workers and their child, elder, or disabled charges are, under any circumstance, complicated ones. Karner's (1998) research on workers providing homecare for the elderly suggests that care laborers who care for other families' dependents can come to be seen as fictive kin and that such relationships, when constructed appropriately, can enable a family member (e.g., the elder) to maintain a sense of the norm of kin providing care. In a parallel fashion, such respite-care workers also derive positive feelings from their work. Authentic expressive bonds between employee care providers and individuals receiving such care and their families should not be dismissed. As Hochschild (2000) argues, "just as global capitalism . . . creates a Third World supply of mothering, so it creates a First World demand for it" (p. 140).

Women's role in care work is at the very center of global dynamics that weave together gender, race, and class; migration, citizenship, and social control; the changing meaning of motherhood; and new constructions of care work and care workers' lives (Zimmerman et al. 2006a). In the following section, I examine the effects of global care chains on transnational parenting.

Transnational Parenting

The concept of networks, linkages, "circles of care" (Abel and Nelson 1990), or global care chains (Hochschild 2000)—systems whereby women care for the children of others while their own children are cared for by women of even lower occupational (and wage) status—is not new. What is new is the extent to which such care chains are now global. Parents participating in transnational labor markets are often doing so in order to provide their families with economic resources that translate into a higher material standard of living and dramatically greater educational, medical, and other quality of life. Does spacial and temporal distance from parent or parents challenge a child's physical or emotional well-being and development in ways that compromise the very advantages the transnational parent seeks to provide?

Third World children in these global care chains should not be described as abandoned or neglected by virtue of the absence of the parent. Many of these children live with either their maternal grandmothers or with aunts or other kin. Such practical arrangements are common among Mexican (Dreby 2006) and other Central American domestic workers in California (Hondagneu-Sotelo and Avila 1997). Furthermore, migrant couples have reported satisfaction with the care their children were receiving and positive relationships with their children's caregivers at home (Dreby 2006). Single mothers who migrate and do not have the option of maternal grandmother care may sometimes place their children with a former husband, the children's father, or with other kin. (Perhaps more scholars should employ another term, such as Grochowski's, 2000, concept of "strategic living communities," to refer to the complex web of family networks across borders.)

Transnational contact between parents and their children can reinforce and strengthen family bonds. Parents and children write letters, telephone, and, increasingly, send e-mail messages to one another. Besides sending portions of their wages home, parents may send clothing, food, medical and school supplies, and other goods home to the family, both on a regular basis and for special holidays and events such as birthdays (Cohen 2000).

Historically, men have been the ones to leave families behind. Children have experienced periodic father absences because of men's occupational demands, military service, or other situations that take them from home, as well as migrant wage labor or forging the path for later immigration of other family members. *Wage fathers* are men who leave families for long periods of time to secure employment (Roopnarine and Gielen 2005). Gielen (1993) has described such work–family patterns for Caribbean men who migrate to (and across) the United States for seasonal agricultural work, Egyptian men who pursue employment in oil industries elsewhere in the Middle East, and Indian men who leave rural for urban areas of greater employment opportunity. These situations deposit greater child-care, household, and other family burdens on women and the older generation left behind.

Dreby (2006) has also examined the impact of transnational fathering on children, fathers, and families, using interviews not only with the adult parents but also with the children, often left home in Mexico. She found that Mexican transnational fathers and mothers responded to the absence from their children in similar ways, by maintaining contact through regular communication with their children and gifting or (the preferred) sending money. However, traditional Mexican gender ideologies emphasize the father's role as financial provider and the mother's role as daily caregiver. Furthermore, these gendered ideologies are connected with honor. A man's migration to increase economic resources for his family is consistent with traditional male gender roles and brings honor. On the other hand, a woman's migration for the same reasons compromises traditional female gender roles and, therefore, a woman's honor.

Not surprisingly, then, Dreby (2006) found that fathers were more likely to lose contact with their children when unable to deliver on their financial obligations. One father reported that he would call his children only when he could give them a money order number for collection. Dreby found that migrant mothers' contact with their children is not dependent on financial remittance but, rather, focuses on the emotional care work they provide for their children, even long distance. The mothers in Dreby's research expressed guilt for leaving their children; fathers almost never did.

Because of the gendered construction of mothering, concerns involving the effects of transnational parenting most often focus on the impact of the absent mother. Transnational mothering is said to "disrupt the notion of family in one place" as women improvise new parenting structures in order to provide for their children and themselves (Hondagneu-Sotelo and Avila 1997:567). These migrant mothers relinquish expectations of living with and relating to their children in a shared space but nonetheless speak of the pain of physical separation from their children (Hondagneu-Sotelo and Avila 1997). Such forms of mothering result from economic forces in the home country, increasingly as a result of globalization.

Once again, gender shapes—and potentially destabilizes even further—the impact of globalization on families. Thus, parents are compromised in their abilities and satisfaction as parents by traditional gender roles. In Dreby's (2006) words: "If transnational fathers fail when they do not send money, transnational mothers fail when their emotional attentions are diverted elsewhere" (p. 52). In fact, the most common pattern for Mexican families has been and remains to be for the father to migrate to the United States, leaving behind his wife and children. Some transnational families begin this way, with the father later sending for the wife to join him, leaving their children behind. Dreby's research indicates that the latter is sometimes at the initiative of the wife, whose emotional distress leads her to pressure her husband for reunification, even if it means leaving their sometimes young children in the care of others in Mexico.

In spite of the risks involved in transnational employment for families and parenting, research in a wide variety of settings demonstrates that children are remarkably resilient. If shared struggle lends itself to family solidarity, children and parents in transnational families may even gain a deeper respect and appreciation for one another. For example, in research on Caribbean adults in New York whose own mothers had earlier immigrated to the United States without them, Wrigley (1995) found that, while the mothers themselves expressed regret at having left their children behind, these adults expressed understanding that their mothers had made the sacrifice of separation in order to give their children a better life.

Parreñas (2002) interviewed 30 children of migrant mothers, 26 children of migrant fathers, and 13 children with two migrant parents. Her findings indicate that, although these children experienced emotional hardships, they did not perceive their mothers as having abandoned them. Children's hardship was reduced when they were enmeshed in supportive extended kin and communities, had open communication with their migrant parent(s), and they understood their parents' limited financial options that led them to work abroad.

Still, children and parents in transnational families do not have the certain satisfactions of everyday/everynight interactions with one another. Although the children in Dreby's (2006) study were by no means abandoned (most were being cared for by their maternal grandmothers), the children—especially older children—revealed emotional distress in the form of difficulty concentrating in school and preoccupation with migrating to join their parents.

Parental absence—especially absence not sustained by conscientious surrogate parenting with the quality of support, communication, and understanding described above—can leave deep wounds. Long periods of physical separation due to a parent's migrant work situation, a parent's absence during war, or other situations can contribute to unfamiliarity, insecurity, and a sense on the part of the child of the parent's indifference. One of the participants in Parreñas's (2002) study described her sense of longing at being separated from her mother:

> There are times when I want to call her, speak to her, cry to her, and I cannot. . . . The only thing I can do is write to her. And I cannot cry through the e-mails and sometimes I just want to cry on her shoulder. (P. 42)

Parents also pay a price for such absences. Some mothers poignantly recount the pain of separation and the reminders that, while they are caring for other people's children, their children are far away.

> When the girl that I take care of calls her mother "Mama," my heart jumps all the time because my children also call me "Mama." I feel the gap caused by our physical separation especially in the morning, when I pack [her] lunch, because that's what I used to do for my children. . . . I begin thinking that this hour I should be taking care of my very own children and not someone else's. . . . The work that I do here is done for my family, but the problem is they are not close to me but are far away in the Philippines. . . . Some days, I just start crying when I am sweeping the floor because I am thinking about my children in the Philippines. Sometimes, when I receive a letter from my children telling me that they are sick, I look up out the window and ask the Lord to look after them and make sure they get better even without me around to care after them. [Starts crying.] If I had wings, I would fly home to my children. Just for a moment, to see my children and take care of their needs, help them, then fly back over here to continue my work. (Parreñas 2002:41–2)

In speaking of her longing for her own children, one woman, a Filipina domestic worker living in Canada, describes herself as "bursting out of loneliness" (Cohen 2000:82).

Hochschild (2001) believes that emotional labor is transmitted along the global care chain. This results in deficits of care when women make positive emotional investments in the children and families of their employers, to the emotional disadvantage of their own at home. Parreñas (2001) refers to this transference of motherly affection from own to employer's children as "displaced mothering" or "diverted mothering." In fact, a criticism of Hochschild's presentation of global care chains is the presumption that mothers in such chains have a finite amount of maternal care that, once expended on another's children, leaves her with little emotional labor to extend to her own children. Zimmerman et al. (2006b) challenge the assumption of such a fixed pool of maternal affection that invariably disadvantages a woman's own children. Instead, they cite research (e.g., Litt 2000) that supports the idea that, first, the children migrant women leave behind are often cared for in an enmeshed kinship group in which the children experience family affection from other family members. Second, Zimmerman et al. argue that the affection for the children of one's employer and one's own children is qualitatively different: "While domestic workers and nannies do form meaningful attachments to their employers' children, these feelings of 'love' in most situations cannot be equated with (or exchanged for) the attachment they have for their own children" (Pp. 19–20).

National governments play a part in risking or assisting the quality of transnational parent–child relationships. Cohen (2000) is critical of the role of governments, through immigration and labor policies, in shaping maladjustment among families in which the mother is a migrant domestic work. Using in-depth interviews with 21 Filipina domestic workers living and working in Canada, Cohen concluded that women's inability to immigrate with their husbands and children destroyed traditional family roles and created "serfdom-like" work environments that required the maintenance of transnational family relations over long distances for many years. In Canada, workers are allowed to sponsor spouses and children after achieving landed immigrant status, but only after 3 years in-country. Policies of family reunification limit such sponsorship to spouses and children and so neglect to take into account the family bonds with parents and other extended kin, a neglect that Cohen charges is Eurocentric. Further, even once unified, the families often experience tension and conflict (Cohen 2000).

In reading the accounts of children of migrant mothers, I am reminded of the literature, prevalent even in the social-scientific literature through the 1960s, of "maternal deprivation." That literature was premised on beliefs that only the biological mother could provide sustaining love and affection to a child and that the outcome of maternal absence was child maladjustment. Likewise, writing on homes "broken" by divorce emphasizes that nothing can substitute for an intact, complete family composed of a mother and a father. The research on transnational parenting remains sufficiently ambiguous to hasten the call for further research in this area.

Zimmerman et al. (2006b:19) remind us that migrant women and the families they leave behind are not merely passive victims. They argue instead for "the persistence (or transcendence) of love" between absent mothers and their children. Many migrant mothers and their children do maintain ties, and the children may well understand and appreciate the rationale behind their mothers' absences.

> I realize that my mother loves us very much. . . . She would just assure us that whenever we have problems to just call her and tell her. [Pauses] . . . I know it has been more difficult for her than for other mothers. (Parreñas 2002:43)

Edgar (2004) also cautions against viewing these transnational families and individuals as expressively bankrupt. Given the dissemination of global information technologies such as the World Wide Web and economies such as budget airfare, spatially disconnected families may be afforded opportunities to maintain contact across space and time at a level greater than that of any other period in history. Karraker and Grochowski (2012) advocate a resiliency approach to family studies. Such an approach has potential value for the study of work–family linkages among global families in particular. For example, transition from postcommunist society has been difficult for Eastern European families. However, using a multiple case study design, Assay (2003) found that former East German and Romanian families possessed qualities of strong families commonly cited in the literature:

- Commitment to the family
- Ability to grow through challenges
- Spending time together

The demands of economic competition in global capitalism seriously tax the balance between work and family, even among families not participating in transnational employment. Giddens, Duneier, and Appelbaum (2006) note the increasing time spouses and parents spend away from home. Average Americans spend more time at their places of employment and less time on vacation than in the past. Americans also spend more time commuting to and from work, school, and other activities away from home (Karraker and Grochowski 2012), all of which translates into less time with family. The most conspicuous increase in hours away from home has been among the mothers of young children. Children in those families now spend more time in child care away from home than at any other point in history.

Hochschild (1997) believes that such changes are related to global competition. She describes the strategies that companies such as Amerco, a profitable Fortune 500 company at the "thriving core of America's globalizing economy" (p. 16), must use to compete globally. One of the key strategies involves raising productivity while lowering wages, benefits, and job security, and increasing hours on the job. Workers in some societies, including those in many Western European countries, have successfully resisted efforts to increase the paid or, in the case of salaried workers, the unpaid work week. However, such a family-friendly tide in Western Europe may be turning.

For example, in 2005, the French National Assembly voted to relax the 35-hour work week rule, allowing workers to work up to 48 hours a week, the maximum work week permitted by the European Union ("France Relaxes 35-Hour Week Rule" 2005). Families throughout the world face inflationary squeezes as wages fail to keep pace with either productivity or inflation (Greenhouse and Leonhardt 2006). Global integration represented by the increasing presence of low-cost goods from China and a reversal in the traditional pattern of global investment (with relatively poorer nations moving into the worldwide economy as net lenders) makes national controls on inflation more difficult (Andrews 2006). Family members are faced with working more to purchase less, scaling back their material ambitions, or increasing their debt.

Yet, as Hochschild (1997) found in the case of Sweden, globally competitive companies and societies can elect family-friendly or work–family-balanced policies. In Sweden, parents are entitled to 10 days of leave in the first 2 months of their child's life. Also, fathers can take leave at 80 percent pay for the first 14 days and 90 percent pay thereafter to care for a sick child. In response to demands from other members of the European Union, however, Sweden has made some reductions in family benefits for working parents. These efforts have been met with some resistance in Sweden (Hochschild 1997), where grassroots groups such as The Children's Lobby, Euronet: The European Children's Network, and Support Stockings organize on behalf of family-friendly policies.

Globalization changes economic arrangements. Transnational employment thus changes families, shifting the roles of women, children, and the elderly, as well as the very foundations of marriage and parenting.

Summary

In societies around the world, including the most patriarchal (e.g., Algeria, Egypt, Jordan, Morocco, Syria, and Tunisia), women's education is the most influential factor shaping their participation in the labor force. Women's employment is shaped by microlevel factors such as family socioeconomics, care duties, and traditionalism, as well as macrolevel forces such as economic development, labor market structure, and urbanization—all factors shaped by globalization (Spierings, Smits, and Verloo 2010).

This chapter has explored another dimension of employment: transnational employment and the transnational families that contribute to the "shuffling about, splitting, and sometimes disintegration of families" (Bryceson and Vuorela 2002:4). Heymann (2006) describes these families as "forgotten," largely overlooked while globalization progresses at a rapid pace. She seeks to reveal the fissures among families and employers and governments across borders and related issues of parental employment and effects on child health and development, family problems and crises, and other concerns.

The situation of transnational families challenges the equation of family as synonymous with household. While members of transnational families live some or most of the time separated from one another, they also may strive to maintain a sense of family, even across national borders. This chapter has examined the impact of transnational employment as a way in which certain economic and family roles are transferred between less-developed and more-developed societies.

The increasing number of migrant domestic and other household workers participating in complex survival circuits demonstrates a way in which globalization contributes to the growing disparities between families in the Third World and those in the First World. These disparities are enmeshed not only in decisions made by families and their members to seek employment abroad but also in national and supranational economic and political policies that severely limit migrant domestic workers' employment and family options. Furthermore, such changes are profoundly gendered, with the potential to impact not only economic relations between domestic workers and their employers but also between migrant workers and their families. Women's increasing participation in the global workforce has not been accompanied by parallel improvements in the status and power of women in societies or in their families.

Care workers are usually women who migrate to more affluent societies, often leaving behind their own families not only to work in domestic employment but also to extend their services to emotional, expressive care work in the households of families in other societies. Like migrant domestic labor, the global distribution of care work responds to economic and political dynamics between First and Third World societies. As care work has become commoditized and marketed, women have left Third World societies for employment in First World societies. Thus, global care chains ensure that families in more-developed societies can draw on a supply of cheap, expendable labor from societies in the less-developed world, while families in the less-developed world are left with a global care deficit—a shortage of women to perform the same functions for their own families in their own countries.

Transnational parenting imposes particular challenges on families. A body of research suggests that children left behind, as well as their parents, experience emotional and other hardships. However, understanding of the impacts of transnational parenting requires cross-cultural sensitivity to kin and community ties, gender dynamics, and the potential for resiliency.

Clearly, more research is needed to ascertain how global demographics, especially migratory labor patterns, impact families in the face of tremendous economic pressures to compete and perform in an increasingly globalized economy. Further study is needed to assess how families who do not share everyday/everynight life in a common space struggle or thrive, shape identities and communities, relate across the family life cycle and across history, and fit into national and transnational social policy paradigms.

A MIGRANT MOTHER'S STORY

Paula Rodriguez

By Joanna Dreby, PhD

Paula, a heavy woman with kind eyes, grew teary when I first asked her if I could interview her about her two children in Mexico. Regardless, she agreed to the interview, which we scheduled for a Tuesday morning. Since Paula worked two full-time jobs at two different fast-food restaurants, that was her only day off from her 70-hour-per-week work schedule. Walking by a dark-blue sheet that converted part of the living room into an extra bedroom, we sat in the meticulously clean kitchen in the first-floor, two-bedroom apartment of a house by the train tracks in an upscale New Jersey town. At the kitchen table, Paula recounted her story.

Paula came to New Jersey about 5 years ago with the help of her sister. Paula was, and is, an undocumented immigrant. Paula has two children, a boy aged 18 and a girl aged 15. Paula is one of six siblings, all of whom are in the United States. She and her sister live in New Jersey; she has a brother in Queens and three brothers in Texas. The family is originally from a little town outside of a small city in the state of Puebla, Mexico. Paula studied the 6 years of *primaria*, or grammar school, and she didn't work after that—she was an *ama de casa*, a housewife.

Suddenly, Paula started to cry, not profusely but by closing her eyes and squinting. She said she felt ashamed about her past. After taking a moment, Paula explained that she had met the father of her children when she was about 18 years old. When her daughter was only 8 months old, he left her.

She felt embarrassed because he left for no reason. He just went away one day and didn't tell her why.

After her boyfriend left, Paula moved in with her cousin Pedro and his wife Blanca in a nearby city. Pedro and Blanca both worked as schoolteachers, and Paula stayed in their home in exchange for housekeeping duties. The couple had a daughter, so Paula helped with child care as well. A little more than a year after Paula's daughter was born, she met four women who were planning to migrate to the United States. She decided to try her luck, as her brothers had done before her, in *el norte*.

Paula went to the state of Washington in 1989 when her son, Mateo, was 4 and her daughter, Cindy, was just 1 year old. She lived with the relatives of one of her travel companions and found a job at McDonald's. As she worked both the opening and closing shifts, Paula was home during the middle of the day and cooked for the family with whom she lived in exchange for her share of the grocery bill. By cutting daily living costs to a minimum, Paula was able to send $150 to $200 a week home for the care of her kids. Paula explained that this remittance was necessary because Blanca had to hire help to care for the children in her absence.

After just 18 months in the United States, Paula went home to Mexico. "I couldn't stand it," she said. "I missed my children way too much. During the time I was away, my daughter forgot about me. But when my son would get on the phone he would ask, 'Mama, when are you coming?' and 'Mama, why did you leave me?'" The adjustment of Paula's children upon her return wasn't automatic. Paula recalled that when she first came home, Cindy didn't recognize her. It took about 2 months of listening to older brother Mateo calling Paula "mama" for little Cindy to follow suit.

Back in Puebla, Paula moved into a bedroom adjoining the kitchen and, as before, took care of the cooking, cleaning, and child care while Blanca and Pedro worked. Her responsibilities expanded slowly over the next 10 years. Blanca and Pedro had another daughter, whom Paula helped raise. Blanca and Pedro also set up a store selling fruits and vegetables in the front of their house, which Paula tended to during the day.

For more than 2 years, Paula planned her second trip north, before eventually migrating again in 1999. Paula patiently waited until her son, Mateo, graduated from the ninth grade; this time she had decided to take him with her. Paula explained that her son wasn't crazy about leaving their home in Mexico. Moreover, she said, "my daughter often asked why [I was going to leave], but I explained to her that there was no future for me in Mexico. There I wasn't able to save any money." Paula didn't want to take her daughter with her for two reasons. First, the expense of crossing for three people, rather than two, was too much. Second, Paula worried about the danger of taking her daughter across the border. "Cindy eventually accepted that I leave, but only with the condition that I go back for her after a few months."

Paula returned to New Jersey, this time with the help of her sister. Within just a day, she started working at a local fast-food restaurant. Mateo was left alone. Paula planned that he would attend high school during the day and spoke to her manager about a part-time position for him in the evenings. But they arrived in New Jersey in July, giving Mateo almost 2 months with little to do. Quickly, Mateo decided he didn't like the United States or where he lived with his mother in New Jersey. He never signed up for high school that fall. Instead, Mateo turned to his uncle in Texas, who offered to take him in and cover all the costs associated with a high school education. Mateo left for Texas that January.

Within 18 months, by attending summer school, Mateo completed the 2 years of high school necessary for his diploma. He still didn't feel good living in the United States, however—"so much that he would call me crying," explained Paula. Mateo decided it would be best to return to Mexico to study. Paula felt bad when her son left for Texas, "mostly because of his rejection after I brought him here. But when he left for Mexico, it hurt more because I knew the separation would be more permanent."

Meanwhile, back in Mexico, Paula's daughter, Cindy, felt jealous about being left behind. "I didn't really realize this, until once when we were talking on the phone, Cindy blurted out, 'Mom, you don't love me because you took Mateo and not me.'" Paula explained to her that it is much more dangerous for a girl on the border and that life in the United States was really no good. "Eventually, she understood that it wasn't that I don't love her, but that I had her best interests in mind."

In 2004, at the time of my initial interview with Paula, Mateo had been back in Mexico for nearly 2 years and almost 5 years had passed since Paula had seen her daughter, Cindy. Mateo, now fluent in English, wanted to get a college degree in tourism. According to Paula, to achieve this end, he still needed 2 more years of high school in Mexico and 4 years of college. Paula calculated 6 more years of schooling for her daughter, who had just started studying at a private high school, financed by Paula's remittances, and who wanted to be a schoolteacher. Working two full-time jobs at the two fast-food restaurants in New Jersey, Paula believed she could finance both children's educations. She expected to continue with her grueling schedule for the 6 years necessary to provide her children with professional degrees that could give them the independence she never had at their age. If all went according to plan, Paula hoped she would be able to return to Mexico eventually for an early retirement.

Epilogue

In 2005, Mateo came back to the United States. Paula had continued to send him money for school until she learned he had dropped out 2 months earlier.

Angry at the deception, she cut him off. Mateo quickly grew frustrated at lack of employment opportunities in Mexico, so he joined his mother, once again, in New Jersey. Later that same year, back in Mexico, Paula's daughter, Cindy, also dropped out of school. At the age of 16, she went to live with her boyfriend and his family while he finished studying to be a teacher.

By 2007, Cindy had married and still lived in Oaxaca. Mateo had moved to Maryland with a girlfriend and had a baby at the age of 21. Despite these changes in her children's lives, Paula continued to work at the same fast-food restaurant and to live in the same first-floor, two-bedroom apartment of a house by the train tracks in an upscale New Jersey town.

Joanna Dreby is an assistant professor of sociology at the State University of New York at Albany. This essay is based on her research on Mexican transnational families, described more fully in her book *Divided by Borders: Mexican Migrants and Their Children* (University of California Press 2010). *Divided by Borders* is the recipient of both the Goode Book Award and the Thomas and Znaniecki Best Book Award from the American Sociological Association.

CRITICAL THINKING QUESTIONS

1. Describe the economic and social conditions that contribute to Third World women leaving their families for employment in First World households.

2. How might Giele and Holst's (2004) predictions regarding adaptation, differentiation, integration, and generalization apply to gender roles in Third World countries?

3. Using the case of Paula Rodriguez, develop a cost/benefit ratio around global care chains for
   - the migrating woman,
   - her family, and
   - her society of origin.

Now develop the same for
   - the employing household,
   - the employing family, and
   - the society in which she is employed.

4. What are the quantitative and qualitative differences between the anguish expressed by transnational families (mothers and their children) and the feelings of guilt or regret expressed by some employed American women.

6

Positioning Families in Global Landscapes

Families, Policies, and Futures

Ronald Bosrock, founding director of the Global Institute at Saint John's University in Collegeville, Minnesota, believes that "globalization can change [the] world for [the] better" (2006:D8). Bosrock acknowledges how far globalization must reach to yield true improvements in the quality of family life but believes that an expanding worldwide economy

> would go a long way toward closing the gap between poor and rich nations. . . . Opening world markets to free trade and the free flow of capital and labor has contributed much toward the weaker countries of the world in the world economy. Globalization has highlighted issues such as the poverty among women, child labor, and the scandalous lack of basic medical care throughout much of the underdeveloped world. (P. D8)

Further, Bosrock argues that global equity and stability are prerequisites to the enjoyment of economic benefits in more-developed societies. The more-developed global North and West have a vested interest in improving economic opportunity in Central American nations and around the world, as well as in reducing the threat of violence in parts of Africa and the Middle East.

In each chapter in *Global Families* I have noted the potential benefits of globalization for families. However, a dominant message of the previous chapters has been the extent to which globalization places families at risk.

I have discussed how global changes in death and disease, fertility, and migration are shaping family structures in ways that impact family dynamics, especially patterns of dependency. I have sought to reveal the extent to which worldwide communication and consumption have dramatic consequences for family norms and values, especially around parenting. I have considered some of the international sources of the greatest family hazards caused by war, human trafficking, and family dislocation. Finally, I have demonstrated how employment transcends traditional definitions of national borders, serving workers' desires to improve their families' economic opportunities, yet often at the expense of the quality of family life in parenting and other family relationships.

In this, the final chapter of *Global Families,* I examine international efforts to improve the quality of life for families across the globe. I describe the work of international and supranational but also regional and national organizations in order to reveal the critical position of a gender-sensitive lens on social policy, including development programs that seek to enhance family well-being. I place family rights in the broader context of human rights and ask: What is the prognosis for the institution and relationships of family in a global society? Where national borders are increasingly contested on political, economic, cultural, and other stages, is the world moving toward a post-family global society, or does family remain a cornerstone for societies, regardless of the global milieu?

Beyond the Second Decade of the Year of the Family

We have passed the second decade since the U.N. Year of the Family was recognized in 1993. Five years later, the United Nations (1998) reiterated the need for a continued emphasis on the needs of families in an era of rapid change, including globalization.

> Rapid changes are underway in the forms and styles of family life. The major changes in societies, such as industrialization, urbanization, secularization, commercialization and *globalization* [italics added], are powerful forces influencing family life. In many parts of the world, children are denied their right to be loved and cared for as well as their right to food, health care and education. Many face domestic violence within their families, the most common form being the gender-based violence. The number of women working outside the home is increasing. The population is aging. The position of the extended family is declining so that the demands on the nuclear family are growing. Unemployment is high and widespread, with catastrophic

consequences for the dignity and self-esteem of both men and women and for family solidarity.

Five years beyond that, the U.N. General Assembly (United Nations 2003) affirmed six objectives:

1. Increase awareness of family issues among governments and in the private sector.

2. Strengthen abilities of national institutions to formulate, implement, and monitor family policies.

3. Stimulate efforts to respond to problems both affecting and affected by families.

4. Undertake reviews and assessments of the conditions and needs of families.

5. Enhance effectiveness and generate new family programs at local, national, and regional levels.

6. Improve collaboration among national and international organizations that support families.

Furthermore, the U.N. Programme on the Family (2003) urges that every social policy on the family should take into account changes facing families in the areas of family structure, aging, migration, and the HIV/AIDS pandemic. Achieving such lofty objectives requires an investment in and by social science that goes beyond culture-specific or comparative research to include study of international, transnational, and global family concerns.

To that end, the United Nations solicited observations of the 2011 International Day of Families around "Confronting Family Poverty and Social Exclusion." The day was an opportunity to recognize that certain families (e.g., large families, migrant families, rural families, single-parent families, and those affected by HIV/AIDS) are more at risk of poverty than are other families. The United Nations called attention to the fact that focusing on families is an effective way to fight poverty in societies and regions, especially if antipoverty strategies focus on child poverty and gender and other inequalities. Finally, the United Nations affirmed not only its own role but also that of civil society in confronting critical social problems (National Council on Family Relations 2011).

In practical terms, what do families and their members need to thrive? Recently, the ChildFund Alliance asked children around the world, "What do you need most?" Their responses ranged from "a ball" to "notebooks, so I can write my lessons" to "breakfast" (Hopfensperger 2011:B3). When asked, "If you had $1, what would you buy?" 45 percent of the children said food and/or water. When asked, "What do you fear most?" 20 percent said they fear death or disease and 15 percent said being hurt by war or violence. If almost half of all children are saying they would spend a dollar on food or water and one out of every three most fears death, disease, or violence, the world has a long way to go in ensuring the basic survival needs of children and their families.

Idealistic declarations and position statements of the United Nations and other supranational organizations are a crucial starting point for achieving international consensus regarding family needs, human rights, and other critical global social values. In developing global consensus, organizations such as the United Nations have the potential to spur improvements in the quality of life for families worldwide. However, in an essay titled "The Global Human Rights of Families," which follows this chapter, Marsha Freeman, director of the International Women's Rights Action Watch at the University of Minnesota Human Rights Center, argues that such public statements can still fall short of resulting in meaningful, assessable social change. Freeman states: "In short, while everyone celebrates the family, few take care of it."[1] As Freeman argues, social policies mean little without enforcement or structural change.

Again, Gendered Family Realities

In 2006, in her Presidential Address before the American Sociological Association, titled "Great Divides: The Cultural, Cognitive, and Social Bases of the Global Subordination of Women," Cynthia Fuchs Epstein (2007) affirmed: "Categorization based on sex is the most basic social divide" (p. 1). Each chapter in *Global Families* has confirmed that the consequences of globalization and effective social change to improve the quality of life for families in today's global world are inextricably bound to issues of gender.

---

[1]For an elaboration on family social policy from a domestic, American perspective, see the final chapter, "From 'Family Values' to 'Valuing Families'," in Karraker and Grochowski's (2012) *Families With Futures: A Survey of Family Studies Into the Twenty-First Century*. That chapter includes a "Principles and Checklist for Assessing the Impact of Policies and Programs on Families," originally adapted by Karen Bogenscheider (2000) from a version published by Theodora Ooms and Stephen Preister and presented at the Family Impact Seminar in Washington, D.C., 1988.

The United Nations in particular has provided a "free space of feminist activism" with global implications (Hawkesworth 2006:112). The U.N. Commission on the Status of Women monitors the status of and works on behalf of women worldwide. The commission has worked with organizations such as the International Labour Organization and the World Health Organization and through international treaties such as Convention for the Suppression of Traffic in Persons to press for improvements in the quality of life for women, girls, and their families. Faith-based organizations such as the U.S. Federation of the Sisters of St. Joseph (see the essay at the end of Chapter 2 on the work of Sisters of St. Joseph in St. Paul, Minnesota) have taken action around human trafficking and other critical issues (McElwee 2011). The Organisation for Economic Co-operation and Development (OECD, 2011) recently embarked on a new project focusing on three key areas: education, employment, and entrepreneurship. The Center for Women Policy Studies (2006), based in Washington, D.C., has recognized the need to build support for U.S. foreign policies that ensure women's human rights around the world in issues such as immigration and poverty, HIV/AIDS, reproductive rights and justice, and human trafficking (including sex trafficking).

While women's political influence remains small, it is growing. The case of Korean–Japanese coalitions to provide recognition and restitution to comfort women, discussed in Chapter 4, testifies to the power of feminist movements that cross national boundaries to effect social change around violence directed at women and their families. Indeed, Seager's (2003) atlas of feminist organizing in the world confirms that in the past decade nations throughout the world—from Afghanistan, Botswana, and Chad through Europe and North America—have enacted legislation to guarantee equal rights to men and women and, in the case of countries such as the Netherlands and South Africa, to gays and lesbians as well. Hawkesworth (2006) quotes a statement from the organization Women in Development Europe: "Feminism in one country is not sustainable—we need feminism on a global scale" (p. 1).

If the article in *The Economist* is correct, the eradication of HIV/AIDS and other global social problems is "a question of money" ("The End of AIDS?" 2011:11) and the struggle is to stop some rich countries giving less. The Netherlands and Spain are cutting their contributions to the Global Fund, and Italy has stopped paying altogether. Clearly, then, global movements can support and advance transnational initiatives, but any really effective response to globalization must involve locally based social movements. Glocally inspired social movements are required.

Women's local participation to fight oppression within regions and countries has a long, albeit sometimes ignored, history. Women have been change agents in sub-Saharan Africa, as rulers and leaders in precolonial Africa, during colonization and post-independence authoritarian regimes in which they were politically marginalized, and as informal and formal agents and coalition builders in the present era (Fallon 2008). In Turkey, where 42 percent of Turkish women older than 15 have suffered physical or sexual violence, women are organizing around such slogans as "no headscarves, no votes" ("Behind the Veil" 2011).

Liu (2007) compares Chinese and Indian women's movements in the wake of the agenda adopted by the U.N. Fourth World Conference and "challenges the dominant assumption that global thinking can substitute for local thinking" (p. 921). Liu's research indicates that, while national women's movements may build from international agenda, the direction and efficacy of national social movements depend on political contexts (e.g., democratic versus authoritarian) unique to each society.

Organizers of global social movements on behalf of women and their families must comprehend the significant divides between global North and South, capitalist and socialist, more or less developed, and among countries constituting diverse cultural, ethnic, racial, religious, and other identities. Snyder's (2006) qualitative study of women's peace organizations meeting at the 1995 Fourth U.N. World Conference on Women reveals that transnational activism among groups representing diverse circumstances is best advanced when the process of intergroup conflict is constructively used to build coalitions leading toward effective and equitable cooperation.

Snyder (2006) argues that a commitment to such transnational, global movements requires, first, examination of inequalities in decision making (such as those that may exist between participants from northern and southern countries), which in turn can provide opportunities to test commitments to coalitions. Second, escalation in long-standing areas of conflict (e.g., around racism) indicates a need to address issues of dominance, which in turn can provide an opportunity for meaningful dialogue. Third, negotiation of priorities, some of which originate in different cultural and ethnic contexts, can increase understanding of differences within coalitions, thereby increasing opportunities for collaboration. Fourth, conflict resolution strategies, such as those that bring indigenous and refugee groups together, can advance the formation of collective identities and relationships for further collaborative efforts.

Thayer's (2010) powerful ethnography of Brazilian women's movements, *Making Transnational Feminism*, suggests that, while very difficult, such social movements can confront and may even transcend class, colonial, gender, heterosexist, and racist barriers between women in the global South and those in the global North. Thayer envisions a feminist counterpublic—an idealized, democratic political space where participants can transcend contradictory power relations, negotiating differences and transforming them into collective power. Global social movements face diverse traditions and agendas, in addition to significant inequalities in experience, power, and resources (such as those seen between the global South and North), but can use inclusive and participatory processes to engage conflict constructively. In doing so, globally oriented social movements have the potential to increase not only their strategic authority but also the depth and complexity of their knowledge surrounding women's, family, and other social issues.

Similar cautions apply to movements to advance the quality of family life worldwide: When it comes to social action, one size cannot fit all. For example, many on the political right would not agree that feminist or gender-based movements will advance pro-family agenda. Likewise, translating concern regarding human rights into effective international law and policy and meaningful social justice around issues addressed by CEDAW, the U.N. Convention on the Elimination of All Forms of Discrimination Against Women (United Nations 1999a), requires knowledge of a society's culture, as well as the voices that are speaking for—and silenced by—that culture (Merry 2005). For example, the success of efforts to require companies to support men's participation in child care in gender-advanced countries such as Sweden rests in a broader sociopolitical context that promotes gender equality. Haas and Hwang (2007) found that father-friendly companies in Sweden had adopted corporate values consistent with the domestic sphere while affirming a high value for the entrée of women into the public sphere. These findings do not bode well for societies such as that of the United States in which the values of corporate culture often compromise family interests and public opinion often seems ambivalent regarding women's participation in the labor force.

Women continue to earn only one tenth of the world's income while laboring two thirds of the world's working hours. Women also continue to constitute the majority (70 percent) of the world's poor (Heyzer, as quoted in Seager 2003:102). However, I hope readers of Global Families share a measure of my optimism for social change. Women are slowly gaining entitlement to and fuller participation in economic, educational, political, religious, and other institutions. Women also are winning self-determination in terms of marriage (including divorce) and reproductive health rights while obtaining more freedom, at least in law, from licensed domestic and sexual violence (Seager 2003). In 1996, the International War Crimes Court (The Hague) indicted eight Bosnian Serb military and police officers in the rape of Muslim women—the first time sexual assault has been addressed separately as a war crime. In 2000, the U.N. Security Council passed a resolution that mandated the equal participation of women in peacekeeping. Other landmarks in women's human rights in the early 21st century include the following:

- Vietnam banned polygamy and dowry.
- Chad made sexual violence, including genital cutting, a criminal offense.
- In Jordan, a new law allowed women to initiate divorce.
- The Scottish Episcopal Church voted to allow women to become bishops.
- Bahrain permitted women to vote and run for all elected offices.
- About 20,000 Colombian women participated in a peace march, demanding an end to the civil war in that country.
- The Norwegian government enacted legislation requiring that companies ensure at least 40 percent of their board members are women. (Seager 2003:102–3)

Rae Lesser Blumberg (1988), a sociologist who has studied and worked with Third World economic development programs, found that the intersection of gender and development provides insights into the interfaces "between macro and micro, between social structures and human lives" (p. 115). Blumberg charges that gender insensitivity characterizes the viewpoint of those in positions of authority who have been, in Blumberg's words, "oblivious to the gender division of labor and rewards within the household." Her analysis indicates that macrolevel development policies to address the African food crisis failed to take into account women's economic place and power at the micro level. These policies set in motion a "chain of consequences" (p. 116) in which women were economically undercut, beginning with diminished abilities and disincentives for women to engage in food cultivation and production.

Lest we forget the role of the individual in social change, some feminist scholars are challenging the economic, political, and cultural emphasis in globalization studies. In *Gender and the Politics of Possibilities: Rethinking Globalization*, Desai (2009) calls attention to the microsocial level to better understand the influence individuals, especially women, can have on the global stage. She argues that "it is women, as cross-border traders, transnational activists, and *Modemmujers* who are shaping processes of globalization in a specifically gendered way" (p. 3). Desai is optimistic that these actors will not only inform scholarship on globalization but will also facilitate social justice movements around the globe.

Epstein (2006) concluded her Presidential Address (cited at the beginning of this section), with a powerful statement regarding the relationship between gender and society:

The most productive societies are those with porous boundaries between categories of people. . . . Small groups of men may prosper by stifling women's potential, but prosperous nations benefit from women's full participation and productivity in societies. (P. 17)

Not only women and societies but their families benefit from women's liberation. Further, as demonstrated in the previous chapters, globalization in the 21st century entails greater movement of families within and across national borders, dramatic culture shifts associated with altered patterns of communication and consumption, greater fluidity in social arrangements resulting from war and other social upheavals, and increases in transnational employment. Globalization may well be just the social process to stimulate the kind of "porous" boundaries of which Epstein spoke.

"Family Returning to East Timor," by M. Kobayashi

Reprinted with permission of the U.N. High Commission on Refugees.

Social Policy, Development, and Family Well-Being

In each of the preceding chapters, I have offered a compendium of research on the many ways families are affected by globalization. In turn, these chapters reveal a pressing need for consideration of family impact when formulating social policies at national, international, and, especially, transnational levels. Based on the research I offer in *Global Families,* a family-sensitive global policy agenda must include six urgent policy priorities, each premised in family impact on a global scale.

1. Accelerate global responses to the HIV/AIDS pandemic, as well as other catastrophic pandemic diseases and malnutrition, while increasing worldwide understanding of the escalating deficits acquired by global societies, from Australia to Zimbabwe, when generations are left without care.

2. Resume global efforts to provide all women and their families with safe, effective reproductive health and technology while addressing social antecedents and consequences that result in imbalanced gender ratios.

3. Revise immigration, refugee, and asylum policies to reduce the uncertainty of family reunification while making visible the assets that women such as those at Sarah's . . . an Oasis for Women (described in the essay at the end of Chapter 2) and their families can contribute to an adopted country.

4. Charge supranational bodies with analyzing the negative effects and promoting the positive effects of global media and consumption, and seek ways to develop sensitivity around the challenges families face as they encounter global culture.

5. Immediately end violence against women and children, including collateral effects of war and during periods of civic unrest, using research that will unmask the patriarchal and other social foundations of rape, trafficking, and other forms of violence.

6. Scrutinize migrant employment practices to reveal the underlying macro-social order underlying migration for work, as well as the manifest and latent consequences for families such as that of Paula Rodriguez (described in the essay at the end of Chapter 5), the home, and host societies.

In each of these areas, I advocate development of family impact statements, along the lines of environmental impact statements. Family ecology and world systems approaches can enable change agents to see families as embedded in interlocking global systems composed of economic, political, cultural, and other social systems, while remaining sensitive to worldwide systems of exploitation and oppression. At the most basic level, policies and practices will need to be premised in a more inclusive definition of family, one that transcends family as a unit formed around a man and a woman and their relations by blood, marriage, or adoption. A global concept of family must be inclusive, making room for the rich array of relationships among children, adults, and elders who are bound together by rights and obligations, perhaps even across time and space.

These initiatives are embedded in social justice, but the means for implementing meaningful change at a global level are complicated. On the global stage, social policy is fundamentally bound to social development and family well-being. Policies that support social development have often linked to improvements in the quality of life for families, but not always. In Eastern Europe in the late 20th century, economic marketization and privatization often meant retrenchment in welfare entitlements and family benefits gained under more authoritarian, socialist regimes. By the early 1980s, nations such as Hungary were moving away from large, comprehensive welfare systems, which included such programs as universal family allowances, a 3-year paid maternity leave grant, and local childrearing assistance grants. Not coincidentally, the International Monetary Fund (IMF), along with the World Bank, urged nations such as Hungary to adopt policies that would restrict eligibility to such welfare programs through the application of means and income tests. Haney (2003) concluded: "The international agencies' reform model targeted national-level social entitlements in an attempt to dismantle the universal tier of the welfare state" (p. 163). The consequence of such vigorously pursued supranational agendas is greater family risk.

Some critics believe governments are incapable or unwilling to engage issues such as transnational migration from the perspectives of those most affected. They see nonstate actors, including nongovernmental organizations (NGOs), as playing a pivotal role in advocating "from the bottom up" to exert pressure on governments and policymakers to take into account the well-being of transnational families (Piper 2003). While doing so, NGOs and other organizations attempting change in the quality of family life on a global scale must first frame societal problems such as poverty and hunger in meaningful ways. As Terezinha da Silva, president of the *Fórum Mulher* (Women's Forum) in Mozambique offers: "I don't like the phrase 'fighting poverty.' Poverty is too wide a topic and it can mean different things to different people" (Moya 2006:22). Poverty is a complex problem, embedded in often disparate economic as well as political, cultural, and other social factors.

These organizations frequently confront additional challenges, including the gendered effects of social problems such as civil wars. Again, da Silva offers that women are most often the collateral victims of war. However, more national and even local organizations such as *Fórum Mulher* are increasing their effectiveness by cooperating and sharing experience and resources with other organizations that focus on women's issues, as well as networking with other NGOs, political groups, government representatives, and trade unions and with academic and donor organizations. The Global Women's Action Network for Children, launched in 2006, is another such organization, bringing together "thoughtful, committed, powerful women from around the world" (Edelman 2006:1) who represent governments and the United Nations, business and nonprofit organizations, cultural and educational groups, and many faith, national, and racial assemblies to work on behalf of the world's children.

Tension between family rights and responsibilities and the national and international bodies that might seek to regulate them may well be fundamental. Sigle-Rushton and Kenney (2004) describe one such area—public policy regarding state provision of publicly funded early childhood education and care. Among the then 15 members of the European Union, only 5 countries (Sweden, Finland, Denmark, Belgium, and France) viewed child care not as a private, family responsibility but a collective, societal responsibility. These five countries offer extensive early childhood education and full day care for a large proportion of children. The child-care programs in these countries are integrated through educational and social-welfare systems, and access is almost universal. In other countries, early childhood education and child care remain the responsibility of parents and the private sector.

Change is on the horizon. Tracking on Hochschild's (1989) argument that little meaningful change has occurred in the ratio of men's breadwinner/caregiver responsibilities, Sigle-Rushton and Kenney (2004) foresee an increase in dual-earner/dual-career families. They already see signs, at least in the European Union, that social policies are changing in response. They cite the 1997 Treaty of Amsterdam, which seeks to make equal opportunities for men and women a basic aim of all policymaking across the European Union. "Gender mainstreaming" appears to have support, as witnessed in nations' increasingly enacting policies that would encourage fathers and mothers to participate more equitably in parental leave and in surveys (e.g., the Employment Options for the Future study) showing that, even with the lost earnings, men would prefer to reduce their hours worked. Such is the case in countries such as Sweden with long-standing support for gender equity in domestic and labor spheres.

Bodies such as the OECD (2006), with a broad commitment to democratic government and the market economy, conduct research on a range of economic and social issues. The OECD's (2002) publication *Babies and Bosses* targets the challenge of balancing work and family life as a global issue and explores how policies in this area contribute to the structure of labor markets and other social outcomes. Family-friendly policies including child care and child-related leave can benefit societies in a variety of ways, including not only improved child development and greater gender equity but also more secure family microeconomics. Other supranational government bodies such as the European Union have adopted policies of gender mainstreaming. Through the European Commission (2006), the European Union is addressing gender inequality in 21 specific areas, including migration, employment, education, trafficking, and development.

How, then, do individual societies around the world measure in terms of some of the indicators of family well-being? The Project on Global Working Families (2011) at Harvard University and McGill University has developed the Work, Family, and Equity Index (WFEI) to measure performance by governments around the world in meeting the needs of working families. The WFEI surveys countries' performance in six policy areas: work schedules and hours; paid leave from work; health; pregnancy, birth, or adoption of a baby; elder care and care for disabled family members; and other family policy.

One important indicator on the WFEI is a guaranteed provision of paid leave for new mothers. On that indicator, the nations of Scandinavia, some nations of the former Soviet Union (e.g., the Russian Federation, Azerbaijan, and Uzbekistan), Japan and South Korea, and certain Western European countries (e.g., Austria, Germany, and the Czech Republic) provide 52 weeks or more of leave for new mothers. Other Western European countries, Canada, and some African and some Asian countries provide at least 14 (but less than 52) weeks of maternity leave. Countries that provide less than 14 weeks of leave are scattered across Central and South America, Africa, and Asia. The United States shares with Liberia, Papua New Guinea, and Sierra Leone the distinction of providing no national policy regarding maternity leave (Project on Global Working Families 2011).

Lawson (2001a) has stated: "Clearly, the global human condition, and especially the well-being of the world's families, is . . . the key problematic for the helping professions of the twenty-first century" (p. 374). Lawson (2001b) offers a framework for family-centered policies and practices applicable to a global world. His framework engages governmental bodies at the local, state, national, and international levels and considers the importance of local mobilization for collective action, matters of place in need and opportunity, global issues of space-time compression, and intercultural contact zones. Lawson's (2001a) futuristic model of social welfare emphasizes the importance of "coordination, synchronization, and alignment" (p. 365).

Many economists and social-policy experts contend that the World Bank and certain other supranational organizations have an almost monopolistic control over strategic policies of global development. Some critics argue that organizations such as the World Bank have transformed themselves into powerful forces with the intent of advancing neoliberal global social policy

(Goldman 2005). Gender-based critiques of the World Bank fault the bank for failing to distribute resources equitably so that women and others previously underrepresented on the global development stage have access to the bank's resources. Other feminist economic theories offer broader critiques of free markets (Strassman 1993), socialism (Folbre 1993), and public/private connections (Jennings 1993). By deconstructing economics (Ferber and Nelson 1993a, 1993b; Williams 1993), questioning classical economic assumptions (England 1993), and taking into account women's experience (Solow 1993) by asking, "Economics for whom?" (Longino 1993), feminist economic theories (Blank 1993) have challenged mainstream economics, organizations such as the World Bank, and the IMF.

A generation ago, the period ushered in by the U.N. Women's Decade in 1976 saw greater appreciation of the connections between women's subordination in the domestic sphere (including women's childbearing, caring, and other family roles) and women's inequality in the broader society. Development theory has long viewed Third World women primarily as reproducers of human capital, but the United Nations (1997) Research Institute for Social Development has called for a "more gender equitable macro-economic agenda." From this perspective population control is critical not only to modernization through demographic transition but also to subsequent economic development and the eventual reduction of poverty, and most certainly to the broader participation of women on the macroeconomic and political stage.

In fact, conformity with World Bank strictures on population control has often been a condition for a country receiving loans from the IMF. By the 1980s structural adjustment policies (SAPs) directed by the World Bank (working closely with the United Nations) aimed for prescriptive population control as a key element in broader development. At the same time, SAPs became associated with cuts in countries' spending on social services and subsidies, to the effect that women are forced to bear increasing responsibilities for health and other care of their family members. Meanwhile, families have been required to assume more of the direct health costs for immunizations and preventive care, as well as for prenatal care and education (Purewal 2001).

Some of the latent dysfunctions wrought by such SAPs have been found to include reduced time in lactation and, consequently, shorter intervals between births. Other consequences include increased morbidity and greater transmission of infectious diseases, and increased infant and child mortality. These changes result in greater strain on the household productive capacities of women, who bear disproportionate responsibility for care of family members (Afshar and Dennis 1992; Purewal 2001; Sparr 1994; Stewart 1991).

The Third World Women's Conference (1998) has mounted efforts to draw attention to the deleterious effects of such policy strategies as shifts away from food subsidies and basic preventative and curative health care and toward the privatization of health care and the influence of transnational corporations in health-related issues. In other words, women too often serve as the "safety net" for decline in development policy support for social welfare programs (Purewal 2001:105), thereby limiting women's ability to care for their families, as well as their ability to achieve literacy and higher education and to derive income from outside the family. At the same time, fertility "disincentives" (e.g., mass sterilization programs, denying food ration cards) in places such as India misrepresent the sources of population growth (in-migration) and permit the exploitation by transnational corporations of markets in less-developed societies. Purewal has been highly critical of traditional World Bank and other initiatives aimed at population control.

> Fertility decline requires that issues of gender equity, poverty, and wealth distribution be seriously addressed. . . . The World Bank has taken the position that "it is possible for fertility to decline . . . without much change in those social, economic, and health variables generally believed to be crucial preconditions for demographic change." (World Bank 1992, as quoted in Purewal 2001:111)

Purewal (2001), Rowbotham (1992), and others charge that SAPs too often represent both a misconceived notion of women's place in development and, in terms of human rights, "the denial of reproductive rights by development and population policies" (Purewal 2001:97). These critics favor, instead, a gender and development approach that emphasizes women's roles in economic production (and income generation), originating not only from their part in the labor force but also from productive activities that maintain the domestic front (Purewal 2001). Such an approach may be more consistent with an acknowledgment of the intersections between family rights and human rights.

Family Rights as Human Rights

The United Nations (2010) Millennium Declaration, adopted in 2000, remains pertinent to the well-being of families today. The declaration entrusts member nations to engage in global partnership around human rights and to

- eradicate extreme poverty and hunger;
- achieve universal primary education;
- promote gender equality and empower women;
- reduce child mortality;
- improve maternal health;
- combat HIV/AIDS, malaria, and other diseases;
- ensure environmental sustainability; and
- build a global partnership for development.

Still, globalization makes citizenship and civic entitlements contested terrain. Land (2004) offers a cogent analysis of the changing definitions of citizenship in law and practice, particularly as they apply to women and children and, by extension, to families. Since 1993, the Women's Human Rights Program of Minnesota Advocates for Human Rights (2006) has joined with organizations in the Commonwealth of Independent States, Central and Eastern Europe, Haiti, Mexico, and Nepal to document violations of women's rights in areas including workplace discrimination and sexual harassment, domestic violence and rape, and sex trafficking. The program has a particular interest in education, rights, and abuses of immigrant and refugee women. Each of these areas impacts not only women and girls but also their families.

In 1990 the U.N. Convention on the Rights of the Child formulated ideals that affirm the protection of basic human rights of those most vulnerable members and, in doing so, also affirm the well-being of families. The convention declared that children have rights to order and regulation in family life and to human dignity in the lives of families (and their members) so they can grow and live productive and rewarding lives (Roopnarine and Gielen 2005:11). The convention built on the Declaration on the Rights of the Child enacted in 1959, which included statements concerning children's civil and political rights, but only with regard to the right to a home and a nationality at birth.

Children's rights have always been understood in the context of social beliefs about children's capacities and their place in the family and society. By the end of the 19th century, patriarchal authority over children was giving way to legislation to protect children, even to the point that in England, by 1889, cruelty and neglect of a child had become a criminal offense. By the middle of the 19th century legislative bodies had begun to establish minimum-age-for-employment laws, as well as laws regarding ages for compulsory education. By the early 20th century, children in France, Germany, and Great Britain gained legal entitlement to school meals and medical inspections. The first attempt to codify these and other rights for children occurred in 1924 when the League of Nations endorsed *Codifying Children's Rights,* although Land (2004) makes clear that this document specified what nations *should* do for children, not any rights to which children could lay claim.

The standards embodied in the Convention on the Rights of the Child, which apply to all persons under 18 years of age, are guided by general principles of nondiscrimination; best interests of the child; right to life, survival, and development; and respect for the views of the child. Articles establish specific civil rights and freedoms, including the right to name and nationality at birth; preservation of identity; access to information; freedom of thought, conscience, and religion; freedom of expression, association, and peaceful assembly; and freedom from violence, abuse, neglect, torture, or cruel and inhuman treatment. Other articles specify children's rights to basic health and welfare, and education, play, leisure, and cultural activities, with special consideration for children with special needs and those in emergency situations such as refugee or war conditions. The convention also specifically denotes children's rights regarding family, including parental responsibilities, rights of children separated from their parents and deprived of family, and adoption procedures, including rights to contact and reunification. Regarding children's right to be free from physical punishment, parental rights to use corporal punishment with their children vary across nations. However, physical punishment of children is now illegal in at least nine European countries (Land 2004).

Today, the U.N. Committee on the Rights of the Child reviews each member nation's progress on children's rights every 5 years. By the year 2000, all member nations had ratified the convention. Two nations, Somalia and the United States, have yet to sign. The unwillingness of American politicians to join the rest of the civilized world in affirming basic human rights of all children is reprehensible, all the more so because of the "pro-family" stance so many American public officials adopt.

From 1951, the European Convention on Human Rights (Articles 8 and 12) grants every European the right to privacy in family life and home and the right to marry (Land 2004). Clearly, international and transnational precedent—or at least inclination—exists to establish globally applicable policies regarding families and their members. In 1995, Euronet was formed by organizations seeking to campaign on behalf of the interests of children in Europe. Euronet was concerned that global issues such as the free movement of children and children's interests in the information revolution in the new European Union were not being adequately addressed. In fact, we have ample evidence that those issues, as well as the global plight of children's education and labor needs, their disadvantaged status as street children and child soldiers, and the particular problems of refugees and child slaves, are not being addressed (see Ansell 2005).

Thus, the rights of children, families, and humanity are inextricably bound. Given the rate at which LGBTQ (lesbian, gay, bisexual, transgender, or questioning) families are forming, being made visible, and becoming politically active on national and transnational stages, the rights of those families and their members must be next on not only the national but also the global political agenda. In a treatise on global justice, Mandle (2006) defines global justice in terms of respect for basic human rights that should guide policy in terms of a wide range of issues, domestically as well as globally.

As Berger and Berger (1983) argue, globalization changes the role of the family with respect to the state. With globalization, the prevalence of transnational economic, political, and other social forces increases, often at the expense of national autonomy. With the rise of global interests, the family no longer serves as the primary agent mediating private and public life. At the same time, families and their members are forced to become more self-reliant (Beck and Beck-Gernsheim 2002).

In some cases, state resistance to globalization can have sobering effects on families denied access to information and new technologies. For example, before the fall of the Soviet Union, with its state-controlled economy, a state decision was made not to import expensive foreign contraceptives or to develop facilities to manufacture modern contraceptives. According to a Soviet state demographer, in 1988 the number of abortions (6,500,000) exceeded the number of live births (Segal 2003).

The national politics of abortion in the United States is another such case. Beginning in the late 1960s in Britain and with the U.S. Supreme Court decision in *Roe v. Wade* in 1973, laws guiding access to abortion trended toward liberalization (Francome 2004). However, Smyth's (2005) analysis of Ireland reveals the extent to which globalization serves as a prism through which to view antiabortion legislation. Smith presents antiabortion legislation as affirmation of Irish ideals for the centrality of family for women but also as resistance to laws that would move Irish practice closer to that of England and as rejection of liberal (American) discourse on individual privacy. Using qualitative analysis of newspaper accounts and parliamentary proceedings, Smyth reveals abortion law as a meaningful symbol of Irish Catholic national—even glocal—culture and identity.

The futures of families in global societies are affected by other transnational movements and, in particular, by movements to advance the cause of women's rights throughout the world. For example, at the ninth Interdisciplinary Congress on Women, held in Seoul, South Korea (June 19–24, 2005), sociologist Esther Ngan-ling Chow and others brought together feminist scholarship that Chow (as cited in Lorber 2005) described as "a prism through which we envision a trans-national, trans-ethnic, trans-lingual, and cross-cultural kind of feminism in both thinking and doing, in both scholarship and practices that go beyond the limitation of one country" (p. 5). While English and Western references still predominate, such conferences can stimulate informed agenda for social policies and also social action around family issues. Such convergence can reveal the extent to which issues previously seen as national or regional become global (Lorber 2005).

Organizations such as International Women's Rights Action Watch (IWRAW 2004) and affiliated bodies of the United Nations have an ongoing charge to monitor and report "implementation of women's human rights under the International Covenant on Economic, Social, and Cultural Rights [a committee of the United Nations]" (p. 7). IWRAW operates in accordance with six other international rights treaties articulated in the U.N.'s Universal Declaration of Human Rights, including treaties dealing with the rights of children and racial discrimination. CEDAW (United Nations 1999a), adopted in 1979, deals with many of the issues addressed in *Global Families*, including equality in marriage and family law (Article 16), employment (Article 11), exploitation (Article 5), and development (Article 3). Although some argue that some of these organizations have been marginalized in larger human rights efforts, organizations such as CEDAW have taken the lead in addressing pressing issues facing families worldwide, including employment and violence, while empowering women and expanding the very notion of human rights (Schöpp-Schilling and Flinterman 2007).

Across the globe, politicians of every persuasion compete for the claim of best representing the interests of families. Familialism refers to the promotion of pro-family ideas and political initiatives ostensibly intended to strengthen families. (Offering couples who complete a course in premarriage counseling a discount on their marriage licenses is an example of familistic legislation.) Too often, familialism is used to provoke opposition to human rights in areas such as access to contraception, abortion, and other health concerns, as well as civil rights for LGBTQ people and their families—and still, across the world, the rights of girls and women. Further, policies sited in the family are not always only or even primarily about family issues. Instead, family "reforms" can serve to advance any number of other agenda, including colonial rule (Haney and Pollard 2003b).

Such familialism is too often ideological metaphor. After all, if the reality of "family" is so contested, what does it mean to be "pro-family"? Karraker and Grochowski (2012) favor shifting the conversation from a rhetoric of "family values" to one of "valuing families." Families do not merely survive but thrive when they have adequate economic resources, nutrient-dense nutrition, access to regular physical activity, healthful environments, good health care (including mental health care), decent housing, freedom from violence of all kinds, and family-friendly workplaces. Furthermore, every family needs a network of family, kin, and friends, along with neighborhoods, community, and schools, to foster a sense of respect and a connection among families and their members. In short, families thrive when the whole society has viable investments in every family.

The Universal Declaration of Human Rights, adopted by the General Assembly of the United Nations in 1948, proclaims the following in Article 16:

1. Men and women of full age, without any limitation due to race, nationality or religion, have the right to marry and to found a family. They are entitled to equal rights as to marriage, during marriage and at its dissolution.

2. Marriage shall be entered into only with the free and full consent of the intending spouses.

3. The family is the natural and fundamental group unit of society and is entitled to protection by society and the State.

Further, in Article 25, the declaration provides these rights:

1. Everyone has the right to a standard of living adequate for the health and well-being of himself and of his family, including food, clothing, housing, and medical care and necessary social services, and the right to security in the event of unemployment, sickness, disability, widowhood, and old age or other lack of livelihood in circumstances beyond his control.

2. Motherhood and childhood are entitled to special care and assistance. All children, whether born in or out of wedlock, shall enjoy the same social protection.

In light of such ambitions, what, then, is the prognosis for family in a global society? In a world in which national borders are increasingly contested on political, economic, cultural, and other stages, are we moving toward a post-family global society or does family remain a cornerstone for societies, regardless of their position in the global milieu?

Conclusions: A Post-Family Global Society?

In *Global Families*, I have demonstrated how globalization places families at substantial risk. At the same time, the social processes of globalization— demographic transitions, transnational employment, worldwide culture shifts, as well as international violence—ensure that family structures will be more diverse and family relationships more flexible, even as they become less localized. The influence of clans and other kin groups will continue to decline, as seen in fewer kin marriages and freer mate selection, greater sexual freedom, wider recognition of women's rights in marriage initiation and family decision making, and the extension of children's rights. These changes lead some to question: What, if anything, will bind people together into intimate, caring bonds in such postmodern, global societies?

While this new world order brings benefits to families, globalization also places families, their members, and, consequently, the greater society at significant risk. People can no longer depend on assumptions, beliefs, and values that traditionally gave certainty and predictability to life and solidarity to social relationships. Meanwhile, the individual is increasingly faced with a complicated set of societal controls and constraints in the form of the educational system, the labor market, and other institutional forces. While such risk can create alliances, personal lives are now constructed in a risky, unpredictable social environment often void of past supports such as kin networks, yet constrained by powerful social forces (Beck and Beck-Gernsheim 2002). Meanwhile, the same trend toward individualization that characterizes societies also characterizes family relationships. In other words, is the family shifting from what Beck and Beck-Gernsheim call "a community of need" to an elective association—that is, a "post-familial family"?

Of course, the situation of families has been evolving, quite noticeably from the end of the 19th century and accelerating beginning in the last half of the 20th century. As men and women can no longer depend on a spouse (or children) to support them in later life, they may make individual choices and plans for their security and lives separate from the family. Beck and Beck-Gernsheim (2002) say that the communal interests represented in the family cannot be taken for granted. Although individual men and women are still linked to the family, the gendered nature of expectations and interests, burdens and opportunities means that individual men and women must create lives of their own. In such post-familial families, the adults and children spend increasing amounts of time outside the home abode, in employment, education, leisure, and entertainment.

As documented in previous chapters, such social trends are exacerbated by globalization. Edgar (2004) agrees that the individualization occurring worldwide has resulted in situations in which "traditional forms of authority have doubtless weakened, and individuals increasingly have to negotiate their own moral stance, plus their relationships and their personal work and family biographies" (p. 7). Of course, individuals and families vary in their ability to manage the risks associated with global restructuring.

Family empowerment is limited by such factors as poverty, religion, and persecution.

But Edgar (2004) is among those who reject such extreme postmodernist positions on the family in a global world. In an article aptly titled "Families as the Crucible of Competence in a Changing Social Ecology," Edgar (1999) described in relevant terms the family's continued centrality as the social location through which both human capital and social capital are acquired. The family remains the pivotal location for acquisition of personal develop and the social network in which the child (and other family members) is embedded, learns skills, and has access to economic and other social resources within the community and beyond, in the national social context. Further, Edgar argues, decisions regarding such family processes as mate selection (including the decision to remain single), parenting, residence, and employment are embedded in systems of resources—negotiations in which the family is a key mediator.

In contrast to this rhetoric, and the debate on what they call the "anti-social family," Barrett and McIntosh (1991) remind us that family, wherever and however it is constructed, has important appeal on several levels involving emotional security for its members. Barrett and McIntosh see the family as, first, "offering a range of emotional and experiential satisfactions not available elsewhere" (p. 21). While *kin*, by ascription, lacks choice and implies constraint, such relations provide an opportunity for a level of psychic support unavailable elsewhere in society. Besides, they contend, there can be pleasure in that which is simply familiar. The appeal of the family also resides in its location as an optimal and rewarding place for bearing and rearing children. Barrett and McIntosh argue that a married couple (or, I add, a constellation of two or more committed adults, whether married or not) can most reliably provide material and social–psychological support for the youngest members of society. That some families fail to do so is that much greater the tragedy of postmodern life.

Barrett and McIntoch (1991) remind us that any model of family is time and culture bound. As discussed in the first chapter, that romantic myth is, in fact, a family form articulated among late 19th century bourgeoisie in Western Europe. To the extent that we hold such an image of the family as the salvation for our social and personal problems, the family as an institution in postmodern, global society is probably doomed.

Can the family not be seen as the "maker of the future," as Boulding (1983) contended a quarter of a century ago? Immigrant family biographies are replete with stories of how families strove to be effective agents for maximizing the resources available to their children and other family members in the communities they called home. As Putnam (2001) argued in

Bowling Alone, the better a family's connections in the community, the better a family's life chances. In a civil society, parents, grandparents, and other family members build social assets through such actions as volunteering and political activity. Such civic engagement builds family assets but also benefits the common good in a civil society. And Edgar (2004) reminds us:

> The family is the filter through which issues such as border protection, terrorism, public transport, and education are interpreted. Moreover public interest in issues changes as cohorts change. . . . [But] kinship is still more important than citizenship, and for most people citizenship has practical meaning [only] through kinship. (P. 14)

Religious leaders are concerned about the extent to which "the world is becoming progressively and pervasively globalized" ("Cardinal Turkson Speaks" 2010:18). In *Familiaris Consortio*, a statement on the role of the Christian family in today's world, the late Pope John Paul II (1981) said:

> [The family now finds its role] extended in a completely new way: it now also involves cooperating for a new international order, since it is only in worldwide solidarity that the enormous and dramatic issues of world justice, the freedom of peoples and the peace of humanity can be dealt with and solved. (P. 74)

Hutton and Giddens (2001) see globalization as testing and complicating families in much the same way as the industrial revolution and urbanization eroded extended family ties. However, in similar ways, globalization also stretches and tests patriarchal control of family members. Globalization's new culture systems, such as the Internet and inexpensive travel back and forth across great distances, likewise will tax family intimacy and authority. Keep in mind, however, that globalization can also expand opportunities for families and their members.

In May 2000, I was introduced to a young man, about age 14, waiting on the steps of the main reception building at Città dei Ragazzi. Founded in 1944 by the late Monsignor John Patrick Carroll-Abbing, Città dei Ragazzi (Boys' Towns, and later Girls' Towns) remains a refuge and a home for children and youth who find themselves alone on the streets of Rome, Italy. Those who find their way to one of the pastoral communities on the outskirts of Rome are "unaccompanied minors"—orphaned, homeless, or displaced. Rather than being separated from their families as armies swept through Italy during World War II, however, the citizens of Boys' and Girls' Towns today are more likely to have fled illegally to Italy from countries across Eastern Europe, Africa, Asia, and the Middle East (Boys' Towns of Italy 2005). In fact, more than half the children and youth served by Boys' and Girls' Towns today are not Catholic, or even Christian, but Muslim (P. S. Moffett, personal communication, 2000). The young man to whom I was introduced wore an expression of anxious anticipation. Originally from Eastern Europe, he had been separated from his family for more than a year. However, an uncle had been located and, on that afternoon, they would be reunited. Nothing else mattered.

More than a decade later, I still think of that young man, who must now be entering his mid-20s. Was he able to reconnect and build meaningful ties with his uncle and perhaps a broader network of extended kin? Has he formed a new family of his own, perhaps in his adopted country of Italy, perhaps in another? Have global demographics, culture, violence, employment, and social policies helped him build family and other assets, or held him back, serving to remind him of his marginal, tenuous place as one of the "others" in his adopted homeland.

Although increasingly diverse, contested, and often at risk, the family continues to receive widespread normative acceptance as a core structure of society. Even among members of societies in which marriage is postponed, deferred, or, as in the case of gays and lesbians, not permitted, new family forms are emerging to ensure that adults and children across the lifespan are enmeshed in ongoing, cooperative, intimate systems, be they of friendship groups, reconstituted families, or even the traditional nuclear, conjugal couple with children. I have faith that individuals, society, and humanity will flourish in the presence of authentic, intimate bonds—even when those bonds are among global families.

Summary

This final chapter offers an examination of the family in an increasingly global society in the second decade beyond the U.N.'s Year of the Family. Social policies that fall short on gender sensitivity have also fallen short of meaningful, assessable social change in the quality of life of families and their members. Meaningful social change is inextricably bound not only to issues of gender but also to social action by organizations that both span supranational, national, and even local, and network to share resources. The greatest urgency for family impact-based social policy at a global level is in the areas of HIV/AIDS, immigration, transnational employment, violence against women and children, and global media and consumption.

Significant improvements in the quality of life of women and their families have been documented across institutional areas and a wide range of countries, but women and their daughters remain the poorest on the planet.

Shamefully, the United States falls toward the bottom of some indices of family policy. Social development can be viewed through a variety of perspectives (e.g., women in development, gender and development), but, again, real enhancement of the lives of families depends on understanding how gender reveals the intersections among micro- and macrosocial forces.

Finally, the argument follows that family rights are human rights, as illustrated by the cases of the politics of human reproduction and the politics of abortion in particular. Transnational movements for the rights of families and their members include the work of organizations such as IWRAW, CEDAW, and the other declarations of the United Nations dealing with children and families. While some scholars continue to emphasize the extent to which globalization is propelling families toward greater disparities between the "haves" and the "have-nots," others emphasize that families remain critical and persistent keystones to society and their members' well-being. In conclusion, although globalization offers a wide range of serious challenges to family structures, functions, and interactions, the evolving family remains a critical, persistent keystone to societal adjustment and individual intimacy and success.

THE GLOBAL HUMAN RIGHTS OF FAMILIES

By Marsha A. Freeman, PhD, JD

All human beings are born into a family. Families may have 2 members or 200. They may or may not receive the protection by their government and their community to which they are entitled according to the universal standards of the Universal Declaration of Human Rights. They may or may not provide adequate nurture and material support to bring children to productive adulthood. They may sacrifice everything to promote the welfare of individual family members whose accomplishments carry honor and wealth, and they may murder members in the name of family honor. Intact or broken, healthy or abusive, honored or rejected, the family is a primary element of human identity.

Late 20th century global developments have placed enormous pressure on families and communities. Pressure on communities and families is not unique in history, but this era's pressures are unique in the level of documentation and analysis focused on them and the resources available to deal with them if political will exists to do so. But governments and other institutions have risen to the occasion inconsistently and with varied results, frequently leaving families and their individual members less well-off and less cohesive than they could be—essentially, less protected than the plain language of the Universal Declaration of Human Rights indicates is their entitlement.

The United Nations declared the International Year of the Family (IYF) in 1994. Considerable rhetoric and some useful research and policy recommendations inevitably result from such United Nations declarations and events. Ten years later, in an IYF anniversary event, close examination of family trends in all regions of the world indicated that while families had changed in some significant ways, the fundamental, global issues that impeded their general health and the ability of individual family members to develop to their full potential remained largely unaddressed.

Ten years is not a long time in which to solve vast, fundamental problems, such as entrenched poverty, the negative impact of globalization on local livelihoods, the HIV/AIDS global epidemic, and patriarchal attitudes. But it is enough time to develop and start to implement intelligent responses. Some progress has in fact occurred, such as programs to lower the rate of new HIV/AIDS cases and to provide cheap and effective treatment, but only in a few countries. In many places school enrollment rates, particularly for girls, are up, attributable to a significant push by donor countries and international agencies. The quality of that education and the real achievement levels, however, are not indicated by the general statistics. And achievement of most of the Millennium Development Goals—adopted by the United Nations in 2000 as a set of reachable targets to reduce poverty, improve health, and increase gender equality by 2015—remains well behind schedule as of 2011.

Policy discussions relating to the family and development generally lack one element that is critical to consistent and sustainable improvement in their well-being: human rights. Both families and individuals within them have a right to protection by the state and by their community. Full realization of human rights would mean that governments and communities pay attention to the distribution of resources, the exercise of freedoms, and the balance of power inside and outside the family unit. To date, no government has a stellar record as to all these issues; even the states with historically excellent social welfare and external human rights records have much to answer for with respect to their minority populations, disabled citizens, gender equality, income distribution, and retrenchment of social benefits.

In short, while everyone celebrates the family, few take care of it.

What Is a Family? And Why Does It Matter?

One of the impediments to good family policy is an imperfect understanding and acceptance of the varied forms of family. Traditionally, "family" refers to persons who are related by blood, marriage, or adoption. This very broad definition can encompass the family formations recognized throughout the world: nuclear (two married parents and their children), extended (multiple generations, multiple wives, siblings, cousins of all degrees), and clan (extended families related to one another). In recent decades, the definition has been challenged to expand, with an increase in one-parent families, unmarried heterosexual partnerships, and, most recently, same-sex partnerships and marriages.

The distinction between family and household is frequently, and unfortunately, blurred in policy discussions. Households may include persons who are not related but who are considered de facto family for purposes of child and elder care and resource sharing. Extended families may share resources and child and elder care but not be in the same household. Blood and marital relations may be legally unrecognized, as in countries where women cannot transmit their citizenship to children or spouses, where the state does not provide for recognition and regulation of certain religious or customary marriages, or where the concept of illegitimacy is preserved by statute or by legally recognized custom. Development economics usually focuses on households rather than on families, discounting cross-household extended family dynamics that have a major impact on income and resource allocations. And development economists have only recently begun to seriously examine intrafamily status and power issues that affect individual and, ultimately, family well-being.

Family or household definitions govern the allocation of public resources and the recognition of rights. In some countries, children of local mothers and foreign fathers, who therefore are deemed not to be citizens, do not have a right to education or health care. "Illegitimate" children may be denied property use or inheritance. In countries in which nuclear families are the norm, grandparents may lose access to the grandchildren in a divorce. In extended-family settings in which children belong to the paternal line, mothers may lose access if they are forced to leave a marriage because of abuse or dowry issues. Children of a same-sex unmarried couple may be denied access to one of the adults in a separation if the nonparent has not legally adopted the child. State support for an elder may be denied if children have stepped in to help financially. Conversely, state support for elders may not exist at all in countries in which family support of elders has always been the norm, even where the extended family is shrinking because of employment or conflict-based migration and decreasing fertility rates. Governments therefore face an enormous challenge to provide for resource allocation and rights recognition on the basis of actual household and family organization, rather than on artificially and traditionally defined household or family models. Few have met all the challenges satisfactorily.

Economic and Social Organization

Families provide social and psychological space for the nurturing of children. They also function as an economic unit, frequently with prescribed economic roles; a political unit, from the family dynasties in democracies to the clan- or ethnicity-based governance of many less-developed countries; and a social unit, enforcing norms of behavior and alliance on both micro and macro levels. At its best, a family provides positive support to its members, encouraging expression of ideas and freedom to develop personal potential. At its worst, a family oppresses its individual members in the name of cultural identity and family cohesion—an excuse for abuse—and conditions social and material support on submission to that abuse.

Members of very poor families, of course, rarely have the choices of personal development and escape from abuse, even with the best of caring relationships. Children are kept home from school to do household or farm chores, forced to work from a very young age, and may be sold into labor or prostitution in another town or across a border. Valuing children for their own potential, no matter how much parents may wish to do so, is an unaffordable luxury. Abused women cannot escape, because they have no way to support themselves and their children outside the family structure. Class exploitation is common; a family's value to the larger society may be only as cheap labor. Families may be broken up by the necessity of migrating to work, leaving children in the care of a single parent or of other family members. Many women left to care for families when men migrate for work have few skills and no individual legal capacity to handle finances or property or to make decisions about the children. When migrant parents return, the family relationships are upended again, as children and other relatives will have evolved in maturity and roles while the workers were away.

Families in less difficult circumstances may also be stressed by conditions of work, as where child care is not supported by the state and family leave policies are narrow. Employment discrimination makes life difficult for many people; even where legal protection is clear, de facto discrimination remains, with a major impact on female workers and families whose members are disabled or are racial, ethnic, or religious minorities.

A human rights approach to policy on family income security and access to basic needs would go much further than the usual rhetoric to truly protect families. Protection of workers from arbitrary treatment and harmful working conditions, a living wage, a safety net for workers in the informal economy, universal primary health care and education, and financial support for persons who cannot work because of age or disability are fundamental human rights for which all governments should provide. Equal access to these basic social and economic goods is critical to family well-being and is required under inter-national law and many national laws. International law, as stated in the International Covenant on Economic, Social and Cultural Rights, requires rich countries to assist poor countries in providing for these basic needs. However, governments are far from universally guaranteeing these rights, and even where rights exist in law and policy, implementation frequently falls short. Consider, for example, the difference between law and reality in the United States with respect to K–12 education, worker rights, and discrimination.

A family is expected to provide for its members' social as well as economic support. In many cultures, individuals are identified first and foremost by their family name and history. Even where family identity is not central, individuals frequently use family as a significant marker for placing themselves and others in a social space. Certainly a child's socialization, which starts with family roles and expectations, is critical to his or her success as an individual and as a member of the larger society. Marriage, educational opportunity, and employ-ment status are deeply affected in all cultures by family ties and identity.

Expanding on the role of families as social space, families and clans have enormous importance as political entities in a number of countries. The head-lines tell us that in Iraq, Afghanistan, Somalia, Yemen, and other states where institutions are in disarray or have failed, clans are the key political authority. In the Occupied Territories in 2007, politically opposed members of a power-ful clan stated that they would settle Fatah-Hamas issues between them-selves, within the clan, since the public authorities were so inept. In more organized states, clans and families may have a particular political heritage and community standing, such that individuals in public life are understood to represent their background as much as they stand for individual positions.

Globalization certainly has had an impact on family size, identity, and abil-ity to provide adequately for family members. Economic migration, pressures on local markets, and shifts in donor priorities have made for physical disloca-tion and disappointed expectations. But globalization also has brought more information to more people, resulting in lower fertility and challenges to oppressive customs such as forced marriage and female genital mutilation, as well as opportunities for women and men to escape the economic dead end of poor villages. People with new information and new opportunities will chal-lenge roles and customs that seem to keep their lives static or disadvan-taged—they will challenge the social space. The social space can expand, or it can resist and either explode or fossilize. Governments and citizens must consider using the energy and opportunities of a changing world to provide greater opportunities for family members and to reexamine oppressive family constructs that keep individuals from making choices to develop their own potential, which ultimately contributes to the well-being of the entire family.

Human Rights and the Family

The family is the natural and fundamental group unit of society and is entitled to protection by society and the State. (Universal Declaration of Human Rights, Article 16.3)

Recognition of the inherent dignity and of the equal and inalienable rights of all members of the human family is the foundation of freedom, justice and peace in the world. (Universal Declaration of Human Rights, preamble)

Families and societies cannot be sustainably successful unless they are built on an ethical infrastructure that accounts for the well-being of all their members. The Universal Declaration of Human Rights (UDHR), adopted in 1948 by the member states of the United Nations, outlines that infrastructure. In the more than 60 years since its adoption, the UDHR and the human rights treaties that derive from its language have been universally accepted, although not totally without reservation, as the standard to which all governments must adhere in developing domestic and, to a certain extent, foreign policy. The failure of individual governments and societies to entirely live up to that standard does not derogate from the standards themselves but indicates the limitations of human nature and political will. Without the standard of the UDHR and the processes of human rights monitoring, governments would be free to deal arbitrarily and cruelly with their citizens and to undermine their material welfare, without any accountability to their citizenry or to the global community. While a country cannot be put in jail, a country can be made to change by the sheer force of international public opinion coupled with advocacy by domestic constituencies empowered by knowing their rights.

While corruption, torture, wealth inequality, discrimination, lack of free expression, and sheer incompetence undermine the enjoyment of human rights in many countries, the international trend since the inception of the UDHR has been toward increased openness and some level of government accountability. Frequently, this change is the result of activism by a relatively small number of people who risk their safety and their lives to press for change. Even where change advocacy does not carry a risk of physical harm, advocates' actions frequently place them at risk of ostracism and social or economic damage. Taking on human rights issues that directly affect the family and its internal dynamic can be particularly risky, as they strike at the heart of identity and intimate power relations.

As the basic unit of society, the family also can be the basic site of oppression. Violence against family members, usually the women and the children, and sometimes elders, is globally endemic. Women experience denial of opportunities for education, employment, health care and healthy spacing of children, property rights, adequate nutrition, and freedom of expression inside the household and in public. Children are beaten, sold into slavery, denied education, sexually exploited by teachers and other adults in their personal circles, and instructed to remain silent at all costs and never to argue with an adult. The scale of these issues is indicated by the adoption of international human rights treaties to deal specifically with discrimination against women (1979) and with the rights of children (1989), when it became clear that their human rights were not adequately articulated and protected under the general treaties—the International Covenant on Civil and Political Rights and the International Covenant on Economic, Social and Cultural Rights.

Dealing with the rights of women and of children is particularly difficult because culture is frequently invoked as an excuse for denial of their rights. Physical and economic oppression of women and the beating of children are defended as necessary to culturally appropriate socialization. The response to that excuse—and it is not a defense but merely an excuse—is that as a matter of fundamental human rights, articulated specifically in the Convention on the Elimination of All Forms of Discrimination Against Women (Article 5), governments are under an obligation to eliminate cultural customs and stereotypes that support inequality and discrimination. Essentially, there is no cultural defense to violation of human rights.

Family members cannot possibly contribute fully to their own family well-being or to the well-being of their community if they are kept enslaved by ignorance, individual poverty, and violence. A family, community, or national regime that is organized on the basis of oppression robs itself, as tremendous political and personal energy and material resources go into maintaining power and privilege, while individuals are prevented from making their full economic and intellectual contribution to society.

Conclusion

Families of all descriptions and sizes are the fundamental social, economic, and political units in which individuals are shaped and on which societies are built. They are universal and indispensable. Not only are governments obligated to protect families, doing so is in their interest. The definition of family for policy and legal purposes should be as expansive as it needs to be to recognize and support individuals' commitments to care for one another, nurture children, and build community.

Family protection requires mobilization of resources to provide for both basic needs, such as primary education, primary health, food security, and housing, and opportunities for intellectual and physical growth. Countries with more resources have a greater responsibility in this respect. Rich countries have a global responsibility to assist poor countries in establishing sufficient family support to help their families develop economically and socially. And all countries involved in the processes of globalization—which means *all countries*—have a responsibility to deal positively with the impact of global markets and cultural change on their families.

Healthy families are the basis of healthy societies that can function well economically and politically. If internal exploitation and violence in the family are accepted as the norm, the larger culture will be exploitive and in some way violent, with a forced cohesion that can be quite fragile. Protecting the family means protecting the individuals within it, and thereby protecting all of society throughout the globe.

Marsha A. Freeman, PhD, JD, is Senior Fellow and Director of the International Women's Rights Action Watch, University of Minnesota Human Rights Center, and Adjunct Professor at the University of Minnesota Law School.

CRITICAL THINKING QUESTIONS

1. Thinking globally, what are the most critical issues facing families today? How is the well-being of families tied to gender?

2. Is globalization leading the world toward a "post-family" condition? Why or why not?

3. Based on what you have learned in reading *Global Families*, what is the likelihood that the young man I met on the steps of Cittá dei Ragazzi is enmeshed in family today? What challenges and opportunities derived from globalization might he have faced?

4. In the essay at the end of this chapter, Marsha Freeman, Director of International Women's Rights Action Watch at the University of Minnesota Human Rights Center, argues, "Not only are governments obligated to protect families; doing so is in their interest." Based on what you have learned about *global families*, what should governments and supranational bodies do to protect families? Why is doing so in the best interests of society?

References

Abdi, C. M. 2007. "Convergence of Civil War and the Religious Right: Reimagining Somali Women." *Signs: Journal of Women in Culture and Society* 33(1):183–207.
———. 2012. "Threatened Identities and Gendered Opportunities: Somali Migration to America." Forthcoming in *Signs: Journal of Women in Culture and Society*.

Abel, E. K. and M. K. Nelson. 1990. *Circles of Care: Work and Identity in Women's Lives*. New York: State University of New York Press.

Achebe, N. 2004. "The Road to Italy: Nigerian Sex Workers at Home and Abroad." *Journal of Women's History* 15(4):178–85.

Adam, B. D. 1995. *The Rise of a Gay and Lesbian Movement*. Rev. ed. New York: Twayne.

Adam, B. D., J. W. Duyvendak, and A. Krouwel. 1999a. *The Global Emergence of Gay and Lesbian Politics: National Imprints of a Worldwide Movement*. Philadelphia, PA: Temple University Press.
———. 1999b. "Introduction." Pp. 1–11 in *The Global Emergence of Gay and Lesbian Politics: National Imprints of a Worldwide Movement*, edited by B. D. Adam, J. W. Duyvendak, and A. Krouwel. Philadelphia, PA: Temple University Press.

Adams, B. N. 2004. "Families and Family Study in International Perspective." *Journal of Marriage and the Family* 66(5):1076–88.

Adams, B. N. and J. Trost, eds. 2005. *Handbook of World Families*. 3rd ed. Thousand Oaks, CA: Sage.

Addams, J. 1910. *Twenty Years at Hull House*. New York: Macmillan.

Adorno, T. 1991. *The Culture Industry: Selected Essays on Mass Culture*. Edited by J. M. Bernstein. London, UK: Routledge.

Afshar, H. and C. Dennis. 1992. *Women and Adjustment Policies in the Third World*. New York: St. Martin's.

Aghajanian, A. 2008. "Family and Change in Iran." Pp. 265–92 in *Families in a Global Context*, edited by C. B. Hennon and S. M. Wilson. New York: Routledge.

Aghajanian, A. and A. L. Moghadas. 1998. "Correlates and Consequences of Divorce in an Iranian City." *Journal of Divorce and Remarriage* 28(3/4):53–71.

Al-Ali, N. 2002. "Loss of Status or New Opportunities? Gender Relations and Transnational Ties Among Bosnia Refugees." Pp. 83–102 in *The Transnational*

Family: New European Frontiers and Global Networks, edited by D. F. Bryceson and U. Vuorela. Oxford, UK: Berg.

Albrow, M. 1997. "The Impact of Globalization on Sociological Concepts: Community, Culture and Milieu." Pp. 20–36 in *Living the Global City: Globalization as Local Process*, edited by J. Eade. London, UK: Routledge.

Allen, J. and D. Massey, eds. 1995. *Geographical Worlds*. Oxford, UK: Oxford University Press.

Allen, K. R. 1989. Single Women/Family Ties: Life Histories of Older Women. Newbury Park, CA: Sage.

Alvi, S., M. D. Schwartz, W. DeKeserdy, and J. Bachaus. 2002. "Victimization and Attitudes Toward Wife Abuse of Impoverished Minority Women." Presented at the annual meeting of the American Society of Criminology, November, Chicago, IL.

Andall, J. 2004. "Acli-Colf and Immigration: Gender, Class, and Ethnicity." *Polis* 18(1): 77–106.

Anderson, B. 2000. *Doing the Dirty Work? The Global Politics of Domestic Labor.* London, UK: Zed Books.

Anderson, B. and J. O'Connell Davidson. 2002. *Trafficking—A Demand Led Problem?* Stockholm, Sweden: Save the Children.

Andrews, E. L. 2006. "Global Trends May Hinder Effort to Curb U.S. Inflation." *New York Times*. Retrieved January 5, 2012 (http://www.nytimes.com/2006/08/28/business/worldbusiness/28fed.html?pagewanted=all).

Angrist, J. D. and J. H. Johnson, IV. 2000. "Effects of Work-Related Absences on Families: Evidence From the Gulf War." *Industrial and Labor Relations Review* 54(1):41–58.

Ansell, N. 2005. *Children, Youth, and Development*. London, UK: Routledge.

Anthias, F. and G. Lazaridis. 2000. "Introduction: Women on the Move in Southern Europe." Pp. 1–13 in *Gender and Migration in Southern Europe: Women on the Move*, edited by F. Anthias and G. Lazaridis. Oxford, UK: Berg.

Appadurai, A. 1996. *Modernity at Large: Cultural Dimensions of Globalization.* Minneapolis: University of Minnesota Press.

Apple, R. 1987. *Mothers and Medicine: A Social History of Infant Feeding, 1890–1950*. Madison: University of Wisconsin Press.

Aries, P. 1960. *L'Enfant et la Vie Familiale sous l'Ancien Régime*. Paris: Librairie Plon.

Askin, K. D. 2001. "Comfort Women: Shifting Shame and Stigma From Victims to Victimizers." *International Criminal Law Review* 1(1/2):5–32.

Assay, S. M. 2003. "Family Strengths in Postcommunist Transition: Romania and the Former East Germany." *Journal of Family and Consumer Science* 95(1):26–32.

Australian Government. 2008. "European Discovery and the Colonization of Australia." Retrieved July 11, 2011 (http://www.cultureandrecreation.gov.au/articles/australianhistory/).

Baber, K. M. and K. R. Allen. 1992. *Women and Families: Feminist Reconstructions.* New York: Guilford.

Baca, M. E. 2006. "Immigrant Children's Roles Open to Interpretation: Kids Acting as Translators Isn't New, but the Long-Term Impact for Them and Their Parents is Mixed at Best." *Star Tribune*, July 23, p. E1.

Bachrach, C. 2001. "Comment: The Puzzling Persistence of Postmodern Fertility Preferences." Pp. 332–8 in *Global Fertility Transition*, edited by R. A. Bulato and J. B. Casterline. New York: Population Council.

Bakan, A. and D. Stasiulis, eds. 1997. *Not One of the Family: Foreign Domestic Workers in Canada*. Toronto, Canada: University of Toronto Press.

Bales, K. 1999. *Disposable People: New Slavery in the Global Economy*. Berkeley: University of California Press.

Balfour, M. C., R. F. Evans, F. W. Notestein, and I. B. Taeuber. 1950. *Public Health and Demography in the Far East: Report of a Survey Trip, September 13–December 13, 1948*. New York: Rockefeller Foundation.

Barber, B. R. 1995. *Jihad vs. McWorld: Terrorism's Challenge to Democracy*. New York: Random House.

Barkawi, T. 2006. *Globalization and War*. Lanham, MD: Rowman & Littlefield.

Barker, D. K. and S. F. Feiner. 2004. *Liberating Economics: Feminist Perspectives on Families, Work, and Globalization*. Ann Arbor: University of Michigan Press.

Barot, R. 2002. "Religion, Migration and Wealth Creation in the Swaminarayan Movement." Pp. 197–213 in *The Transnational Family: New European Frontiers and Global Networks*, edited by D. F. Bryceson and U. Vuorela. Oxford, UK: Berg.

Barrett, M. and M. McIntosh. 1991. *The Anti-Social Family*. 2nd ed. London, UK: Verso.

Barry, K. 1995. *The Prostitution of Sexuality*. New York: New York University Press.

Baudrillard, J. 1988. *Jean Baudrillard: Selected Writings*. Stanford, CA: Stanford University Press.

———. 1989. *America*. London, UK: Verso.

———. 1990. *Fatal Strategies*. New York: Semiotext(e).

Bauman, Z. 1992. *Intimations of Postmodernity*. London, UK: Routledge.

———. 1998. *Globalization: The Human Consequences*. New York: Columbia University Press.

———. 2001. *The Individualized Society*. Cambridge, UK: Polity.

———. 2003. *Liquid Love: On the Frailty of Human Bonds*. Cambridge, UK: Blackwell.

———. 2004. *Wasted Lives: Modernity and Its Outcasts*. Cambridge, UK: Blackwell.

———. 2007. *Liquid Times: Living in an Age of Uncertainty*. Cambridge, UK: Polity.

BBC News. 2006. "Dutch Government Backs Burqa Ban." Retrieved November 17, 2006 (http://news.bbc.co.uk/2/hi/europe/6159046.stm).

Beck, U. 1992. *Risk Society: Towards a New Modernity*. Translated by M. Ritter. Newbury Park, CA: Sage.

———. 1998. *Democracy Without Enemies*. Cambridge, UK: Polity.

———. 2000. *The Brave New World of Work*. Translated by P. Camiller. Cambridge, UK: Polity.

———. 2001. "Living Your Own Life in a Runaway World: Individualisation, Globalisation, and Politics." Pp. 164–74 in *Global Capitalism*, edited by W. Hutton and A. Giddens. New York: New Press.

Beck, U. and E. Beck-Gernsheim. 2002. *Individualization: Institutionalized Individualism and Its Social and Political Consequences*. Newbury Park, CA: Sage.

———. 2004. "Families in a Runaway World." Pp. 499–514 in *The Blackwell Companion to the Sociology of Families*, edited by J. Scott, J. K. Treas, and M. Richards. Cambridge, UK: Cambridge University Press.

———. 2010. "Passage to Hope: Marriage, Migration, and the Need for a Cosmopolitan Turn in Family Research." *Journal of Family Theory & Review* 2(4):401–14.

Beck-Gernsheim, E. 2001. "Household-Migrant Women and Marriage-Migrant Women in a Globalizing World." Pp. 61–80 in *Women and Social Transformation*, edited by E. Beck-Gernsheim, J. Butler, and L. Puigvert. Oxford, UK: Berg.

Beck-Gernsheim, E., J. Butler, and L. Puigvert. 2001. *Women and Social Transformation*. Translated by J. Vaida. New York: Peter Lang.

"Behind the Veil." 2011. *The Economist*, May 14, p. 68.

Bengtson, V. L., A. C. Acock, K. R. Allen, P. Dilworth-Andersons, and D. M. Klein, eds. 2005. *Sourcebook of Family Theory and Research*. Thousand Oaks, CA: Sage.

Berger, P. and B. L. Berger. 1983. *The War Over the Family: Capturing the Middle Ground*. London, UK: Hutchinson.

Bergmann, M. S. and M. E. Jucovy, eds. 1982/1990. *Generations of the Holocaust*. New York: Columbia University Press.

Bernardotti, A., V. Capecchi, and P. Pinto. 1994. "L'Osservatorio delle Immigrazioni del Comune di Bologna: Un Servizio per chi Vuole Documentarsi e Conoscere." *Osservatorio* 0(November):2–3. As translated by and quoted in Orsini-Jones and Gattulo (2000).

Bhagwati, J. N. 2004. *In Defense of Globalization*. New York: Oxford University Press.

Billington, R., J. Hockey, and S. Strawbridge. 1998. *Exploring Self and Society*. Basingstoke, UK: Macmillan.

Bilsen, K. and H. de Witte. 2001. "Waarom Worden Individuen Actief Binnen een Extreem-Rechtse Organisatie? Integratie van de Beschikbare Literatuur in een Hypothetische Kader ter Verklaring van Extreem-Rechts Militantisme." *Tijdschrift voor Sociologie* 22(1):37–62.

Binnie, J. 2004. *The Globalization of Sexuality*. Thousand Oaks, CA: Sage.

Blank, J. 2003. "Sex Trafficking: An Exploratory Study Interviewing Traffickers." Master of Arts thesis, Department of Criminology, Middlesex University, London, UK.

Blank, R. M. 1993. "What Should Mainstream Economists Learn From Feminist Theory?" Pp. 133–43 in *Beyond Economic Man: Feminist Theory and Economics*, edited by M. A. Ferber and J. A. Nelson. Chicago, IL: University of Chicago Press.

Bliss, K. E. 2004. "A Right to Live as Gente Decente: Sex Work, Family Life, and Collective Identity in Early-Twentieth-Century Mexico." *Journal of Women's History* 15(4):164–9.

Blumberg, R. L. 1988. "Gender Stratification, Economic Development, and the African Food Crisis: Paradigm and Praxis in Nigeria." Pp. 115–37 in *Social Structures and Human Lives*, edited by M. W. Riley. Vol. 1, American Sociological Association Presidential Series: Social Change and the Life Course. Newbury Park, CA: Sage.

Bodnar, J. 1987. *The Transplanted: A History of Immigrants in Urban America*. Bloomington: Indiana University Press.

Bogenscheider, K. 2000. "Has Family Policy Come of Age? A Decade Review of the State of U.S. Family Policy in the 1990s." *Journal of Marriage and the Family* 62(4):1136–59.

Booth, A., A. C. Crouter, and N. Landale, eds. 1997. *Immigration and the Family: Research and Policy on U.S. Immigrants*. Mahwah, NJ: Lawrence Erlbaum.

Bose, C. E. 2006a. "Immigration 'Reform': Gender, Migration, Citizenship and SWS." *Gender & Society* 20(5):569–75.

———. 2006b. "Puerto Rico, Globalization, and Gender Issues." *SWS Network News* XXIII(1):4–5.

Bose, C. E. and M. Kim. 2009. *Global Gender Research: Transnational Perspectives*. New York: Routledge.

Bosrock, R. M. 2006. "Globalization Can Change World for Better." *Star Tribune*, December 25, p. D8.

Boss, P. 2006. *Loss, Trauma, and Resilience: Therapeutic Work With Ambiguous Loss*. New York: Norton Professional Books.

Boulding, E. 1983. "Familia Faber: The Family as Maker of the Future." *Journal of Marriage and the Family* 45(2):257–66.

Bourdieu, P. 1998. *Practical Reason: On the Theory of Action*. Cambridge, UK: Polity.

Boyer, R. and D. Drache, eds. 1996. *States Against Markets: The Limits of Globalization*. London, UK: Routledge.

Boys' Towns of Italy. 2005. "Boys' Towns of Italy, Inc." Retrieved January 6, 2012 (http://www.boystownofitaly.org/pdf/boys%20brochure.pdf).

Brajsa-Zganec, A. 2005. "The Long-Term Effects of War Experiences on Children's Depression in the Republic of Croatia." *Child Abuse and Neglect* 29(1):31–43.

Brantley, C. 2003. "Colonial Africa: Transforming Families for Their Own Benefit (and Ours)." Pp. 139–55 in *Families in a New World: Gender, Politics and State Development in a Global Context*, edited by L. Haney and L. Pollard. New York: Routledge.

Briggs, L. 2003. "Familiar Territory: Prostitution, Empires, and the Question of U.S. Imperialism in Puerto Rico, 1849–1916." Pp. 40–63 in *Families in a New World: Gender, Politics and State Development in a Global Context*, edited by L. Haney and L. Pollard. New York: Routledge.

Britner, P. A., D. Mossler, and I.-M. Eigsti. 2008. "International Adoption: Risk and Resilience." *National Council on Family Relations Report* 53(3):F8–F9.

Brown, David. 2011. "Diabetes Becoming Alarmingly Common Worldwide, New Study Finds." *Washington Post*, June 26. Retrieved June 28, 2011 (http://www.washingtonpost.com/national/health-science/diabetes-becoming-alarmingly-common-worldwide-new-study-finds/2011/06/24/AGMkaFlH_story.html).

Browning, D. S. 2003. *Marriage and Modernization: How Globalization Threatens Marriage and What to Do About It*. Grand Rapids, MI: William B. Erdmans.

Brownmiller, S. 1975. *Against Our Will: Men, Women, and Rape*. New York: Simon & Schuster.

Bryceson, D. F. and U. Vuorela. 2002. "Transnational Families in the Twenty-First Century." Pp. 3–30 in *The Transnational Family: New Frontiers and Global Networks*, edited by D. F. Bryceson and U. Vuorela. Oxford, UK: Berg.

Bubloz, M. M. and M. S. Sontag. 1993. "Human Ecology Theory." Pp. 419–48 in *Sourcebook of Family Theories and Methods: A Contextual Approach*, edited by P. G. Boss, W. J. Doherty, R. LaRossa, W. R. Schumm, and S. K. Steinmetz. New York: Plenum.

Bulato, R. A. 2001. "Introduction." Pp. 1–14 in *Global Fertility Transition*, edited by R. A. Bulato and J. B. Casterline. New York: Population Council.

Butron, M. A. G. 2001. "The Effects of Free-Market Globalization on Women's Lives." Pp. 43–50 in *Globalization and Its Victims*, edited by J. Sobrino and F. Wilfred. London, UK: SCM-Canterbury.

Cainkar, L. A. 2011. *Homeland Insecurity: The Arab American and Muslim Experience After 9/11*. New York: Russell Sage.

Caldwell, J. C. 2001. "The Globalization of Fertility Behavior." Pp. 93–115 in *Global Fertility Transition*, edited by R. A. Bulato and J. B. Casterline. New York: Population Council.

———. 2004. "Social Upheaval and Fertility Decline." *Journal of Family History* 29(4):382–406.

"Cardinal Turkson Speaks on Caritas in Veritate." 2010. *Perspectives Magazine* 11(2):18–9.

"The Case Against Globaloney." 2011. *The Economist*, April 23, p. 72.

Castells, M. 2000. *The Rise of the Network Society*. 2nd ed. Oxford, UK: Blackwell.

———. 2004. *The Power of Identity*. 2nd ed. Malden, MA: Blackwell.

Center for Women Policy Studies. 2006. *News From the Center for Women Policy Studies*, Winter. Retrieved January 6, 2012 (http://www.centerwomenpolicy.org/news/newsletter/documents/CWPSnews-Winter2006.pdf).

Chang, G. 2000. *Disposable Domestics: Immigrant Women Workers in the Global Economy*. Cambridge, MA: South End.

Chang, I. 1997. *The Rape of Nanking: The Forgotten Holocaust of WWII*. New York: Basic.

Chant, S. 1997. *Women Headed Households: Diversity and Dynamics in the Developing World*. New York: St. Martin's.

Chaplin, D. 1978. "Domestic Service and Industrialization." *Comparative Studies in Sociology* 1:97–127.

Chart, S. 2000. "Men in Crisis? Reflections on Masculinities, Work and Family in North-West Costa Rica." *European Journal of Development Research* 12(2):350–8.

Chee, M. W. L. 2005. *Taiwanese American Transnational Families: Women and Kin Work*. London, UK: Taylor & Francis.

Chell-Robinson, V. 2000. "Female Migrants in Italy: Coping in a Country of New Immigration." Pp. 103–23 in *Gender and Migration in Southern Europe: Women on the Move*, edited by F. Anthias and G. Lazaridis. Oxford, UK: Berg.

Christensen, H. T., ed. 1964. *Handbook of Marriage and the Family*. Chicago, IL: Rand McNally.

Chu, C. Y. C., Y. Xie, and R. R. Yu. 2011. "Coresidence With Elderly Parents: A Comparative Study of Southeast China and Taiwan." *Journal of Marriage and the Family* 73(1):120–35.

Chu, H. 2011. "Rupert Murdoch's News Corp. Drops Bid for BSkyB." *Los Angeles Times*, July 13. Retrieved July 13, 2011 (http://www.latimes.com/news/nation world/world/la-fg-britain-murdoch-20110714,0,655495.story).

Chung, C. S. 1995. "Korean Women Drafted for Military Sexual Slavery by Japan." Pp. 11–32 in *True Stories of the Korean Comfort Women*, edited by K. Howard. London, UK: Cassell.

———. 1997. "The Origin and Development of the Military Sexual Slavery Problem in Imperial Japan." *Positions* 5(1):219–53.

Clarke-Stewart, A. 1993. *Daycare*. Rev. ed. Cambridge, MA: Harvard University Press.

Coale, A. J. 1973. "The Demographic Transition." Pp. 53–72 in *International Population Conference, Liège, 1973*. Vol. 1. Liège, Belgium: IUSSP. As cited in Caldwell 2001.

Cochrane, A. and K. Pain. 2000. "A Globalizing Society?" Pp. 5–46 in *A Globalizing World? Culture, Economics, Politics*, edited by D. Held. London: Routledge.

Cockburn, C. 2004. "The Continuum of Violence: A Gender Perspective on War and Peace." Pp. 24–44 in *Sites of Violence: Gender and Conflict Zones*, edited by W. Giles and J. Hyndman. Berkeley: University of California Press.

Cohen, R. 1997. *Global Diasporas: An Introduction*. Seattle: University of Washington Press.

————. 2000. "Mom Is a Stranger: The Negative Impact of Immigration Policies on the Family Life of Filipina Domestic Workers." *Canadian Ethnic Studies* 32(3):76–88.

Cohen, S. K. 2006. "The Experience of the Jewish Family in the Nazi Ghetto: Kovno—A Study." *Journal of Family History* 31(3):267–88.

Collins, D. 2009. "'We're There and Queer': Homonormative Mobility and Lived Experience Among Gay Expatriates in Manila." *Gender & Society* 23(4):465–93.

Collins, P. H. 1990. Black Feminist Thought: Knowledge, Consciousness, and the Politics of Empowerment. Boston, MA: Unwin Hyman.

Comunian, A. L. 2005. "The Italian Family: Past and Present." Pp. 225–41 in *Families in Global Perspective*, edited by L. Jaipul, L. Roopnarine, and U. P. Gielen. Boston, MA: Pearson.

Constable, N. 2002. "Filipina Workers in Hong Kong Homes: Household Rules and Relations." Pp. 115–41 in *Global Women: Nannies, Maids, and Sex Workers in the New Economy*, edited by B. Ehrenreich and A. R. Hochschild. New York: Metropolitan/Owl of Henry Holt.

Cooke, L. P. and J. Baxter. 2010. "'Families' in International Context: Comparing Institutional Effects Across Western Societies." *Journal of Marriage and the Family* 72(3):516–36.

Coontz, S. 1992. *The Way We Never Were: Americans and the Nostalgia Trap*. New York: Basic Books.

————. 1997. *The Way We Really Are: Coming to Terms With America's Changing Families*. New York: Basic Books.

————. 2005. *Marriage, a History: How Love Conquered Marriage*. New York: Penguin.

Coser, L. 1973. "Servants: The Obsolescence of an Occupational Role." *Social Forces* 52(1):31–40.

Cowan, R. S. 1983. *More Work for Mother: The Ironies of Household Technology From the Open Hearth to the Microwave*. New York: Basic Books.

Craig, L. and K. Mullan. 2010. "Parenthood, Gender, and Work–Family Time in the United States, Australia, Italy, France, and Denmark." *Journal of Marriage and the Family* 72(5):1344–61.

Crowley, M., D. T. Lichter, and Z. Qian. 2006. "Beyond Gateway Cities: Economic Restructuring and Poverty Among Mexican Immigrant Families and Children." *Family Relations* 55(3):345–60.

Cruz-Malavé, A. and M. F. Manalansan, IV. 2002. "Dissident Sexualities/Alternative Globalism." Pp. 1–10 in *Queer Globalizations: Citizenship and the Afterlife of Colonialism*, edited by A. Cruz-Malavé and M. F. Manalansan, IV. New York: New York University Press.

Currier, A. 2010. "Political Homophobia in Postcolonial Namibia." *Gender & Society* 24(1):110–29.

d'Addio, A. C. and M. M. d'Ercole. 2005. *Trends and Determinants of Fertility Rates in OECD Countries: The Role of Policies*. Organization of Economic Cooperation and Development. Working Paper 27. Retrieved December 20, 2006 (http://www.oecd.org/dataoecd/7/33/35304751.pdf).

Dalla, R. L. and A. Christensen. 2005. "Latino Immigrants Describe Residence in Rural Midwestern Meatpacking Communities: A Longitudinal Assessment of Social and Economic Change." *Hispanic Journal of Behavioral Sciences* 27(1):23–42.

Dalla, R. L., F. Villarruel, S. C. Cramer, and G. Gonzalez-Kruger. 2004. "Examining Strengths and Challenges of Rapid Rural Immigration." *Great Plains Research* 14:231–51.

Darkwah, A. K. 2009. "Trading Goes Global: Ghanaian Market Women in an Era of Globalization." Pp. 41–8 in *Global Gender Research: Transnational Perspectives*, edited by C. Bose and M. Kim. New York: Routledge.

Davidson, J. O. 2006. *Children in the Global Sex Trade*. Cambridge, UK: Polity.

Denmark, D. 2005. "Mass Media and Media Power in Australia." Pp. 220–39 in *Australian Social Attitudes: The First Report*, edited by S. Wilson, G. Meagher, R. Gibson, D. Denmark, and M. Western. Sydney, Australia: University of New South Wales Press.

Desai, M. 2009. *Gender and the Politics of Possibilities: Rethinking Globalization*. Lanham, MD: Rowman & Littlefield.

Diekmann, A. and H. Engelhardt. 1999. "The Social Inheritance of Divorce: Effects of Parent's Family Type in Postwar Germany." *American Sociological Review* 64(6):783–93.

Dill, B. T. 1994. *Across the Boundaries of Race and Class: An Exploration of the Relationship Between Work and Family Among Black Female Domestic Servants*. New York: Garland.

Dobratz, B., L. K. Waldner, and T. Buzzell. 2012. *Power, Politics, and Society: An Introduction to Political Sociology*. Boston, MA: Allyn & Bacon.

"Dolls No More American Whore." 2002. *Newsweek*, March 25, p. 5. Retrieved September 11, 2006 (http://plinks.ebscohost.com).

Doole, C. 2000. "Australia Attacked Over Aborigine Treatment." Retrieved July 11, 2011 (http://news.bbc.co.uk/2/hi/asia-pacific/845400.stm).

Dorow, S. K. 2006. *Transnational Adoption: A Cultural Economy of Race, Gender, and Kinship*. New York: New York University Press.

Dreby, J. 2006. "Honor and Virtue: Mexican Parenting in the Transnational Context." *Gender & Society* 20(1):32–59.

Dribe, M. and M. Stanfors. 2009. "Does Parenthood Strengthen a Traditional Household Division of Labor? Evidence from Sweden." *Journal of Marriage and the Family* 71(1):33–45.

Durkheim, E. 1897/1951. *Suicide*. Translated by J. A. Spaulding and G. Simpson. New York: Free Press.

Duyvendak, J. W. 1995. "From Revolution to Involution: The Disappearance of the Gay Movement in France." *Journal of Homosexuality* 29(4):369–85.

Edelman, M. W. 2006. "Child Watch™ Column: The Global Women's Action Network for Children." Retrieved January 6, 2012 (http://cdf.childrensdefense.org/site/News2?page=NewsArticle&id=7010).

Edgar, D. 1999. "Families as the Crucible of Competence in a Changing Social Ecology." Pp. 109–29 in *Learning to Cope: Developing as a Person in Complex Societies*, edited by E. Frydenberg. Oxford, UK: Oxford University Press.

———. 2004. "Globalization and Western Bias in Family Sociology." Pp. 3–16 in *The Blackwell Companion to the Sociology of Families*, edited by J. Scott, J. K. Treas, and M. Richards. Cambridge, UK: Cambridge University Press.

Ehrenreich, B. and A. R. Hochschild. 2002. *Global Women: Nannies, Maids, and Sex Workers in the New Economy*. New York: Metropolitan/Owl of Henry Holt.

Ehrlich, P. R. 1968. *The Population Bomb*. New York: Ballantine Books.

Eisenstein, Z. 2004. *Against Empire: Feminisms, Racism, and the West*. London, UK: Zed Books.

Eitzen, D. S. and M. Baca Zinn. 2011. "Globalization: An Introduction." Pp. 1–9 in *Globalization: The Transformation of Social Worlds*. 3rd ed., edited by D. S. Eitzen and M. Baca Zinn. Belmont, CA: Wadsworth.

Elder, G. 1974. *Children of the Great Depression*. Chicago, IL: University of Chicago Press.

Elder, G. and E. C. Clipp. 1988. "War Experience and Social Ties: Influences Across Forty Years in Men's Lives." Pp. 306–27 in *Social Structures and Human Lives*, edited by M. W. Riley. Newbury Park, CA: Sage.

"The End of AIDS?" 2011. *The Economist*, June 4, p. 11.

Ender, M. G. 2000. "Beyond Adolescence: The Experiences of Adult Children of Military Parents." Pp. 241–55 in *The Military Family: A Practice Guide for Human Service Providers*, edited by J. Martin, L. Rosen, and L. Sparacino. Westport, CT: Praeger.

———, ed. 2002. *Military Brats and Other Global Nomads: Growing Up in Organization Families*. Westport, CT: Praeger.

———. 2006. "Voices From the Backseat: Growing Up in Military Families." Pp. 138–66 in *Military Life: The Psychology of Serving in Peace and Combat*. Vol. 3, The Military Family. Westport, CT: Praeger.

———. 2009. *American Soldiers in Iraq: McSoldiers or Innovative Professionals?* New York: Routledge.

Ender, M. G., K. Campbell, T. Davis, and P. Michaelis. 2007. "Greedy Media: Army Families, Embedded Reporting, and the War in Iraq." *Sociological Focus* 40(1):48–71.

England, P. 1993. "The Separative Self: Androcentric Bias in Neoclassical Arguments." Pp. 23–36 in *Beyond Economic Man: Feminist Theory and Economics*, edited by M. A. Ferber and J. A. Nelson. Chicago, IL: University of Chicago Press.

Epstein, C. F. 2007. "Great Divides: The Cultural, Cognitive, and Social Bases of the Global Subordination of Women." *American Sociological Review* 72(1):1–22.

Esacove, E. W. 2010. "Love Matches: Heteronormality, Modernity, and AIDS Prevention in Malawi." *Gender & Society* 24(1):83–109.

Esser, R. 2003. "'Language No Obstacle': War Brides in the German Press, 1945–49." *Women's History Review* 12(4):577–603.

European Commission. 2006. "Gender Equality." Retrieved August 8, 2006 (http://ec
.europa.eu/employment_soci/gender_equality/gender_mainstreaming/gender_ove).

Evans, A. and E. Gray. 2005. "What Makes an Australian Family?" Pp. 12–29 in
Australian Social Attitudes: The First Report, edited by S. Wilson, G. Meagher,
R. Gibson, D. Denemark, and M. Western. Sydney, Australia: University of New
South Wales Press.

Ewing, K. P. 2011. *Being and Belonging: Muslims in the United States Since 9/11.*
New York: Russell Sage.

Fahim, K. 2011. "Slap to a Man's Pride Set Off Tumult in Tunisia." *New York Times,*
January 21. Retrieved July 13, 2011 (http://www.nytimes.com/2011/01/22/
world/africa/22sidi.html?pagewanted=all).

Fairlie, R. W., R. A. London, R. Rosner, and M. Pastor. 2006. *Crossing the Divide:
Immigrant Youth and Digital Disparity in California.* Center for Justice,
Tolerance, and Community, University of California, Santa Cruz. Retrieved
December 8, 2006 (http://cjtc.ucsc.edu/docs/digital.pdf).

Fallon, K. M. 2008. *Democracy and the Rise of Women's Movements in Sub-Saharan
Africa.* Baltimore, MD: The Johns Hopkins University Press.

Faramarz, S. 2005. "Plight of Women Adds to France's Immigrant Woes." *Star
Tribune* (Associated Press), November 18, p. A20.

Farber, B. 1971. *Kinship and Class: A Midwestern Study.* New York: Basic Books.

Farwell, N. 2004. "War Rape: New Conceptualizations and Responses." *Affilia*
19(4): 389–403.

Featherstone, M. 1990. "Global Culture: An Introduction." *Theory, Culture and
Society* 7:1–14.

———. 1991. *Consumer Culture and Postmodernism.* London, UK: Sage.

Ferber, M. A. and J. A. Nelson, eds. 1993a. *Beyond Economic Man: Feminist Theory
and Economics.* Chicago, IL: University of Chicago Press.

———. 1993b. "Introduction: The Social Construction of Economics and the Social
Construction of Gender." Pp. 1–22 in *Beyond Economic Man: Feminist Theory
and Economics,* edited by M. A. Ferber and J. A. Nelson. Chicago, IL: University
of Chicago Press.

Field, N. 1997. "War and Apology: Japan, Asia, the Fiftieth, and After." *Positions*
5(1):1–49.

"Fighting Road Kill." 2011. *The Economist,* May 12, p. 77.

Fischer, A. K. and L. Srole. 1978. "Antecedents and Consequences of Residential
Mobility: The Midtown Manhattan Longitudinal Study." Presented at the annual
meetings of the International Sociological Association, August, Uppsala, Sweden.

Flusty, S. 2004. *De-Coca-Colonization: Making the Globe From the Inside Out.* New
York: Routledge.

Folbre, N. 1993. "Socialism, Feminist and Scientific." Pp. 94–110 in *Beyond
Economic Man: Feminist Theory and Economics,* edited by M. A. Ferber and
J. A. Nelson. Chicago, IL: University of Chicago Press.

Foner, N. 1997. "The Immigrant Family: Cultural Legacies and Cultural Changes."
International Migration Review 31(4):961–74.

———. 2000. *From Ellis Island to JFK: New York's Two Great Waves of Immigration.*
New Haven, CT: Yale University Press.

Footrakoon, O. 2000. "Lived Experiences of Thai War Brides in Mixed Thai-
American Families in the United States." PhD dissertation, Department of
History, University of Minnesota, Minneapolis.

"France Relaxes 35-Hour Week Rule." 2005. BBC News. Retrieved January 19, 2006 (http://news.bbc.co.uk/1/hi/world/europe/4373167.stm).

Francome, C. 2004. *Abortion in the USA and the UK*. Burlington, VT: Ashgate.

Frankel, G. and C. Whitlock. 2005. "London Probe Extends Abroad." *Washington Post*, July 16. Retrieved July 21, 2005 (http://www.washingtonpost.com/wp-dyn/content/article/2005/07/15/AR2005071500547.html).

Freeman, J. M. and N. D. Hū. 2003. *Voices From the Camps: Vietnamese Children Seeking Asylum*. Seattle: University of Washington Press.

Furlong, A. and F. Cartmel. 1997. *Young People and Social Change: Individualization and Risk in Late Modern Society*. Buckingham, UK: Open University Press.

"The Future of Mobility." 2011. *The Economist*, May 26. Retrieved July 13, 2011 (http://www.economist.com/node/18741382).

Gabilondo, J. 2002. "Like Blood for Chocolate, Like Queers for Vampires." Pp. 236–363 in *Queer Globalizations: Citizenship and the Afterlife of Colonialism*, edited by A. Cruz-Malavé and M. F. Manalansan, IV. New York: New York University Press.

Gamburd, M. 2000. *The Kitchen Spoon's Handle: Transnationalism and Sri Lankan Migrant Housemaids*. Ithaca, NY: Cornell University Press.

Gdadebo, P., A. R. Rayman-Read, and S. J. Heymann. 2003. "Biological and Social Risks Entwined: The Case of AIDS in Africa." Pp. 31–51 in *Global Inequalities at Work: Work's Impact on the Health of Individuals, Families, and Societies*, edited by S. J. Heymann. New York: Oxford University Press.

Genovese, E. D. 1974. *Roll, Jordan, Roll: The World the Slaves Made*. New York: Pantheon.

Gentleman, A. 2008. "India Nurtures Business of Surrogate Motherhood." *New York Times*, March 10. Retrieved March 10, 2009 (http://www.nytimes.com/2008/03/10/world/asia/10surrogate.html?hp).

George, S. 1999. *The Lugano Report: On Preserving Capitalism in the Twenty-First Century*. Sterling, VA: Pluto.

"Germany Beefs Up Benefits to Bolster the Nation's Birth Rate." 2007. *Star Tribune*, January 4, p. A16.

Gerner, M. E. and F. L. Perry, Jr. 2002. "Gender Differences in Cultural Acceptance and Career Orientation Among Internationally Mobile and Noninternationally Mobile Adolescents." Pp. 165–92 in *Military Brats and Other Global Nomads: Growing Up in Organization Families*, edited by M. G. Ender. Westport, CT: Praeger.

"Getting On." 2011. *The Economist*, June 25, pp. 15–16.

Giddens, A. 1991. *Modernity and Self-Identity: Self and Society in the Modern Age*. Cambridge, UK: Polity.

———. 1992. *The Transformation of Intimacy: Sexuality, Love, and Eroticism in Modern Societies*. Cambridge, UK: Polity.

———. 2000. *Runaway World: How Globalization is Reshaping Our Lives*. New York: Routledge.

———. 2001. "The Global Revolution in Family and Personal Life." Pp. 17–23 in *Family in Transition*. 11th ed., edited by A. S. Skolnick and J. H. Skolnick. Boston, MA: Allyn & Bacon.

Giddens, A., M. Duneier, and R. P. Appelbaum. 2006. *Essentials of Sociology*. New York: W. W. Norton.

Giele, J. Z. 2004. "Women and Men as Agents of Change in Their Own Lives."
Pp. 299–317 in *Changing Life Patterns in Western Industrial Societies*. Vol. 8,
Advances in Life Course Research, edited by J. Z. Giele and E. Holst. Oxford,
UK: Elsevier.

Giele, J. Z. and E. Holst. 2004. "New Life Patterns and Changing Gender Roles."
Pp. 3–22 in *Changing Life Patterns in Western Industrial Societies*. Vol. 8,
Advances in Life Course Research, edited by J. Z. Giele and E. Holst. Oxford,
UK: Elsevier.

Gielen, U. P. 1993. "Gender Roles in Traditional Tibetan Cultures." Pp. 413–37 in
International Handbook on Gender Roles, edited by L. L. Adler. Westport, CT:
Greenwood.

Giglio, M. 2011. "The Cyberactivists Who Helped Topple a Dictator." *Newsweek*,
January 15. Retrieved June 30, 2011 (http://www.newsweek.com/2011/01/15/
tunisia-protests-the-facebook-revolution.html).

Gil, A. G., W. A. Vega, and J. M. Dimas. 1994. "Acculturative Stress and Personal
Adjustment Among Hispanic Adolescent Boys." *Journal of Community
Psychology* 22(1):43–54.

Glele-Ahanhanzo, M. 2002. "Racism, Racial Discrimination, Xenophobia and All
Forms of Discrimination." *Economic and Social Council Report*, February 12,
2002. Retrieved July 11, 2011 (http://www.unhchr.ch/Huridocda/Huridoca
.nsf/0/d7d491c643c20b21c1256b84005a41d0?Opendocument).

Glenn, E. N. 1986. *Issei, Nisei, War Bride: Three Generations of Japanese American
Women in Domestic Service*. Philadelphia, PA: Temple University Press.

Glick, J. E. 2010. "Connecting Complex Processes: A Decade of Research on
Immigrant Families." *Journal of Marriage and the Family* 72(3):498–515.

Global Alliance Against Traffic in Women. 2001. *Human Rights and Trafficking in
Persons: A Handbook*. Bangkok, Thailand: Indochina Publishing.

Goldin, I., G. Cameron, and M. Balarajan. 2011. *Exceptional People: How Migration
Shaped Our World and Will Define Our Future*. Princeton, NJ: Princeton
University Press.

Goldman, M. 2005. *Imperial Nature: The World Bank and Struggles for Social Justice
in the Age of Globalization*. New Haven, CT: Yale University Press.

Gonzales, N. A., J. Deardorff, D. Formoso, A. Barr, and M. Barrerra, Jr. 2006.
"Family Mediators of the Relation Between Acculturation and Adolescent
Mental Health." *Family Relations* 55(3):318–30.

Gonzales, N. A., G. P. Knight, A. Morgan-Saenz, and A. Sirolli. 2002. "Acculturation
and the Mental Health of Latino Youth: An Integration and Critique of the
Literature." Pp. 45–74 in *Latino Children and Families in the United States:
Current Research and Future Directions*, edited by J. Contreras, A. Neal-Barnett,
and K. Kerns. Westport, CT: Praeger.

Goode, W. J. 1963. *World Revolution and Family Patterns*. New York: Free
Press.

Goodkind, D. 1997. "The Vietnamese Double Marriage Squeeze." *International
Migration Review* 1(117):108–27.

Gornick, J. D. and M. K. Meyers. 2004. "Welfare Regimes in Relation to Paid Work
and Care." Pp. 45–67 in *Changing Life Patterns in Western Industrial Societies*.
Vol. 8, Advances in Life Course Research, edited by J. Z. Giele and E. Holst. New
York: Elsevier.

Granot, H. 1995. "Impact of the Gulf War on Marriage and Divorce in Israel." *International Journal of Sociology of the Family* 25(2):39–46.

Greenhouse, S. and Leonhardt, D. 2006. "Real Wages Fail to Match a Rise in Productivity." *New York Times*. Retrieved January 5, 2012 (http://www.nytimes.com/2006/08/28/business/28wages.html?pagewanted=all).

Greenstein, T. N. 2006. "Domestic (In)Justice: National Context, Family Satisfaction, and Fairness in the Division of Household Labor." Paper presented at the annual meeting of the American Sociological Association, August, Montréal, Canada.

Greider, W. 1997. *One World, Ready or Not: The Manic Logic of Global Capitalism.* New York: Simon & Schuster.

Grochowski, J. R. 2000. "Families as 'Strategic Living Communities.'" Paper presented at the annual meeting of the American Academy of Health Behavior, September 2000, Santa Fe, NM.

Gunewardena, N. and A. Kingsolver. 2007. "Introduction." Pp. 3–22 in *The Gender of Globalization: Women Navigating Cultural and Economic Marginalities*, edited by N. Gunewardena and A. Kingsolver. New York: School for Advanced Research Press.

Gupta, S. 1999. "The Effects of Transitions in Marital Status on Men's Performance of Housework." *Journal of Marriage and the Family* 61(3):700–11.

Haas, L. and C. P. Hwang. 2007. "Gender and Organizational Culture: Correlates of Companies' Responsiveness to Fathers in Sweden." *Gender & Society* 21(1):52–79.

Hagan, J. and W. Rymond-Richmond. 2009. *Darfur and the Crime of Genocide.* New York: Cambridge University Press.

Haksun, K. 1995. "Bitter Memories I Am Loath to Recall." Pp. 32–40 in *True Stories of the Korean Comfort Women*, edited by K. Howard. London, UK: Cassell.

Hampton, K. N. and B. Wellman. 2004. "Long Distance Community in the Network Society: Contact and Support Beyond Netville." Pp. 94–107 in *The Family Experience: A Reader in Cultural Diversity.* 4th ed., edited by M. Hutter. Boston, MA: Pearson.

Hamwi, M. 2006. "Sending Babies Abroad." *Newsweek*, November 13, p. 17.

Hancock, L. 2002. "The Care Crunch: Changing Work, Families and Welfare in Australia." *Critical Social Policy* 22(1):119–40.

Haney, L. 2003. "Welfare Reform With a Familial Face: Reconstituting State and Domestic Relations in Post-Socialist Eastern Europe." Pp. 159–78 in *Families in a New World: Gender, Politics and State Development in a Global Context*, edited by L. Haney and L. Pollard. New York: Routledge.

Haney, L. and L. Pollard, eds. 2003a. *Families of a New World: Gender, Politics, and State Development in a Global Context.* New York: Routledge.

———. 2003b. "In a Family Way: Theorizing State and Familial Relations." Pp. 1–14 in *Families of a New World: Gender, Politics, and State Development in a Global Context*, edited by L. Haney and L. Pollard. New York: Routledge.

Hardt, M. and A. Negri. 2000. *Empire.* Cambridge, MA: Harvard University Press.

———. 2004. *Multitude, War, and Democracy in the Age of Empire.* New York: Penguin.

Hareven, T. K. 1977. "Family Time and Historical Time." *Daedalus* 97(2):385–96.

———. 1982. *Family Time and Industrial Time: The Relationship Between the Family and Work in a New England Industrial Community.* Cambridge, UK: Cambridge University Press.

————. 2000. *Families, History, and Social Change: Life-Course and Cross-Cultural Perspectives*. Boulder, CO: Westview.

Hawkesworth, M. E. 2006. *Globalization and Feminist Activism*. Lanham, MD: Rowman & Littlefield.

Held, D., H. McGrew, D. Goldblatt, and J. Perraton. 1999. *Global Transformations: Politics, Economics, and Culture*. Cambridge, UK: Polity.

Hennon, C. B. and S. M. Wilson, eds. 2008. *Families in a Global Context*. New York: Routledge.

Herbert, W. 1996. *Foreign Workers and Law Enforcement in Japan*. London, UK: Kegan Paul International.

Herman, E. and R. McChesney. 1997. *The Global Media: The New Missionaries of Corporate Capitalism*. London, UK: Cassell.

Heymann, J. 2006. *Forgotten Families: Ending the Growing Crisis Confronting Children and Working Parents in the Global Economy*. Oxford, UK: Oxford University Press.

Hicks, G. 1995. *The Comfort Women: Japan's Brutal Regime of Enforced Prostitution in the Second World War*. New York: W. W. Norton.

Hightower, K. and H. Scherer. 2007. *Help! I'm a Military Spouse—I Want a Life Too!: How to Craft a Life for You as You Move With the Military*. 2nd ed. Dulles, VA: Potomac.

Hill, R. and R. H. Rodgers. 1964. "The Developmental Approach." Pp. 171–211 in *Handbook of Marriage and the Family*, edited by H. T. Christensen. Chicago, IL: Rand McNally.

Hirst, P. and G. Thompson. 1992. "The Problem of 'Globalization': International Economic Relations, National Economic Management, and the Formation of Trading Blocs." *Economy and Society* 21(4):357–96.

Hochschild, A. R. 1989. *The Second Shift: Working Parents and the Revolution at Home*. New York: Viking.

————. 1997. *The Time Bind: When Work Becomes Home and Home Becomes Work*. New York: Metropolitan.

————. 2000. "Global Care Chains and Emotional Surplus Value." Pp. 130–46 in *On the Edge: Living With Global Capitalism*, edited by W. Hutton and A. Giddens. London, UK: Jonathan Cape.

————. 2001. "The Nanny Chain." *American Prospect* 11(4). Retrieved January 5, 2012 (http://prospect.org/article/nanny-chain).

Hollinger, M. A. 2007. "Ethical Reflections for a Globalized Family Curriculum." Pp. 244–78 in *Cultural Diversity and Families*, edited by B. S. Trask and R. R. Hamon. Thousand Oaks, CA: Sage.

Hondagneu-Sotelo, P. 2001. *Doméstica: Immigrant Workers Cleaning and Caring in the Shadows of Affluence*. Berkeley: University of California Press.

Hondagneu-Sotelo, P. and E. Avila. 1997. "'I'm Here, but I'm There': The Meanings of Latina Transnational Motherhood." *Gender & Society* 5(2):548–71.

Hook, J. 2006. "Care in Context: Men's Unpaid Work in 20 Countries, 1965–2003." *American Sociological Review* 71(4):639–60.

Hopfensperger, J. 2006. "A Freeze in the Nursing Pipeline." *Star Tribune*, December 2, pp. A1, A21.

————. 2011. "Survey: What Do Poor Kids Need?" *Star Tribune*, January 18, p. B3.

Hosek, J. 2002. *Married to the Military: The Employment of Earnings of Military Wives Compared With Those of Civilian Wives*. Santa Monica, CA: Rand.

Hotakainen, R. 2011. "Concern Grows Over 'Epidemic' Veteran Suicide Rate." *News Tribune*. Retrieved July 4, 2011 (http://www.thenewstribune.com/2011/05/26/1680716/concern-grows-over-epidemic-veteran.html).

Hovey, J. D. and C. A. King. 1996. "Acculturative Stress, Depressions, and Suicidal Ideation Among Immigrant and Second-Generation Latino Adolescents." *Journal of the American Academy of Child and Adolescent Psychology* 35(9):1183–92.

"How to Survive Double Deployment." 2003. *USAA Magazine*, March, pp. 20–1.

Howard, K., ed. 1995. *True Stories of the Korean Comfort Women*. London, UK: Cassell.

Huang, S. and B. S. A. Yeoh. 1996. "Ties That Bind: State Policy and Migrant Female Domestic Helpers in Singapore." *Geoforum* 27:479–93.

Huebner, A. J. and J. A. Mancini. 2005. *Adjustments Among Adolescents in Military Families When a Parent Is Deployed: Final Report to the Military Family Research Institute and Department of Defense Quality of Life Office*. South Bend, IN: Purdue University Press.

Huebner, A. J., J. A. Mancini, G. L. Bowen, and D. K. Orthner. 2009. "Shadowed by War: Building Community Capacity to Support Military Families." *Family Relations* 58(2):216–28.

Hughes, D. M. 2001a. "Globalization, Information Technology, and Sexual Exploitation of Women and Children." *Rain and Thunder: A Radical Feminist Journal of Discussion and Activism* 13(Winter):1–3.

———. 2001b. "The 'Natasha' Trade: Transnational Sex Trafficking." *National Institute of Justice Journal* 246(January):8–15.

Human Rights Law Centre. 2011. "Australian Fronts: UN to Defend Human Rights Record." Retrieved July 11, 2011 (http://www.hrlc.org.au/content/topics/international-human-rights-mechanisms/australian-fronts-un-to-defend-human-rights-record-8-june-2011/).

———. 2006. "Occupied Palestinian Territories: Authorities Must Address Violence Against Women and Girls; Inadequate Laws and Policies Deny Victims Justice." Retrieved November 9, 2006 (http://hrw.org/english/docs/2006/11/07/palab14496.htm).

Huntington, S. P. 1996. *The Clash of Civilizations and the Remaking of World Order*. New York: Simon & Schuster.

Hutter, M. 1981. *The Changing Family: Comparative Perspectives*. New York: Wiley.

———. 1986–1987. "Immigrant Families in the City." *The Gallatin Review* 6:60–9.

Hutton, W. and A. Giddens, eds. 2001. *On the Edge: Living With Global Capitalism*. London, UK: Vintage.

Hylmö, A. 2002. "'Other' Expatriate Adolescents: A Postmodern Approach to Understanding Expatriate Adolescents Among Non-U.S. Children." Pp. 193–210 in *Military Brats and Other Global Nomads: Growing Up in Organization Families*, edited by M. G. Ender. Westport, CT: Praeger.

Immigrant Law Center. 2003. *Non-Citizen Women and Children: A Vulnerable Population*. St. Paul, MN.

Inclan, J. 2003. "Class, Culture, and Gender Contradictions in Couples Therapy With Immigrant Families." Pp. 333–48 in *Feminist Family Therapy: Empowerment and Social Location*, edited by L. B. Silverstein and T. J. Goodrich. Washington, DC: American Psychological Association.

Inglis, C. 2004. "Australia's Continuing Transformation." Retrieved July 11, 2011 (http://www.migrationinformation.org/Feature/display.cfm?ID=242).

Ingoldsby, B. B. and S. Smith. 2006. *Families in Global and Multicultural Perspective.* 2nd ed. Thousand Oaks, CA: Sage.

Ingoldsby, B. B., S. Smith, and J. E. Miller. 2004. *Exploring Family Theories.* Los Angeles, CA: Roxbury.

International Organization for Migration. 2011. Retrieved December 29, 2011 (http://www.iom.int/jahia/jsp/index.jsp).

International Women's Rights Action Watch (IWRAW). 2004. *Equality and Women's Economic, Social, and Cultural Rights: A Guide to Implementation and Monitoring Under the International Covenant on Economic, Social and Cultural Rights.* Minneapolis, MN.

Itzin, C. 1992. "Social Construction of Sexual Inequality." Pp. 57–75 in *Pornography, Women, Violence, and Civil Liberties: A Radical New View*, edited by C. Itzin. Oxford, UK: Oxford University.

Iwao, S. 2001. "Japan's Battle of the Sexes: The Search for Common Ground." Pp. 114–18 in *Family in Transition.* 11th ed., edited by A. S. Skolnick and J. H. Skolnick. Boston, MA: Allyn & Bacon.

Izuhara, M. and H. Shibata. 2002. "Breaking the Generational Contract? Japanese Migration and Old-Age Care in Britain." Pp. 155–69 in *The Transnational Family: New European Frontiers and Global Networks*, edited by D. F. Bryceson and U. Vuorela. Oxford, UK: Berg.

Jackson, R. M. 2001. "Destined for Equality." Pp. 81–8 in *Family in Transition.* 11th ed., edited by A. S. Skolnick and J. H. Skolnick. Boston, MA: Allyn & Bacon.

Jacobson, H. 2008. *Culture Keeping: White Mothers, International Adoption, and the Negotiation of Family Difference.* Nashville, TN: Vanderbilt University Press.

James, P. 2006. "Review of *Australian Social Attitudes: The First Report* edited by S. Wilson, G. Meagher, R. Gibson, D. Denemark, and M. Western." *Australian Humanities Review*, April (38). Retrieved December 15, 2006 (http://www.lib.latrobe.edu.au/AHR/archive/Issue-April-2006/james).

Jasso, G. 1997. "Migration and the Dynamics of Family Phenomena." Pp. 63–77 in *Immigration and the Family: Research and Policy on U.S. Immigrants*, edited by A. Booth, A. C. Crouter, and N. Landale. Mahwah, NJ: Lawrence Erlbaum.

Jelin, E. 2004. "The Family in Argentina: Modernity, Economic Crisis, and Politics." Pp. 391–413 in *Handbook of World Families*, edited by B. N. Adams and J. Trost. Thousand Oaks, CA: Sage.

Jennings, A. L. 1993. "Public or Private? Institutional Economics and Feminism." Pp. 111–30 in *Beyond Economic Man: Feminist Theory and Economics*, edited by M. A. Ferber and J. A. Nelson. Chicago, IL: University of Chicago Press.

Johnson, M. M. 1989. "Feminism and the Theories of Talcott Parsons." Pp. 101–18 in *Feminism and Sociological Theory*, edited by R. A Wallace. Newbury Park, CA: Sage.

Joseph, M. 2002. "Family Affairs: The Discourse of Global/Localizations." Pp. 71–99 in *Queer Globalizations: Citizenship and the Afterlife of Colonialism*, edited by A. Cruz-Malavé and M. F. Manalansan, IV. New York: New York University Press.

Journal of Marriage and the Family. 2004. Special Issue: International Perspectives on Families and Social Change 66(5).

Kallis, A. A. 2005. "From the Editor: Remembering (the Shoah) and Forgetting (the Itsembambor)." *Journal of Genocide Research* 7(1):5–29.

Kamerman, S. B. and A. J. Kahn. 1997. *Family Change and Family Policies in Great Britain, Canada, New Zealand, and the United States.* New York: Oxford University Press.

Kandido-Jaksic, M. 1999. "Ethnically-Mixed Marriages and Social Distance Towards Members of Some Ex-Yugoslav Nations." *Sociologija* 41(2):103–24.

Karner, T. X. 1998. "Professional Caring: Homecare Workers as Fictive Kin." *Journal of Aging Studies* 12(1):69–83.

Karney, B. R. and J. S. Crown. 2006. *Families Under Stress: An Assessment of Data, Theory, and Research on Marriage and Divorce in the Military.* Santa Monica, CA: Rand Corporation, National Defense Research Institute.

Karraker [Wilkes], M. W. 1975. *Occupation and Anomia in the Rural South: 1960–1970.* Master's thesis, Department of Rural Sociology, North Carolina State University, Raleigh, NC.

———. 2004. "The Stranger and Marginality, Sociation and Social Processes: Concepts for Globalizing Knowledge Around Issues of Transnational Immigration." Presented at the International Education Seminar on Immigration in Western Europe, June, Berlin, Germany, and Marseilles and Paris, France.

———. 2006. "Competition, Conflict, Accommodation, and Assimilation: Applications of Robert Park's Social Processes to International Migration." Presented at the annual meeting of the British Sociological Society, April, Harrogate, UK.

Karraker, M. W. and J. R. Grochowski. 2012. *Families With Futures: A Survey of Family Studies Into the Twenty-First Century.* 2nd ed. London, UK: Routledge.

Katragadda, C. P. and R. Tidwell. 1998. "Rural Hispanic Adolescents at Risk for Depressive Symptoms." *Journal of Applied Social Psychology* 28(20):1916–30.

Kellermann, N. P. F. 2001. "Perceived Parental Rearing Behavior in Children of Holocaust Survivors." *Israel Journal of Psychiatry* 38(1):58–68.

Khalidi, R. 2011. "The Arab Spring." *The Nation*, May 3. Retrieved July 13, 2011 (http://www.thenation.com/article/158991/arab-spring).

Kilbride, P. and J. Kilbride. 1990. *Changing Family Life in East Africa: Women and Children at Risk.* University Park: Pennsylvania State University Press.

Killian, C. 2006. *North African Women in France: Gender, Culture, and Identity.* Stanford, CA: Stanford University Press.

Kirk, D. 1996. "Demographic Transition Theory." *Population Studies* 50(3):361–87.

Korteweg, A. C. 2008. "The Sharia Debate in Ontario: Gender, Islam, and Representations of Muslim Women's Agency." *Gender & Society* 22(4):434–54.

Koser, K. 2009. "Why Migration Matters." *Current History* 108(717):147–53.

Kraut, R., M. Paterson, V. Lundmark, S. Kiesler, T. Mukopadhyay, and W. Schlerlis. 1998. "Internet Paradox: A Social Technology That Reduces Social Involvement and Psychological Well-Being?" *American Psychologist* 53(9):1017–31.

Krell, R., P. Suedfeld, and E. Soriano. 2004. "Child Holocaust Survivors as Parents: A Transgenerational Perspective." *American Journal of Orthopsychiatry* 74(4):402–508.

Kristoff, N. D. 2009. "Obama and UNFPA." *On the Ground* (*New York Times* blog). Retrieved June 29, 2011 (http://kristof.blogs.nytimes.com/tag/barack-obama/).

Kristoff, N. D. and S. WuDunn. 2009. *Half the Sky: Turning Oppression Into Opportunity for Women Worldwide*. New York: Knopf.

Krohn, I. R. 1998. "Holocaust Scatters Family in '30s, Reunion Gathers It Back Together." Retrieved January 2, 2012 (http://www.jweekly.com/article/full/9533/holocaust-scatters-family-in-30s-reunion-gathers-it-back-together/).

Kroska, A. 2004. "Divisions of Domestic Work: Revising and Expanding the Theoretical Explanations." *Journal of Family Issues* 25(7):900–32.

Kŭmju, H. 1995. "I Want to Live Without Being Treated With Contempt." Pp. 70–9 in *True Stories of the Korean Comfort Women*, edited by K. Howard. London, UK: Cassell.

Kunovich, R. M. and C. Deitelbaum. 2004. "Ethnic Conflict, Group Polarization, and Gender Attitudes in Croatia." *Journal of Marriage and the Family* 66(5):1089–1107.

LaFraniere, S. 2006. "Sex Abuse of Girls is Stubborn Scourge of Africa." *New York Times*, December 1. Retrieved December 1, 2006 (http://www.nytimes.com/2006/12/01/world/africa/01madagascar.html?ei+5070&en+dld65).

Laliberte, D., B. Laplante, and V. Piche. 2003. "The Impact of Forced Migration on Marital Life in Chad." *European Journal of Population/Revue Européenne de Demographie* 19(4):413–35.

Land, H. 2004. "Children, Families, States, and Changing Citizenship." Pp. 54–68 in *The Blackwell Companion to the Sociology of Families*, edited by J. Scott, J. Treas, and M. Richards. Malden, MA: Blackwell.

Landale, N. S. 1997. "Immigration and the Family: An Overview." Pp. 281–91 in *Immigration and the Family: Research and Policy on U.S. Immigrants*, edited by A. Booth, A. C. Crouter, and N. Landale. Mahwah, NJ: Lawrence Erlbaum.

Larney, B. E. 1994. "Children of World War II in Germany: A Life Course Analysis." PhD dissertation, Department of Sociology, Arizona State University, Phoenix.

Lash, S. and C. Lury. 2006. *Global Culture Industry*. Oxford, UK: Blackwell.

Lawler, E. J., S. R. Thye, and J. Yoon. 2011. *Social Commitments in a Depersonalized World*. New York: Russell Sage.

Lawson, H. A. 2001a. "Globalization, Flows of Culture and People, and New-Century Frameworks for Family-Centered Policies, Practices, and Development." Pp. 338–76 in *Family-Centered Policies and Practices: International Implications*, edited by K. Briar-Lawson, H. A. Lawson, and C. B. Hennan, with A. R. Jones. New York: Columbia University Press.

———. 2001b. "Introducing Globalization's Challenges and Opportunities and Analyzing Economic Globalization and Liberalization." Pp. 293–337 in *Family-Centered Policies and Practices*, edited by K. Briar-Lawson, H. A. Lawson, and C. B. Hennon, with A. R. Jones. New York: Columbia University Press.

Lee, D. R. 1998. "Mail Fantasy: Global Sexual Exploitation in the Mail-Order Bride Industry and Proposed Legal Solutions." *Asian Law Review* 5(1):139–79.

Lee, K. S. 2010. "Gender, Care Work, and the Complexity of Family Membership in Japan." *Gender & Society* 24(5):647–71.

Leeder, E. J. 2004. *The Family in Global Perspective: A Gendered Journey*. Thousand Oaks, CA: Sage.

Legarde, E., M. S. van der Loeff, C. Enel, B. Holmgren, R. Dray-Spira, G. Pison, J. P. Piau, V. Delaunay, S. M'Boup, I. Ndoye, M. Pellicer, H. Whittle, and P. Aaby. 2003. "Mobility and the Spread of Human Immunodeficiency Virus into Rural Areas of West Africa." *International Journal of Epidemiology* 32:744–52.

Lemberger, J., ed. 1995. *A Global Perspective on Working With Holocaust Survivors and the Second Generation.* Jerusalem, Israel: JDC–Brookdale Institute of Gerontology and Human Development.

Lemert, C. and A. Elliott. 2006. *Deadly Worlds: The Emotional Costs of Globalization.* Lanham, MD: Rowman and Littlefield.

Lengermann, P. M. and G. Niebrugge. 2010a. "Contemporary Feminist Theories." Pp. 193–228 in *Contemporary Sociological Theory and Its Classical Roots.* 3rd ed., edited by G. Ritzer. New York: McGraw-Hill.

———. 2010b. "Feminism and Postmodern Social Theory." Pp. 264–65 in *Contemporary Sociological Theory and Its Classical Roots.* 3rd ed., edited by G. Ritzer. New York: McGraw-Hill.

Leung, H.-C. and K.-M. Lee. 2005. "Immigration Controls, Life-Course Coordination, and Livelihood Strategies: A Study of Families Living Across the Mainland–Hong Kong Border." *Journal of Family and Economic Issues* 26(4):487–507.

Levine, P. 2004. "'A Multitude of Unchaste Women': Prostitution in the British Empire." *Journal of Women's History* 15(4):159–63.

Lipovetsky, G. and S. Charles. 2005. *Hypermodern Times: Themes for the 21st Century.* Translated by A. Brown. Cambridge, UK: Polity.

Litt, J. 2000. *Medicalized Motherhood: Perspectives From the Lives of African-American and Jewish Women.* New Brunswick, NJ: Rutgers University Press.

Liu, D. 2007. "When Do National Movements Adopt or Reject International Agenda? A Comparative Analysis of the Chinese and Indian Women's Movements." *American Sociological Review* 71(6):921–42.

Longino, H. E. 1993. "Economics for Whom?" Pp. 158–68 in *Beyond Economic Man: Feminist Theory and Economics*, edited by M. A. Ferber and J. A. Nelson. Chicago, IL: University of Chicago Press.

Lopata, H. Z. 1971. *Occupation Housewife.* Westport, CT: Greenwood.

Lorber, J. 2005. "Women's Worlds 2005 Seoul, South Korea." *SWS Network News* XXII(3):5–8.

Lorentzen, L. A. and J. Turpin, eds. 1998. *The Women and War Reader.* New York: New York University Press.

Lukose, R. A. 2009. *Liberalization's Children: Gender, Youth, and Consumer Citizenship in Globalizing India.* Durham, NC: Duke University Press.

MacAskill, E. 2007. "UN Clashes With Iraq on Civilian Death Toll." 2007. *The Guardian*, January 17. Retrieved January 27, 2012 (http://www.guardian.co.uk/world/2007/jan/17/iraq.ewenmacaskill).

MacKay, H. 2000. "The Globalization of Culture?" Pp. 47–84 in *A Globalizing World: Culture, Economics, Politics*, edited by D. Held. London, UK: Routledge.

Mandle, J. 2006. *Global Justice: An Introduction.* Cambridge, UK: Polity.

Marchand, M. H. and A. S. Runyan, eds. 2000. *Gender and Global Restructuring: Sightings, Sites, and Resistances.* London, UK: Routledge.

Markus, A., J. Jupp, and P. McDonald. 2009. *Australia's Immigration Revolution.* Crows Nest, NSW, Australia: Allen & Unwin.

Marling, W. H. 2006. *How "American" Is Globalization?* Baltimore, MD: The Johns Hopkins University Press.

Marsh, I., G. Meagher, and S. Wilson. 2005. "Are Australians Open to Globalisation?" Pp. 240–57 in *Australian Social Attitudes: The First Report*, edited by S. Wilson, G. Meagher, R. Gibson, D. Denemark, and M. Western. Sydney, Australia: University of New South Wales Press.

Marsh, J. R. 2008. "Womb Outsourcing Threatens International Adoptions." Retrieved June 29, 2011 (http://www.childlaw.us/2008/03/womb-outsourcing -threatens-int.html).

Martinez, C. R., Jr. 2006. "Effects of Differential Family Acculturation on Latino Adolescent Substance Use." *Family Relations* 55(3):306–17.

Marty, M. E. and R. S. Appleby. 1991. *Fundamentalism Observed*. Vol. I, The Fundamentalism Project. Chicago, IL: University of Chicago Press.

Mascia-Lees, F. E. 2010. *Gender & Difference in a Globalizing World*. Long Grove, IL: Waveland.

Massey, D. 1994. *Space, Place, and Gender*. Minneapolis: University of Minnesota Press.

———, ed. 2010. *New Faces in New Places: The Changing Geography of American Immigration*. New York: Russell Sage.

Mattelart, A. 1994. *Mapping World Communication: War, Progress, Culture*. Translated by S. Emanuel and J. A. Cohen. Minneapolis: University of Minnesota Press.

Mayer, K. U. 1988. "German Survivors of World War II: The Impact on the Life Course of the Collective Experience of Birth Cohorts." Pp. 229–46 in *Social Structures and Human Lives*, edited by M. W. Riley. Newbury Park, CA: Sage.

McCluskey, K. C., ed. 1994. *Notes From a Traveling Childhood: Reading for Internationally Mobile Parents*. Washington, DC: Foreign Service Youth Foundation.

McCorry, P. 1984. "The Lost Rosary; or, Our Irish Girls, Their Trials, Temptations, and Triumphs." Pp. 153–9 in *The Exiles of Erin: Nineteenth-Century Irish-American Fiction*, edited by C. Fanning. Notre Dame, IN: University of Notre Dame Press.

McCubbin, H. I., B. B. Dahl, P. J. Metres, Jr., E. J. Hunter, and J. A. Plag, eds. 1974. *Family Separation and Reunion: Families of Prisoners of War and Servicemen Missing in Action*. San Diego, CA: Center for Prisoner of War Studies, Naval Health Research Center.

McElwee, J. J. 2011. "Religious Community Publicly Backs Embattled Sr. Elizabeth Johnson." *National Catholic Reporter*, July 14. Retrieved January 6, 2012 (http://ncronline.org/news/women-religious/religious-community-publicly-backs -embattled-sr-elizabeth-johnson).

McGregor, J. H. S. 2006. *Venice From the Ground Up*. Cambridge, MA: Belknap Press of Harvard University Press.

McLuhan, M. 1964. *Understanding Media*. New York: McGraw-Hill.

McMahon, K. and J. Stanger. 2002. *Speaking Out: Three Narratives of Women Trafficked to the United States*. Los Angeles, CA: Coalition to Abolish Slavery and Trafficking.

Meissner, D. M., R. D. Hormats, A. G. Walker, and S. Ogata. 1993. *International Migration Challenges in a New Era: Policy Perspectives and Priorities for Europe, Japan, North America, and the International Community*. New York: Trilateral Commission.

Mendoza, K. R. 2003. "Freeing the 'Slaves of Destiny': The Lolas of the Filipino Comfort Women Movement." *Cultural Dynamics* 15(3):247–66.

Merry, S. E. 2005. *Human Rights and Gender Violence: Translating International Law Into Local Justice.* Chicago, IL: University of Chicago Press.

Merton, R. K. 1968. *Social Theory and Social Structure*, enl. ed. New York: Free Press.

Meyer, M. H., ed. 2000. *Care Work: Gender, Labor and the Welfare State.* New York: Routledge.

Mies, M. 1994. "Gender and Global Capitalism." Pp. 107–122 in *Capitalism and Development*, edited by L. Sklar. New York: Routledge.

Miles, S. 2000. *Youth Lifestyles in a Changing World.* Buckingham, UK: Open University Press.

Miller, C. R. and E. W. Butler. 1966. "Anomia and Eunomia: A Methodological Evaluation of Leo Srole's Anomia Scale." *American Sociological Review* 31(3):400–06.

Miller, D. 1997. *Capitalism: An Ethnographic Approach.* Oxford, UK: Berg.

Min, P. G. 2003. "Korean 'Comfort Women': The Intersection of Colonial Power, Gender, and Class." *Gender & Society* 17(6):938–57.

Minnesota Advocates for Human Rights. 2004. *The Government Response to Domestic Violence Against Refugee and Immigrant Women in the Minneapolis/St. Paul Metropolitan Area: A Human Rights Report.* Minneapolis, MN.

———. 2006. "Women's Human Rights Program." Retrieved January 6, 2012 (http://www.theadvocatesforhumanrights.org/Women_s_Human_Rights_Program.html).

Miyoshi, M. 1993. "A Borderless World? From Colonialism to Transnationalism and the Decline of the Nation-State." *Critical Inquiry* 19(Summer):726–51.

Mizruchi, E. H. 1960. "Social Structure and Anomia in a Small City." *American Sociological Review* 25(5):645–54.

Mohanty, C., A. Russo, and L. Torres. 1991. *Third World Women and the Politics of Feminism.* Bloomington: Indiana University Press.

Moore, M. 2006. "As Europe Grows Grayer, France Devises a Baby Boom." *Washington Post*, October 18, p. A01. Retrieved December 26, 2011 (http://www.washingtonpost.com/wp-dyn/content/article/2006/10/17/AR2006101701652.html).

Moreno, J. C. 2002. "Entering Into the Realm of 'the Other': A Few Suggestions for Crossing Boundaries of Human Difference." Presented at the annual meeting of the Minnesota Council of Family Relations, December, St. Paul.

Morley, D. 1986. *Family Television: Cultural Power and Domestic Leisure.* London, UK: Comedia.

Morley, D. and K. Robins. 1995. *Spaces of Identity: Global Media, Electronic Landscapes, and Cultural Boundaries.* London, UK: Routledge.

Moses, A. 2004. *Genocide and Settler Society: Frontier Violence and Stolen Indigenous Children in Australian History.* Vol. 6. New York: Berghahn.

Moya, F.-N. 2006. "Fighting Poverty by Another Name." *Mail and Guardian*, July 28–August 3, p. 22.

Mulhall, E. 2009. "Women Warriors: Supporting She 'Who Has Borne the Battle.'" *Iraq and Afghanistan Veterans of America Issue Report*, October. Retrieved July 4, 2011 (http://media.iava.org/IAVA_WomensReport_2009.pdf).

Murdock, G. P. 1949. *Social Structure.* New York: Macmillan.

————. 1982. *Outline of Cultural Materials.* New Haven, CT: Human Relations Area Files.

Muroi, H. and N. Sasaki. 1997. "Tourism and Prostitution in Japan." Pp. 180–219 in *Gender, Work, and Tourism,* edited by M. T. Sinclair. London, UK: Routledge.

Nairn, T. and P. James. 2005. *Global Matrix: Nationalism, Globalism and State-Terrorism.* London, UK: Pluto.

Naples, N. A. and M. Desai, eds. 2002. *Women's Activism and Globalization: Linking Local Struggles and Transnational Politics.* London: Routledge.

Nashef, Y. 1992. *The Psychological Impact of the Intifada on Palestinian Children Living in Refugee Camps in the West Bank, as Reflected in Their Dreams, Drawings and Behavior.* Frankfurt am Main, Germany: Peter Lang.

National Council on Family Relations. 2011. "United Nations Observes the International Day of Families." Retrieved May 12, 2011 (http://www.ncfr.org/news/united-nations-observes-international-day-families).

Nayak, A. 2003. *Race, Place, and Globalization: Youth Cultures in a Changing World.* Oxford, UK: Berg.

Nederveen Pieterse, J. 2004. *Globalization and Culture: Global Mélange.* Lanham, MD: Rowman & Littlefield.

Nozaki, Y. 2001. "Feminism, Nationalism, and the Japanese Textbook Controversy Over 'Comfort Women.'" Pp. 170–89 in *Feminism and Antiracism: International Struggles for Justice,* edited by F. W Twine and K. M. Blee. New York: New York University Press.

Oakley, A. 1974. *The Sociology of Housework.* New York: Pantheon.

Obama, B. 2006. *The Audacity of Hope: Thoughts on Reclaiming the American Dream.* New York: Crown.

Ode, K. 2007. "Foreign Adoptions Decline as Rules Shift." *Star Tribune,* January 14, pp. A1, A13.

Office of the Registrar General and Census Commissioner, India. 2010–2011. "Census Data 2001, India at a Glance, Sex Ratio." Retrieved June 28, 2011 (http://censusindia.gov.in/Census_Data_2001/India_at_glance/fsex.aspx).

Ohmae, K. 1995. *The End of the Nation State.* New York: Free Press.

Oishi, N. 2005. *Women in Motion: Globalization, State Policies, and Labor Migration in Asia.* Stanford, CA: Stanford University Press.

Okpun, Y. 1995. "Taken Away at Twelve." Pp. 95–103 in *True Stories of the Korean Comfort Women,* edited by K. Howard. London, UK: Cassell.

Ollenburger, J. C. and H. A. Moore. 1998. *A Sociology of Women: The Intersection of Patriarchy, Capitalism, and Colonization.* 2nd ed. Upper Saddle River, NJ: Prentice Hall.

Ong, A. 1999. *Flexible Citizenship: The Cultural Logics of Transnationality.* Durham, NC: Duke University Press.

Ono, H. and J. Berg. 2010. "Homogamy and Intermarriage of Japanese and Japanese Americans with Whites Surrounding World War II." *Journal of Marriage and the Family* 72(5):1249–62.

Orecklin, M. 2002. "Puppet Politics." *Time,* September 30. Retrieved September 11, 2006 (http://www.time.com/time/magazine/article/0,9171,1003371–3,00.html).

Organisation for Economic Co-operation and Development (OECD). 2002. *Babies and Bosses: Reconciling Work and Family Life.* Vol. 1, Australia, Denmark and the Netherlands. Paris, France: OECD.

————. 2006. "About the Organisation for Economic Co-operation and Development (OECD)." Retrieved December 20, 2006 (http://www.oecd.org/pages/0,3417 ,en_36734052_36734103_1_1_1_1_1,00.html).

————. 2011. *Gender Equality in Education, Employment, and Entrepreneurship.* Retrieved July 10, 2011 (http://www.oecd.org/dataoecd/7/5/48111145.pdf).

Orsini-Jones, M. and F. Gattullo. 2000. "Migrant Women in Italy: National Trends and Local Perspectives." Pp. 125–44 in *Gender and Migration in Southern Europe: Women on the Move*, edited by F. Anthias and G. Lazaridis. Oxford, UK: Berg.

Palriwala, R. and P. Uberoi. 2008. "Exploring the Links: Gender Issues in Marriage and Migration." Pp. 23–62 in *Marriage, Migration, and Gender*, edited by R. Palriwala and P. Uberoi. London, UK: Sage.

Park, I. J. K. 2007. "Enculturation of Korean American Adolescents Within Family and Cultural Contexts: The Mediating Role of Ethnic Identity." *Family Relations* 56(4):403–12.

Park, R. E. 1950. *Race and Culture.* New York: Free Press.

————. 1952. *Human Communities.* New York: Free Press.

Parra-Cardona, J. R., L. A. Bulock, D. R. Imig, F. A. Villaruel, and S. J. Gold. 2006. "'Trabajando Duro Todos Los Días': Learning from the Life Experiences of Mexican-Origin Migrant Families." *Family Relations* 59(3):361–75.

Parreñas, R. S. 2000. "Migrant Filipina Domestic Workers and the International Division of Reproductive Labor." *Gender & Society* 14(4):560–80.

————. 2001. *Servants of Globalization: Women, Migration, and Domestic Work.* Stanford, CA: Stanford University Press.

————. 2002. "The Care Crisis in the Philippines: Children and Transnational Families in the New Global Economy." Pp. 39–54 in *Global Women: Nannies, Maids, and Sex Workers in the New Economy*, edited by B. Ehrenreich and A. R. Hochschild. New York: Metropolitan/Owl.

Parsons, T. 1966. *Societies: Evolutionary and Comparative Perspectives.* Englewood Cliffs, NJ: Prentice Hall.

Partnership for a New American Economy. 2011. "The 'New American' Fortune 500." Retrieved June 29, 2011 (http://www.renewoureconomy.org/sites/all/ themes/pnae/img/new-american-fortune-500-june-2011.pdf).

Pavalko, E. K. and G. H. Elder, Jr. 1990. "World War II and Divorce: A Life-Course Perspective." *American Journal of Sociology* 95(5):1213–34.

Pearce, R. L. D. 2002. "Children's International Relocation and the Developmental Process." Pp. 145–65 in *Military Brats and Other Global Nomads: Growing Up in Organization Families*, edited by M. G. Ender. Westport, CT: Praeger.

Peskin, H. 1981. "Observations on the First International Conference on Children of Holocaust Survivors." *Family Process* 20(4):391–4.

Pew Research Center. 2011a. "The Future of the Global Muslim Population: Projections for 2010–2030." Retrieved May 11, 2011 (http://pewforum.org/ The-Future-of-the-Global-Muslim-Population.aspx).

————. 2011b. "Muslim Americans: Middle Class and Mostly Mainstream." Retrieved May 11, 2011 (http://pewforum.org/Politics-and-Elections/Little-Support-for-Terrorism-Among-Muslim-Americans.aspx).

————. 2011c. "98% vs. 64%—TV: Have It but Could Live Without It." Retrieved July 13, 2011 (http://pewresearch.org/databank/dailynumber/?NumberID=687)

Picard, A. 2006. "Gathering Opens With Focus on AIDS Prevention." *The Globe and Mail*, August 14, pp. A1, A11.

P'ilgi, M. 1995. "I So Much Wanted to Study." Pp. 80–7 in *True Stories of the Korean Comfort Women*, edited by K. Howard. London, UK: Cassell.

Piper, N. 2000. "Globalization, Gender, and Migration: The Case of International Marriage in Japan." Pp. 205–25 in *Towards a Gendered Political Economy*, edited by J. Cook, J. Roberts, and G. Waylen. London, UK: Macmillan.

———. 2001. "Transnational Women's Activism in Japan and Korea: The Unresolved Issue of Military Sexual Slavery." *Global Networks* 1(2):155–70.

———. 2003. "Bridging Gender, Migration, and Governance: Theoretical Possibilities in the Asian Context." *Asian and Pacific Migration Journal* 12(1–2):21–48.

Pitts, J. R. 1964. "The Structural-Functional Approach." Pp. 51–124 in *Handbook of Marriage and the Family*, edited by H. T. Christensen. Chicago, IL: Rand McNally.

Pollard, L. 2003. "The Promise of Things to Come: The Image of the Modern Family in State-Building, Colonial Occupation, and Revolution in Egypt, 1805–1922." Pp. 17–39 in *Families in a New World: Gender, Politics and State Development in a Global Context*, edited by L. Haney and L. Pollard. New York: Routledge.

"Pope Extols Virtues of Traditional Families in a Changing Spain." 2006. *Star Tribune*, July 11, p. A9.

Pope John Paul II. 1981. *Familiaris Consortio: The Role of the Christian Family in the Modern World*. Vatican translation. Boston, MA: Pauline Books and Media.

Population Research Institute. 1999. "Money for Nothing: Why the United States Should Not Resume UNFPA Funding." Retrieved June 28, 2011 (http://pop.org/content/money-for-nothing-why-the-united-states-should-not-resume-unfpa-funding-889).

Portes, A. and M. Zhou. 1993. "The New Second Generation: Segmented Assimilation and Its Variants." *Annals of the American Association of Political and Social Science* 530(November):74–96.

Project on Global Working Families. 2006. "Work, Family and HIV." Retrieved December 26, 2011 (http://www.hsph.harvard.edu/globalworkingfamilies/HIV.htm).

———. 2011. "Work, Family, and Equity Labour Initiative." Retrieved January 6, 2012 (http://www.mcgill.ca/ihsp/research/labour/wfei).

Purewal, N. K. 2001. "New Roots for Rights: Women's Responses to Population and Development Policies." Pp. 96–117 in *Women Resist Globalization*, edited by S. Rowbotham and S. Linkogle. London, UK: Zed Books.

Purkayastha, B. 2005. *Negotiating Ethnicity: South Asian Americans Traverse a Transnational World*. New Brunswick, NJ: Rutgers University Press.

Putnam, R., with L. M. Feldstein and D. Cohen. 2001. *Bowling Alone: The Collapse and Revival of American Community*. New York: Simon & Schuster.

Quah, S. R. 2008. *Families in Asia: Home and Kin*. 2nd ed. New York: Routledge.

Quester, G. H. 1990. "The Psychological Effects of Bombing on Civilian Populations: Wars of the Past." Pp. 201–14 in *Psychological Dimensions of War*, edited by B. Glad. Newbury Park, CA: Sage.

Quotations Page. 2007. Retrieved January 15, 2007 (http://www.quotationspage.com/search.php3?Search=the+future+belongs&startsearch=Search&Author=Eleanor+Roosevelt&C=coles&C=poorc&C=lindsly&C=net&C=devils&C=contrib).

Ray, L. 2006. *Globalization and Everyday Life.* New York: Routledge.

Rheingold, H. 1993. *The Virtual Community.* Reading, MA: Addison-Wesley.

Richmond, A. 1994. *Global Apartheid: Refugees, Racism, and the New World Order.* Toronto, Canada: Oxford University Press.

Riley, N. E. and K. E. Van Vleet. 2011. *Making Families Through Adoption.* Thousand Oaks, CA: Pine Forge.

Rippi, S. 2003. "Kompensation oder Konflikt? Zur Erklärung negativer Einstellungen zur Zuwanderung." Instit Soziologie, Universität Chemnitz, Germany.

Ritzer, G. 1993. *The McDonaldization of Society: An Investigation Into the Changing Character of Contemporary Social Life.* Newbury Park, CA: Pine Forge.

———. 1995. *Expressing America: A Critique of the Increasingly Global Credit Card Society.* Thousand Oaks, CA: Pine Forge.

———. 1996. *The McDonaldization of Society.* Rev. ed. Thousand Oaks, CA: Pine Forge.

———. 2004a. *The Globalization of Nothing.* Thousand Oaks, CA: Pine Forge.

———. 2004b. *The McDonaldization of Society.* Rev. New Century ed. Thousand Oaks, CA: Pine Forge.

———. 2005a. *Enchantment in a Disenchanted World: Revolutionizing the Means of Consumption.* 2nd ed. Thousand Oaks, CA: Pine Forge.

———. 2005b. "The 'New' Means of Consumption: A Postmodern Analysis." Pp. 280–98 in *Illuminating Social Life: Classical and Contemporary Theory Revisited.* 3rd ed., edited by P. Kivisto. Thousand Oaks, CA: Pine Forge.

———. 2007. *Contemporary Sociological Theory and Its Classical Roots.* 2nd ed. New York: McGraw Hill.

———. 2010. *Contemporary Social Theory & Its Classical Roots: The Basics.* 3rd ed. New York: McGraw Hill.

Robertson, R. 1990. "Mapping the Global Condition: Globalization as the Central Concept." *Theory, Culture, and Society* 7(1):15–30.

———. 1995. "Glocalization: Time-Space and Homogeneity-Heterogeneity." Pp. 25–44 in *Global Modernities*, edited by M. Featherstone, S. Lash, and R. Robertson. Thousand Oaks, CA: Sage.

Robila, M., ed. 2004. *Families in Eastern Europe.* New York: Elsevier.

Roeder, V. D. and A. V. Millard. 2000. "Gender and Employment Among Latino Migrant Farmworkers in Michigan." Working Paper No. 52. Michigan State University, Julian Samora Research Institute, Ann Arbor, MI. Retrieved January 16, 2007 (http://www.jsri.msu.edu/RandS/research/wps/wp52abs.html).

Romero, M. 1992. *Maid in the U.S.A.* New York: Routledge.

Roopnarine, J. L. and M. Shin. 2003. "Caribbean Immigrants from English-Speaking Countries: Socio-Historical Forces, Migratory Patterns, and Psychological Issues in Family Functioning." Pp. 123–42 in *Migration, Immigration, and Emigration in International Perspectives*, edited by L. L. Adler and U. P. Gielen. Westport, CT: Greenwood.

Roopnarine, J. L. and U. P. Gielen. 2005. "Families in Global Perspective: An Introduction." Pp. 3–13 in *Families in Global Perspectives*, edited by J. L. Roopnarine and U. P. Gielen. Boston, MA: Pearson.

Rosen, E. I. 2002. *Making Sweatshops: The Globalization of the U.S. Apparel Industry.* Berkeley: University of California Press.

Rosenau, J. N. 1997. *Along the Domestic Frontier: Exploring Governance in a Turbulent World.* Cambridge, UK: Cambridge University Press.

———. 2003. *Distant Proximities: Dynamics Beyond Globalization.* Princeton, NJ: Princeton University Press.

Rosenthal, G. 2000. "Social Transformation in the Context of Familial Experience: Biographical Consequences of a Denied Past in the Soviet Union." Pp. 115–38 in *Biographies and the Division of Europe,* edited by R. Breckner, D. Kalekin-Fischman, and I. Miethe. Opladen, Germany: Leske and Budrich.

———. 2002a. "Introduction. Family History: Life Stories." *History of the Family: An International Quarterly* 7(2):175–82.

———. 2002b. "Veiling and Denying the Past: The Dialogue in Families of Holocaust Survivors and Families of Nazi Perpetrators." *History of the Family: An International Quarterly* 7(2):225–38.

Rosero-Bixby, L. 2001. "Comment: Population Programs and Fertility." Pp. 205–9 in *Global Fertility Transition,* edited by R. A. Bulato and J. B. Casterline. New York: Population Council.

Rostow, W. W. 1961. *The Stages of Economic Growth.* Cambridge, UK: Cambridge University Press.

Rothenberg, D. 1998. *With These Hands: The Hidden World of Migrant Farmworkers Today.* New York: Harcourt Brace.

Rotheram-Borus, M. J. 1989. "Ethnic Differences in Adolescents' Identity Status and Associated Behavioral Problems." *Journal of Adolescence* 12(4):361–74.

Rowbotham, S. 1992. *Women in Movement: Feminism and Social Action.* London, UK: Routledge.

Roy, A. 2003. *War Talk.* Cambridge, MA: South End.

Ruff-O'Herne, J. 2008. *Fifty Years of Silence: The Extraordinary Memoir of a War Rape Survivor.* Sydney, NSW, Australia: William Heinemann.

Ruger, W., S. E. Wilson, and S. L. Waddoups. 2002. "Warfare and Welfare: Military Service, Combat, and Marital Dissolution." *Armed Forces and Society* 29(1):85–107.

Ruiz-Casares, M. 2010. "Kin and Youths in the Social Networks of Youth-Headed Households in Namibia." *Journal of Marriage and the Family* 72(5):1408–25.

Rumbaut, R. G. 1997. "Ties That Bind: Immigration and Immigrant Families in the United States." Pp. 3–46 in *Immigration and the Family: Research and Policy on U.S. Immigrants,* edited by A. Booth, A. C. Crouter, and N. Landale. Mahwah, NJ: Lawrence Erlbaum.

"Rupert Murdock." 2011. *New York Times,* March 4. Retrieved July 1, 2011 (http://topics.nytimes.com/top/reference/timestopics/people/m/rupert_murdoch/index.html?scp=1&sq=global%20media%20control&st=cse).

Safa, H. I. 2002. "Women and Globalization: Lessons From the Dominican Republic." Pp. 141–56 in *The Spaces of Neoliberalism: Land, Place and Family in Latin America,* edited by J. Chase. Bloomfield, CT: Kumarian.

Said, E. W. 1978. *Orientalism.* New York: Pantheon.

Salzinger, L. 2003. *Gender in Production: Making Workers in Mexico's Global Factories.* Berkeley, CA: University of California Press.

Sangok, Y. 1995. "I Came Home but Lost My Family." Pp. 124–33 in *True Stories of the Korean Comfort Women,* edited by K. Howard. London, UK: Cassell.

Sanminiatelli, M. 2007. "Italy Accuses 2,000 of Human Trafficking." Retrieved January 26, 2007 (http://www.nytimes.com/2007/01/25/world/europe/25italy.html).

Sarker, S. and E. N. De. 2002. *Trans-Status Subjects: Gender in the Globalization of South and Southeast Asia*. Durham, NC: Duke University Press.

Sassen, S. 2002. "Global Cities and Survival Circuits." Pp. 254–74 in *Global Women: Nannies, Maids, and Sex Workers in the New Economy*, edited by B. Ehrenreich and A. R. Hochschild. New York: Metropolitan/Owl.

Saxena, P. C., A. Kulczycki, and R. Jurdi. 2004. "Nuptiality Transitions and Marriage Squeeze in Lebanon: Consequences of Sixteen Years of Civil War." *Journal of Comparative Family Issues* 35(2):251–8.

"Scarred by History: The Rape of Nanjing." 2005. Retrieved December 31, 2006 (http://news.bbc.co.uk/2/hi/asia-pacific/223038.stm).

Schiller, N. G., L. Basch, and C. Blanc-Szanton. 1992a. "Towards a Definition of Transnationalism: Introductory Remarks and Research Questions." Pp. ix–xiv in *Towards a Transnational Perspective on Migration: Race, Class, Ethnicity, and Nationalism Reconsidered*, edited by N. G. Schiller, L. Basch, and C. Blanc-Szanton. *Annals of the New York Academy of Sciences* 645(July 6). New York: The New York Academy of Sciences.

———. 1992b. "Transnationalism: A New Analytic Framework for Understanding Migration." Pp. 1–24 in *Towards a Transnational Perspective on Migration: Race, Class, Ethnicity, and Nationalism Reconsidered*, edited by N. G. Schiller, L. Basch, and C. Blanc-Szanton. *Annals of the New York Academy of Sciences* 645(July 6). New York: The New York Academy of Sciences.

Schmalzbauer, L. 2009. "Gender on a New Frontier: Mexican Migration in the Rural Mountain West." *Gender & Society* 23(6):747–67.

Schmickle, S. 2006. "Old Habits vs. New Hungers." *Star Tribune*, July 11, pp. A1, A7.

Schmitt, J. and J. Wadsworth. 2006. "Changing Patterns in the Relative Economic Performance of Immigrants to Great Britain and the United States, 1980." Center for Economic Performance Working Paper 1422, April. Retrieved January 3, 2012 (http://www.cepr.net/documents/publications/immigration_2006_04.pdf).

Schöpp-Schilling, H. B. and C. Flinterman, eds. 2007. *The Circle of Empowerment: Thirty-Five Years of the UN Committee on the Elimination of Discrimination Against Women*. New York: Feminist Press.

Schwartzberg, B. 2004. "'Lots of Them Did That': Desertion, Bigamy, and Marital Fidelity in Late-Nineteenth-Century America." *Journal of Social History* 37(3): 573–600.

Scott, D. 2000. "Embracing What Works: Building Communities That Strengthen Families." *Children Australia* 25(2):4–9.

Scott, J., J. Treas, and M. Richards, eds. 2004. *The Blackwell Companion to the Sociology of Families*. Oxford, UK: Blackwell.

Seager, J. 2003. *The Penguin Atlas of Women in the World*. New York: Penguin.

Segal, S. J. 2003. *Under the Banyan Tree: A Population Scientist's Odyssey*. New York: Oxford University Press.

Shah, A. 2007. "New Kid on the Block." *Star Tribune*, January 7, pp. E1, E3.

Shaw, A. 2004. "Immigrant Families in the UK." Pp. 270–85 in *The Blackwell Companion to the Sociology of Families*, edited by J Scott, J. Treas, and M. Richards. Oxford, UK: Blackwell.

Shea, N. 1954. *The Army Wife*. 3rd rev. ed. New York: Harper and Brothers.

Sheng, X. 2004. "Chinese Families." Pp. 99–128 in *Handbook of World Families*, edited by B. N. Adams and J. Trost. Thousand Oaks, CA: Sage.

Shircliff, E. J. and J. M. Shandra. 2011. "Non-Governmental Organizations, Democracy, and HIV Prevalence: A Cross-National Analysis." *Sociological Inquiry* 81(2):143–73.

Sigle-Rushton, W. and C. Kenney. 2004. "Public Policy and Families." Pp. 457–77 in *The Blackwell Companion to the Sociology of Families*, edited by J. Scott, J. Treas, and M. Richards. Malden, MA: Blackwell.

Silverstein, L. B. and C. F. Auerbach. 2005. "(Post)modern Families." Pp. 33–47 in *Families in Global Perspectives*, edited by J. L. Roopnarine and U. P. Gielen. Boston, MA: Allyn & Bacon.

Singh, J. P. 2004. "The Contemporary Indian Family." Pp. 129–66 in *Handbook of World Families*, edited by B. N. Adams and J. Trost. Thousand Oaks, CA: Sage.

Sirjamaki, J. 1964. "The Institutional Approach." Pp. 33–50 in *Handbook of Marriage and the Family*, edited by H. T. Christensen. Chicago, IL: Rand McNally.

Sklair, L. 2002. *Globalization: Capitalism and Its Alternatives*. Oxford, UK: Oxford University Press.

Skolnick, A. S. and J. H. Skolnick. 2001. *Family in Transition*. 11th ed. Boston, MA: Allyn & Bacon.

Slouka, M. 1995. *War of the Worlds: Cyberspace and the High-Tech Assault on Reality*. New York: Basic Books.

Smith, A. D. 1990. "Towards a Global Culture?" *Theory, Culture, & Society* 7:171–91.

Smyth, L. 2005. *Abortion and Nation: The Politics of Reproduction in Contemporary Ireland*. Burlington, VT: Ashgate.

Snyder, A. 2006. "Fostering Transnational Dialogue: Lessons Learned From Women Peace Activists." *Globalization* 3(1):31–47.

Soh, C. S. 2000a. "From Imperial Gifts to Sex Slaves: Theorizing Symbolic Representations of the 'Comfort Women.'" *Social Science Japan Journal* 3(1): 59–76.

———. 2000b. "Human Rights and the 'Comfort Women.'" *Peace Review* 12(1): 123–9.

———. 2004. "Aspiring to Craft Modern Gendered Selves: 'Comfort Women' and Chongsindair in Late Colonial Korea." *Critical Asian Studies* 36(2):175–98.

Solow, R. M. 1993. "Feminist Theory, Women's Experience, and Economics." Pp. 153–7 in *Beyond Economic Man: Feminist Theory and Economics*, edited by M. A. Ferber and J. A. Nelson. Chicago, IL: University of Chicago Press.

Sørenson, A. 2004. "Economic Relations Between Women and Men: New Realities and the Re-Interpretation of Dependence." Pp. 281–97 in *Changing Life Patterns in Western Industrial Societies*. Vol. 8, Advances in Life Course Research, edited by J. Z. Giele and E. Holst. New York: Elsevier.

Sparr, P., ed. 1994. *Mortgaging Women's Lives: Feminist Critiques of Structural Adjustment*. London, UK: Zed Books.

Spencer-Walters, T. 2008. "Family Patterns in Sierra Leone." Pp. 153–80 in *Families in a Global Context*, edited by C. B. Hennon and S. M. Wilson. New York: Routledge.

Spierings, N., J. Smits, and M. Verloo. 2010. "Micro- and Macrolevel Determinants of Women's Employment in Six Arab Countries." *Journal of Marriage and the Family* 72(5):1391–1407.

Spybey, T. 1996. *Globalization and World Society*. Cambridge, UK: Polity.

Srole, L. 1956. "Social Integration and Certain Corollaries: An Exploratory Study." *American Sociological Review* 21(6):709–16.

Stack, C. B. 1974. *All Our Kin: Strategies for Survival in a Black Community*. New York: Harper and Row.

Standing, G. 2001. "Care Work: Overcoming Insecurity and Neglect." Pp. 15–31 in *Care Work: The Quest for Security*, edited by M. Daly. Geneva, Switzerland: International Labour Organization.

Stanger, J. E. 2005. "Children of Holocaust Survivors: A Life-History Study." PhD dissertation, Department of Humanistic Studies, State University of New York, Albany.

Stein, Gertrude. 1937/1973. *Everybody's Autobiography*. New York: Vintage.

Stevenson, B. 1991. "Distress and Discord in Virginia Slave Families." Pp. 103–24 in *In Joy and in Sorrow: Women, Family, and Marriage in the Victorian South*, edited by C. Bleser. New York: Oxford University Press.

Stewart, F. 1991. "The Many Faces of Development." *World Development* 19(12):1847–64.

Strasser, S. 1982. *Never Done: A History of American Housework*. New York: Pantheon.

Strassman, D. 1993. "Not a Free Market: The Rhetoric of Disciplinary Authority in Economics." Pp. 54–68 in *Beyond Economic Man: Feminist Theory and Economics*, edited by M. A. Ferber and J. A. Nelson. Chicago, IL: University of Chicago Press.

Stryker, S. 1964. "The Interactional and Situational Approaches." Pp. 125–70 in *Handbook of Marriage and the Family*, edited by H. T. Christensen. Chicago, IL: Rand McNally.

Sunok, Y. 1995. "It Makes Me Sad That I Can't Have Children." Pp. 115–23 in *True Stories of the Korean Comfort Women*, edited by K. Howard. London, UK: Cassell.

T'aesŏn, K. 1995. "Death and Crisis." Pp. 151–7 in *True Stories of the Korean Comfort Women*, edited by K. Howard. London, UK: Cassell.

Tambe, A. 2005. "The Elusive Ingénue: A Transnational Feminist Analysis of European Prostitution in Colonial Bombay." *Gender & Society* 19(2):160–79.

Thai, H.-C. 2002. "Clashing Dreams: Highly Educated Overseas Brides and Low-Wage U.S. Husbands." Pp. 230–53 in *Global Woman: Nannies, Maids, and Sex Workers in the New Economy*, edited by B. Ehrenreich and A. R. Hochschild. New York: Metropolitan/Owl.

Thayer, M. 2010. *Making Transnational Feminism*. New York: Routledge.

Thomas, W. I. and F. Znaniecki. 1927. *The Polish Peasant in Europe and America*. New York: Knopf.

Tilly, L. A. and J. W. Scott. 1990. *Women, Work and Family*. New York: Routledge.

Timera, M. 2002. "Righteous or Rebellious? Social Trajectory of Sahelian Youth in France." Pp. 147–54 in *The Transnational Family: New European Frontiers and Global Networks*, edited by D. F. Bryceson and U. Vuorela. Oxford, UK: Berg.

Tomlinson, J. 1999. *Globalization and Culture*. Chicago, IL: University of Chicago Press.

Toro-Morn, M. I. 1995. "Gender, Class, Family, and Migration: Puerto Rican Women in Chicago." *Gender & Society* 9(6):712–26.

"Tough Times, Longer Waits Lead to Lower International Adoption Rates in America." 2010. *The Washington Times*, August 2. Retrieved June 29, 2011 (http://communities.washingtontimes.com/neighborhood/red-thread-adoptive-family-forum/2010/aug/2/tough-times-longer-waits-lead-lower-international/).

"Trafficking in Persons Report 2006." 2006. *Stop Trafficking! Anti-Human Trafficking Newsletter*, 4(7).

Trask, B. S. 2010. *Globalization and Families: Accelerated Systemic Social Change*. New York: Springer.

Trask, B. S. and R. R. Hamon. 2007. *Cultural Diversity and Families*. Thousand Oaks, CA: Sage.

Tremblay, G. 1992. "Is Quebec Culture Doomed to Become American?" *Canadian Journal of Communication* 17(2). Retrieved September 11, 2006 (http://www.cjc-online.ca/viewarticle.php?id=86&layout=html).

Troshynski, E. and J. Blank. 2008. "Sex Trafficking: An Exploratory Study Interviewing Traffickers." *Trends in Organized Crime. Special Topic: Interviewing Organized Criminals* 11(1):30–41.

Truong, T.-D. 1990. *Sex, Money, and Morality: Prostitution and Tourism in Southeast Asia*. London, UK: Zed Books.

Tryhorn, C. 2009. "Nice Talking to You . . . Mobile Phone Use Passes Milestone." *The Guardian*, March 3. Retrieved July 1, 2011 (http://www.guardian.co.uk/technology/2009/mar/03/mobile-phones1).

Tung, C. 2000. "The Cost of Caring: The Social Reproductive Labor of Filipina Live-In Home Health Caregivers." *Frontiers: A Journal of Women's Studies* 21(1/2):61–82.

Turpin, J. and L. A. Lorentzen, eds. 1996. *The Gendered New World Order: Militarism, Development, and the Environment*. New York: Routledge.

Twine, F. W. 2011. *Outsourcing the Womb: Race, Class, and Gestational Surrogacy in a Global Market*. New York: Routledge.

United Nations. 1948. *The Universal Declaration of Human Rights*. Retrieved January 6, 2012 (http://www.un.org/en/documents/udhr/).

———. 1997. *Working Towards a More Gender Equitable Macro-Economic Agenda*. Report of a conference held in Rajendrapur, Bangladesh, November 26–28. Geneva, Switzerland: U.N. Research Institute for Social Development.

———. 1998. "International Day of Families." Retrieved January 6, 2012 (http://social.un.org/index/Family/InternationalObservances/InternationalDayofFamilies/1998/Backg98.aspx).

———. 1998/1999 (updated). United Nations Workshop on Technology and Families Report. Retrieved December 18, 2006 (http://www.un.org/esa/socdev/family/Meetings/FamTech/FamTec.htm).

———. 1999a. *Assessing the Status of Women: A Guide to Reporting Under the Convention on the Elimination of All Forms of Discrimination Against Women*. New York: United Nations Division for the Advancement of Women, Department of Social and Economic Affairs.

———. 1999b. *Globalization With a Human Face*. Retrieved July 9, 2011 (http://hdr.undp.org/reports/global/1999/en/).

———. 2003. *Families in the Process of Development*. New York: United Nations Division for Social Policy and Development. Retrieved November 21, 2005 (http://www.un.org/esa/socdev/family).

————. 2005. *The Role of Information and Communication Technologies in Global Development: Analysis and Policy Recommendations.* New York: U.N. External Publications Office.

————. 2010. *The Millennium Development Goals Report, 2010.* Retrieved January 2, 2012 (http://www.un.org/millenniumgoals/pdf/MDG%20Report%20 2010%20En%20r15%20-low%20res%2020100615%20-.pdf).

————. 2011. "Uniting for Universal Access: Towards Zero New HIV Infections, Zero Discrimination and Zero AIDS-Related Deaths." Retrieved May 12, 2011 (http://www.who.int/hiv/pub/unsg_report_20110331.pdf).

U.N. Children's Fund (UNICEF). 2000. *Protocol to Prevent, Suppress and Punish Trafficking in Persons, Especially Women and Children, Supplementing the United Nations Convention Against Transnational Organized Crime.* New York: United Nations.

————. 2004. *Trafficking in Human Beings, Especially Women and Children in Africa.* Florence, Italy: Innocenti Insight.

————. 2010. "Child Trafficking." Retrieved July 4, 2011 (http://www.unicef.org/ protection/index_exploitation.html).

U.N. Department of Economic and Social Affairs (UNDESA). 2011. "World Population Prospects: The 2010 Revision." Retrieved June 28, 2011 (http://esa .un.org/unpd/wpp/index.htm).

U.N. Economic and Social Commission for Asia and the Pacific (UNESCAP). 2011. "Gender and Globalization." Retrieved July 7, 2011 (http://www.unescap.org/ esid/gad/issues/Globalization/index.asp).

U.N. Educational, Scientific, and Cultural Organization (UNESCO). 1999. *Statistical Yearbook, 1999* (updated 2005). Retrieved December 30, 2011 (http://www .unevoc.unesco.org/pubscoll.php?akt=id&st=&id=1073&lg=en).

————. 2003a. *Proceedings of the International Symposium on Culture Statistics, Montréal, 21 to 23 October 2002.* Retrieved December 29, 2011 (http://www .uis.unesco.org/StatisticalCapacityBuilding/Workshop%20Documents/ Culture%20workshop%20dox/International%20Symposium_Montreal%20 2002.pdf).

————. 2003b. "World Television Day Celebrated Today." Retrieved July 1, 2011 (http://portal.unesco.org/ci/en/ev.php-URL_ID=13630&URL_DO=DO_ TOPIC&URL_SECTION=201.html).

————. 2005. *International Flows of Selected Cultural Goods and Services, 1994– 2003: Defining and Capturing the Flows of Global Cultural Trade.* Retrieved December 29, 2011 (http://unesdoc.unesco.org/images/0014/001428/142812e .pdf).

————. 2008. "Number of Cell Phone Subscribers to Hit 4 Billion This Year, UN Says." Retrieved July 1, 2011 (http://portal.unesco.org/ci/en/ev.php-URL_ ID=27530&URL_DO=DO_TOPIC&URL_SECTION=201.html).

————. 2010. *Mobile Learning for Quality Education and Social Inclusion.* Retrieved July 1, 2011 (http://unesdoc.unesco.org/images/0019/001921/192144e.pdf).

U.N. High Commission on Refugees (UNHCR). 2011. *UNHCR Global Trends 2010.* Retrieved July 4, 2011 (http://www.unhcr.org/4dfa11499.html).

U.N. Human Rights Council. 2011. *Report of the Special Rapporteur on the Promotion and Protection of Right to Freedom of Opinion and Expression, Frank LaRue.* Retrieved July 1, 2011 (http://www2.ohchr.org/english/bodies/ hrcouncil/docs/17session/A.HRC.17.27_en.pdf)

U.N. International Telecommunications Union (UNITU). 2011. "Key Global Telecom Indicators for the World Telecommunication Service Sector." Retrieved July 13, 2011 (http://www.itu.int/ITU-D/ict/statistics/at_glance/KeyTelecom2010.html).

U.N. News Centre. 2010. "Mobile Telephones More Common Than Toilets in India, UN Report Finds." Retrieved July 1, 2011 (http://www.un.org/apps/news/story.asp?NewsID=34369&Cr=mdg&Cr1=).

U.N. Office on Drugs and Crime (UNODC). 2009. *Global Report on Trafficking in Persons*. Retrieved July 4, 2011 (http://www.unodc.org/documents/human-trafficking/Global_Report_on_TIP.pdf).

———. 2011. "Human Trafficking." Retrieved July 4, 2011 (http://www.unodc.org/unodc/en/human-trafficking/what-is-human-trafficking.html).

U.N. Programme on the Family. 2003. "Families in the Process of Development: Major Trends Affecting Families World-Wide." Retrieved June 1, 2006 (http://www.un.org/esa/socdev/family/majortrends.htm).

Upton, R. 2003. "'Women Have No Tribe': Connecting Carework, Gender, and Migration in an Era of HIV/AIDS in Botswana." *Gender & Society* 17(2): 314–22.

U.S. Bureau of the Census. 2006. "Table 6: Immigrants Admitted by Class of Admissions: 1990–2004." *Statistical Abstract of the United States: 2006*. Washington, DC: United States Government Printing Office.

———. 2011. "Table 48: Persons Obtaining Legal Permanent Resident Status by Class of Admission: 2000–2008." *Statistical Abstract of the United States: 2010*. Retrieved June 29, 2011 (http://www.census.gov/compendia/statab/2011/tables/11s0048.pdf).

U.S. Bureau of International Information Programs. 2003. "World AIDS Day 2003 Marks a 'Turning Point' in Pandemic, Powell Says." Retrieved December 3, 2006 (http://usinfo.org/wf-archive/2003/031128/epf504.htm).

U.S. Central Intelligence Agency. 2011. *The World Factbook*. Retrieved July 11, 2011 (http://www.cia.gov/library/publications/the-world-factbook/geos/as.html).

U.S. Department of Defense. 2011. "Operation Iraqi Freedom Military Deaths, March 19, 2003 through May 31, 2011." Retrieved July 4, 2011 (http://siadapp.dmdc.osd.mil/personnel/CASUALTY/oif-deaths-total.pdf).

U.S. Holocaust Memorial Museum. 2006a. "Beyond Every Name a Story: Miriam (Rot) Eshel. Part I, Introduction." Retrieved January 2, 2012 (http://www.ushmm.org/wlc/en/article.php?ModuleId=10006810).

———. 2006b. "Beyond Every Name a Story: Miriam (Rot) Eshel. Part II, After the Holocaust." Retrieved January 2, 2012 (http://www.ushmm.org/wlc/en/article.php?ModuleId=10006811).

———. 2006c. "Beyond Every Name a Story: Miriam (Rot) Eshel. Whence Your Strength." Retrieved January 2, 2012 (http://www.ushmm.org/wlc/en/article.php?ModuleId=10006812).

———. 2006d. "Burundi: Overview." Retrieved December 31, 2006 (http://www.ushmm.org/conscience/alert/burundi/contents/01-overview/).

———. 2006e. "Chechnya, Russia: Overview." Retrieved December 31, 2006 (http://www.ushmm.org/conscience/alert/chechnya/contents/01-overview/).

———. 2006f. "Children During the Holocaust." Retrieved December 31, 2006 (http://www.ushmm.org/wlc/article.php?lang=en&ModuleId=10005142).

———. 2006g. "DR Congo: Overview." Retrieved December 31, 2006 (http://www.ushmm.org/conscience/alert/congo/contents/01-overview/).

────. 2006h. "The Holocaust." Retrieved December 31, 2006 (http://www.ushmm .org/wlc/article/php?lang=en&ModuleId+10005143).

────. 2006i. "Rwanda: Overview." Retrieved December 31, 2006 (http://www .ushmm.org/conscience/alert/rwanda/contents/01-overview/).

────. 2006j. "Sudan: Overview." Retrieved December 31, 2006 (http://www .ushmm.org/conscience/alert/darfur/contents/01-overview/).

────. 2006k. "What Is Genocide?" Retrieved December 31, 2006 (http://www .ushmm.org/genocide/take_action/genocide).

Vandegrift, D. 2008. "'This Isn't Paradise—I Work Here': Global Restructuring, the Tourism Industry, and Women Workers in Caribbean Costa Rica." *Gender & Society* 22(6):778–98.

Vanek, J. 1974. "Time Spent in Housework." *Scientific American* 231 (November):116–20.

Vélez-Ibáñez, C. G. 2004. "Regions of Refuge in the United States: Issues, Problems, and Concerns for the Future of Mexican-Origin Populations in the United States." *Human Organization* 63(1):1–20.

Veseth, M. 2005. *Globaloney: Unraveling the Myths of Globalization.* Lanham, MD: Rowman & Littlefield.

Vincent, S. 2000. "Flexible Families: Capitalist Development and Crisis in Rural Peru." *Journal of Comparative Family Studies* 31(2):155–70.

Wainwright, M. 2006. "Tribunal Dismisses Case of Muslim Woman Ordered Not to Teach in Veil." *Manchester Guardian*, October 20. Retrieved January 27, 2012 (http://www.guardian.co.uk/uk/2006/oct/20/politics.schools1).

Walby, S. 2009. *Globalization and Inequalities: Complexity and Contested Modernity.* Thousand Oaks, CA: Sage.

Wallerstein, I. 1990. "Culture as the Ideological Battleground of the Modern World-System." *Theory, Culture & Society* 7(1):31–55.

────. 1996. *Historical Capitalism With Capitalist Civilization.* New York: W. W. Norton.

Walsh, D. 2006. "The Third Parent: What Do We Know? And What Do We Need to Know About the Role Popular Media Plays in Family Process?" Plenary address presented at the annual meeting of the National Council on Family Relations, November, Minneapolis, MN.

"War Crimes Court." 2007. *Star Tribune*, January 29, p. A15.

Ward, K. 1990. "Introduction and Overview." Pp. 1–24 in *Women Workers and Global Restructuring*, edited by K. Ward. Ithaca, NY: Industrial and Labor Relations Press of Cornell University.

"War's Overlooked Victims." 2011. *The Economist*, January 15, pp. 63–5.

Washington, J. 2011. "For Minorities, a New 'Digital Divide' Seen." Pew Internet, January 11. Retrieved July 1, 2011 (http://www.pewinternet.org/Media -Mentions/2011/For-minorities-new-digital-divide-seen.aspx).

Waters, M. 1994. "Ethnic and Racial Identities Among Second-Generation Black Immigrants in New York City." *International Immigration Review* 28(4):795–820.

West, E. 2004. *Chains of Love: Slave Couples in Antebellum South Carolina.* Urbana: University of Illinois Press.

White, J. M. 2005. *Advancing Family Theories.* Thousand Oaks, CA: Sage.

White, J. M. and D. M. Klein. 2007. *Family Theories.* 3rd ed. Thousand Oaks, CA: Sage.

White, L. 2004. "True Confessions." *Journal of Women's History* 15(4):142–44.

Williams, R. M. 1993. "Race, Deconstruction, and the Emergent Agenda of Feminist Economic Theory." Pp. 144–52 in *Beyond Economic Man: Feminist Theory and Economics*, edited by M. A. Ferber and J. A. Nelson. Chicago, IL: University of Chicago Press.

Williams, T. K. 1991. "Marriage Between Japanese Women and U.S. Servicemen Since World War II." *Amerasia Journal* 17(1):135–54.

Wilson, S. M. and C. B. Hennon. 2008. "Emerging Trends for Family Scholarship Across Societies." Pp. 495–514 in *Families in a Global Context*, edited by C. B. Hennon and S. M. Wilson. New York: Routledge.

Wilson, S., G. Meagher, R. Gibson, D. Denemark, and M. Western. 2005. *Australian Social Attitudes: The First Report*. Sydney, Australia: University of New South Wales.

Wilson, T. D. 2009. *Women's Migration Networks in Mexico and Beyond*. Albuquerque: University of New Mexico Press.

Wolton, D. 1998. *Au dela de l'Internet (Over the Internet)*. Paris, France: La Decouverte.

World Bank. 1992. *Population and the World Bank: Implications From Eight Case Studies*. Washington, DC.

World Health Organization. 2009. "Global Summary of the AIDS Epidemic, 2009." Retrieved June 28, 2011 (http://www.who.int/hiv/data/2009_global_summary.png).

———. 2011a. "Fact File: 10 Facts on HIV/AIDS." Retrieved June 28, 2011 (http://www.who.int/features/factfiles/hiv/facts/en/index6.html).

———. 2011b. "Fact Sheet: Infectious Diseases." Retrieved June 28, 2011 (http://www.who.int/topics/infectious_diseases/factsheets/en/index.html).

———. 2011c. "Fact Sheet: The Top 10 Causes of Death." Retrieved June 28, 2011 (http://www.who.int/mediacentre/factsheets/fs310/en/).

———. 2011d. "HIV/AIDS." Retrieved May 12, 2011 (http://www.who.int/ceh/risks/otherisks/en/index2.html).

———. 2011e. "HIV Treatment Reaching 6.6 Million People, but Majority Still in Need." Retrieved June 28, 2011 (http://www.who.int/mediacentre/news/releases/2011/hivtreatement_20110603/en/index.html).

———. 2011f. "Prevention of Blindness and Visual Impairment." Retrieved June 28, 2011 (http://www.who.int/blindness/causes/priority/en/index2.html).

Wrigley, J. 1995. *Other People's Children: An Intimate Account of the Dilemmas Facing Middle-Class Parents and the Women They Hire to Raise Their Children*. New York: Basic Books.

Yang, H. 1997. "Revisiting the Issue of Korean 'Military Comfort Women': The Question of Truth and Positionality." *Positions* 5(1):51–71.

Yang, W.-S., and M. C.-W. Lu. 2010. *Asian Cross-Border Marriage Migration: Demographic Patterns and Social Issues*. Amsterdam, the Netherlands: Amsterdam University Press.

Yi, Z. 2002. "A Demographic Analysis of Family Households in China, 1982–1995." *Journal of Comparative Family Studies* 33(1):15–34.

Yongnyŏ, Y. 1995. "I Thought I Would Die." Pp. 143–150 in *True Stories of the Korean Comfort Women*, edited by K. Howard. London, UK: Cassell.

Yongsu, Y. 1995. "Return My Youth to Me." Pp. 88–94 in *True Stories of the Korean Comfort Women*, edited by K. Howard. London, UK: Cassell.

Yŏngsuk, Y. 1995. "I Will No Longer Harbor Resentment." Pp. 50–7 in *True Stories of the Korean Comfort Women*, edited by K. Howard. London, UK: Cassell.

Zimmerman, M. K., J. S. Litt, and C. E. Bose. 2006a. *Global Dimensions of Gender and Carework*. Stanford, CA: Stanford University Press.

Zimmerman, M. K., J. S. Litt, and C. E. Bose. 2006b. "Globalization and Multiple Crises of Care." Pp. 9–29 in *Global Dimensions of Gender and Carework*, by M. K. Zimmerman, J. S. Litt, and C. E. Bose. Stanford, CA: Stanford University Press.

Index

Note: Italicized page numbers indicate illustrations.

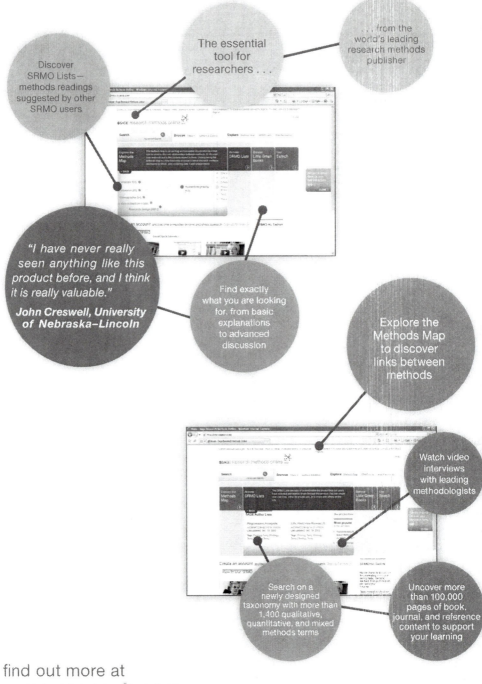

ⓢSAGE researchmethods
The Essential Online Tool for Researchers

The essential tool for researchers . . .

. . . from the world's leading research methods publisher

Discover SRMO Lists— methods readings suggested by other SRMO users

"I have never really seen anything like this product before, and I think it is really valuable."

John Creswell, University of Nebraska–Lincoln

Find exactly what you are looking for, from basic explanations to advanced discussion

Explore the Methods Map to discover links between methods

Watch video interviews with leading methodologists

Search on a newly designed taxonomy with more than 1,400 qualitative, quantitative, and mixed methods terms

Uncover more than 100,000 pages of book, journal, and reference content to support your learning

find out more at
srmo.sagepub.com